HOMESCHOOLING

what to do when you want to quit

Affording the Extras **13**

When you want to quit because money is scarce and extra-curriculars are expensive

An Introvert's Perspective **21**

When you want to quit because your personality craves alone time

When You're Feeling Behind **27**

When you want to quit because you don't feel on track

Falling Behind on Lessons **33**

When you want to quit because you are struggling to catch up

Because You Work at Home **37**

When you want to quit because work deadlines are always looming

Making Homeschooling and Working From Home...Work **47**

When you want to quit because working makes life too hectic

The Overwhelmed Highway **59**

When you want to quit because everything about homeschooling is just draining

Mary Poppins' Advice For Homeschooling Little Ones **65**

When you want to quit because the littles are wearing you out

When You're an Exhausted Mom of Many Littles **73**

When you want to quit because the littles are STILL wearing you out

How to Cope When Homeschooling Means Isolation for Mom **85**

When you want to quit because you feel like you are on your own

A Lonely (but not so lonely) Homeschool Journey .. **89**

When you want to quit because you crave a community

Fighting Fears with Faith 97

When you want to quit because you feel inadequate to teach

Feeling Inadequate to Homeschool High School 103

When you want to quit because teaching the higher levels scares you

Homeschooling High School 111

When you want to quit because teaching the higher levels REALLY scares you

When You Feel That Public School Would Be Better 131

When you want to quit because your kids might learn more at school

Feeling Under-Appreciated as a Homeschool Mom 137

When you want to quit because you don't feel valued as a mom

Homeschooling When You Feel Unappreciated 143

When you want to quit because no one understands how hard you work

Homeschooling with a Traveling Husband 153

When you want to quit because your husband is always away on business

Flying Solo When Dad Travels or Works Late 161

When you want to quit because your husband's job is demanding

When Mom Has Meltdowns 169

When you want to quit because YOU are the emotional one

When the Bottom Falls Out 183

When you want to quit because everything around you is crumbling

Running Errands with Little Helpers 189

When you want to quit because the day-to-day is too overwhelming

When Your Kids Are Intense 195

When you want to quit because your kids are challenging to teach

Homeschooling An Intense Child 205

When you want to quit because your kids are overexcitable

Homeschooling Outliers 215

When you want to quit because your kids don't seem to fit in

Homeschooling Through A Health Crisis 223

When you want to quit because medical issues are always in the way

Homeschooling Through a Move 233

When you want to quit because there is no room for homeschooling among the boxes

Homeschooling through Job Loss or Financial Crisis 239

When you want to quit because financial obstacles are in the way

Homeschooling While Pregnant 249

When you want to quit because your pregnancy is high risk or challenging

Homeschooling While Pregnant 253

When you want to quit because pregnancy causes your bus wheels to fall off

When You're Longing for Quiet 257

When you want to quit because the noise is too overwhelming

When Your Husband Doesn't Approve 267

When you want to quit because your husband rejects your ideas

Facing Judgment and Stereotypes from Outsiders .273

When you want to quit because you feel judgmental eyes everywhere

When Your Heart Is No Longer In It 277

When you want to quit because the joy has vanished

When your Spirit is Eager but the Flesh is Weak.... 287

When you want to quit because your body is giving out

Homeschool Moms Have No Down Time! 303

When you want to quit because you treasure your kids, but want to be alone

When Family and Friends Turn Up the Pressure .. 309

When you want to quit because the raised eyebrows become too much

Spending So Much Time in the Kitchen.................. 315

When you want to quit because you feel like all you ever do is cook

Help! I'm No Good With Record-Keeping 321

When you want to quit because organization is your nemesis

Help! I Homeschool and My House is a Mess!........ 327

When you want to quit because you crave a tidy home

Cleaning While Homeschooling 335

When you want to quit because the messes are out of control

The House is a Mess! Balancing Homeschool and Housework 341

When you want to quit because the messes are STILL out of control

The Stress of Choosing Curriculum.......................345

When you want to quit because the options are overwhelming

Balancing Homeschool with a Special-Needs Child 349

When you want to quit because your child has needs you struggle with meeting

Trying to Balance Homeschooling with a Child with Special Needs..353

When you want to quit because juggling therapy and homeschooling is too much

Homeschooling an Unmotivated Student **361**

When you want to quit because your child lacks ambition

When You Feel Like Homeschooling is Breaking Your Marriage **369**

When you want to quit because your marriage is in jeopardy

Help! How Can I Discipline My Children? **379**

When you want to quit because your kids are unruly

When the Kids Don't Obey.....................................**391**

When you want to quit because your kids do not respect you

When Homeschooling Looks Like Climbing Mount Everest **397**

When you want to quit because life keeps throwing you curveballs

Homeschooling Through Hard Times or a Death in the Family **405**

When you want to quit because the hard times keep adding up

Homeschooling with Bickering Kids **411**

When you want to quit because your kids don't like each other

When You Feel Like You're Doing a Terrible Job ... **417**

When you want to quit because you have doubts about all your abilities

When Your Kid Hates School **423**

When you want to quit because your kid flat out refuses to do school

What If You Feel Like You're Doing Too Little? **433**

When you want to quit because you feel too relaxed

Am I Pushing My Kids Too Much? **437**

When you want to quit because you wonder if you are overly pushy

Introduction
Erica Arndt

I'll never forget our first day of homeschooling. I was so excited, and so was my daughter. She was only 3 at the time, so she didn't really know what was headed her way and honestly neither did I! We had started early with her because I was eager. I decorated our dining room like a school room with fun wall hangings and lots of color. And I had certainly a vision of what I thought homeschooling should look like. *(I imagined my children studying quietly, making fun history and art projects, and snuggled up on the couch reading together.)*

What I didn't foresee was how hard homeschooling would turn out to be. It also never occurred to me that my doe-eyed babe wouldn't necessarily share my enthusiasm for school work. Especially when she had to do school and her younger brother was free to play and enjoy life.

It ended up taking a few years into our homeschooling journey before we really found a routine that worked well for us. We tried more than one room set-up, we switched curriculum and started over with something new, we had awesome days, and we had awful days.

But eventually we found our homeschooling groove, and slowly it became our norm. We've been successfully homeschooling for 9 years now but like most homeschoolers I have to say that we've had our ups and downs.

Whether you're just starting out, or a seasoned homeschooler, discouragement hits us all at one point or another. We all doubt our decisions from time to time. We all have experienced good days along with bad days. And we've all seen the flashing lights of that yellow bus and considered for just a quick moment about putting our kids on it.

I want to encourage you...
Hang in there.
You are not alone.
Remember, tomorrow is a new day.
Don't give up.
Don't flag down the yellow bus.

Homeschooling is an ongoing and rewarding process. The time and energy you have committed to devoting to your children's future won't return void. You might have days when it seems like nothing is going well, and your patience will be pushed to the limits.

But you'll also witness moments when your children are flourishing. You'll begin to see glimpses of where this journey is leading and the benefits to your family will become apparent as well. As you witness the bonds created within your family, you'll be thankful that you took the leap. Homeschooling rewards come in baby steps, but you'll know when you see them, and they'll warm your heart and motivate you to persevere.

One thing we like to do to help stave off discouragement and remind us why we chose this journey to begin with, is refer back to our homeschooling vision statement. Years ago when we first started homeschooling we created a vision for our homeschool. It listed things like what our long term goals for our children were and what we wanted to teach them in regards to character, academics, social skills, and spiritual wisdom. We listed what we wanted our children to be like as adults and what the overall goal of our decision to homeschool was. Essentially it was a list to help us choose our homeschooling path.

It's funny because although we made that vision as more of a list of why we would homeschool, it turned into an encouragement for us further down the road when discouragement hit. Just like everyone we've doubted our decision to homeschool. And it was helpful to be able to look back on our goals and vision and get encouragement from our own words to stay focused on our path.

Keep in mind as you're reading through this book that there is no such thing as the perfect parent. We are all just trying to do what is best for our family. Your homeschool won't necessarily look like mine and your methods will probably be different too. But hopefully you'll be inspired to make any changes you need to make your homeschool successful and be encouraged to keep on your chosen path.

Homeschooling isn't for the faint of heart. It requires strength, commitment, consistency, flexibility, and most of all patience. But steady on my dear friend! As you read through this book know that these nuggets of wisdom come from many homeschooling parents who have blazed the trail before you. We've struggled just like you will and we've overcome obstacles just like you will. We wanted to give you some tips and tricks that we wish we had and that will hopefully help alleviate your fears and concerns. But mostly we came together as a group of homeschooling parents to provide you with helpful tools to stay on the homeschooling course, to encourage you, and to let you know that you are not alone on this journey!

Affording the Extras
Dianna Kennedy

The flexibility of a homeschool schedule opens up a world of possibilities outside of your day-to-day curriculum. Extracurricular activities can offer homeschool students a way to meet new friends, explore their passions, try something new, or simply blow off steam.

For some families, extracurricular adventures simply aren't a big part of their lives. For others, the benefits of these activities rank higher on the priority list.

Once you've given some thought to what type of extras you want to explore and how you'll fit the extras into your schedule, the next hurdle is cost. As a mother of many, I can tell you that I spend more on my children's sports and enrichment programs than I do on our homeschooling curriculum.

I'm looking at it as an investment into our children's lives, but as we bring up more children, we're having to take a serious look at how to balance our children's interests and our budget. I'll share the ideas that we've pursued to help ease the strain on our checkbook.

Be choosy

My children would love to do everything I've ever suggested to them – sports, music, art, nature classes and more. You have to accept the fact that you simply cannot do everything. Take an honest look at the activity or class you're considering and evaluate how it would improve your life.

Don't force your interests on your children

I would have loved to learn how to play the piano when I was a child, but that doesn't mean my sons want to tackle those lessons. You'll have to swallow some of your interests and let them lead.

Set limits

We do this in our school for scheduling sanity as well as for budgetary concerns. If you set a limit of one activity per season, you'll build more downtime into your lives, as well as save some money.

Don't succumb to pressure

There's no law that says that you have to involve your children in a certain number of activities in order to educate them properly. Try not to get caught up in the never-ending struggle of keeping up with everyone else. Consider your family's individual needs and close your eyes to everyone else.

Shop around

Extracurricular activities don't have to be expensive. By shopping around, you may find a cheaper alternative that fits your family budget.

Consider these ideas for extracurricular activities:

- **Library:** Have you scanned your local library's offerings? Looking at some of the libraries in my area, I'm seeing arts and crafts projects for teens, story times, family story times, and more. A majority of these programs are free or extremely low-cost.

- **Community parks and recreational leagues:** Most cities have some sort of community parks and recreational leagues that offer sports like baseball, football and more.

- **4-H:** For youth ages 9-19, 4-H is the largest youth organization in the world. You'll find areas such as cooking, equestrian sports, shooting sports, farming and more for your children to explore.

- **Public schools:** Your mileage may vary, but in some areas, homeschool children are allowed to participate in the local public school's activities. My daughter is in her second year of participating in Girls on the Run, a national program to teach girls to be runners for life. I saw the flyer at the local school, made the call, and she's had a blast.

- **Churches:** If your church is associated with a school, there may be an athletics program in which your children can become involved. I've had a great experience with Upward Sports, which has locations all over the country for soccer, basketball, flag football, volleyball, cheerleading and more. This program is usually sponsored by a local church. Churches are also wonderful resources for music lessons and children's choir.

- **Homeschool co-ops:** In our area, homeschool co-ops offer a variety of enrichment classes and even sports. My sons took a CrossFit class last year at our homeschool co-op and loved it. Through the co-op, it was less than half the cost than if we had gone through the CrossFit studio.

- **Community colleges:** Take a look at your local community college. Some offer adult learning experiences – classes like pottery, yoga, water aerobics and more. There may be an age requirement, so these classes may be more appropriate for teens.

- **Local newspaper:** Check your newspaper for activities and events to fit your budget.

- **Poll your friends:** Ask your friends and find out where they're taking their kids for classes or sports. Chances are, they're as budget-conscious as you.

Also, consider your friend and family as potential coaches or teachers. Do you have a friend who is an artist? Chat her up about teaching an art class to a group of homeschoolers.

More bang for your buck

If you have multiple children, you may want to consider activities that charge as a family, that put a cap on family expenses, or that offer a discount for multiple children. In our local American Heritage Girls troop, there is a discounted rate for families with more than one daughter involved.

Another idea for saving money? Find activities that the entire family can attend. I know friends who take tae kwon do together, or others who have every child on the swim team during the summer.

Be a volunteer

If there's a sport or activity that seems cost-prohibitive to you, ask about volunteering. My daughter has been riding for the past four years. Riding horses isn't on the list of cheap activities, but we make it work by volunteering. Rachel earns partial credit toward her lessons by volunteering, and learns the value of service.

Don't forget the cost of gear

When considering the cost of a sport or activity, don't overlook the gear, equipment or uniforms. Soccer is relatively cheap, only requiring a ball, shin guards and cleats. If your child wants to pursue horseback riding, they will eventually need a helmet, riding boots, gloves and pants.

Some equipment and gear can be handed down, while others will have to be purchased new for each child. You can search children's consignment stores, consignment sales, eBay and Craigslist for used equipment.

Ask for a discount

I've had luck in the past when I've asked about a homeschooling discount, or rates for multiple children. You may be turned down, but you won't know until you ask.

Consider it a gift

If your extended family asks about gift ideas for Christmas or birthdays, what about asking for money or gift certificates toward lessons, sports gear, or camps?

I know our family would appreciate a clutter-free gift that helps our children enjoy their passions. Grandparents usually want a child to unwrap something, but I think that a small Christmas ornament of a horse, along with money for lessons, would please my horse-loving daughter more than anything else under the tree.

Affording the extras doesn't have to be stressful. Try putting some of these ideas into place and don't forget to have fun!

An Introvert's Perspective
Tonia Lyons

Homeschooling is hard work and, when you are an introvert at home with a houseful of kids (or even just one), you can really begin to feel the pressure. It is so very easy to push yourself to continue and "be on" all the time for everyone, but it doesn't come without a cost. Introverts NEED alone time. That is how you recharge and refresh yourself. When you have your children home with you all day, it is so easy to ignore that need for time alone.

What is an introvert?

An introvert is someone who is recharged by being alone. They generally don't like large crowds or making small talk (we really want to know how you are when we ask you!). They do prefer to plan ahead. They can be lots of fun – but only with people they are comfortable with.

They are not socially awkward or shy, nor do they dislike people. But spending time with groups of people or talking for awhile can drain an introverted person. This applies to homeschooling moms too.

Why you need to create some space for yourself

Spending most of the day teaching your children and maintaining your home can be exhausting for an introverted mom. You are doing your family a disservice by not taking the time you need for yourself. I'm not saying you should throw out the schoolbooks and let your kids sit in front of the television set all day. But you must learn to create intentional moments of peace and quiet (I know it's hard to find that time!) for yourself and even for your children.

If you continue to push yourself and don't create those quiet moments, your body and mind will begin to suffer as well. This can lead to a host of issues, including stress, anger and digestive issues. It will also cause homeschooling burnout. Being a mom and a teacher is a big job!

Create a daily routine that includes quiet moments

The first step is to create a schedule that works for your family. There's no need to schedule every available moment, but a basic daily routine that has quiet moments built in throughout the day (your introverted children will thank you!) will help you manage your life but still create still moments.

There are three times during the day that are easy and manageable, even for busy households.

1. Set wakeup times. To make sure I get that alone time in the morning, my daughter is not allowed out of bed before 7 a.m. Set specific "out of bed" times for your kids – if they are early risers, teach them to stay in bed with a book or a few quiet toys until it's time to get out of bed.

Plan to get up 30 minutes before they do so you can have a few minutes of peace and prayer time to start your day right.

2. Set bedtimes. I confess that we are pretty loose with bedtimes around here since I have just one. But we all do much better with a relaxing bedtime routine that has us each in our quiet space before bed. Read to your kids, tuck them in, and go have your own quiet evening.

3. Daily quiet time. All your kids will benefit from 30 minutes or an hour of daily quiet time. Allow napping, reading, quiet individual play time, audio books, drawing – this is a great time to work on habits of quietness and learning to play alone. Teach it from an early age and institute a daily 30-minute quiet break after lunch, and fairly soon it will become routine (and something your kids will look forward to – especially your little introverts).

By creating a consistent schedule that allows for quiet moments throughout the day, you are providing some breathing room for yourself, as well as time for your children that will teach them to be creative and respectful of the boundaries that everyone needs in their lives.

Healthy habits for the homeschool mom

We get so busy, as homeschooling moms, that it's easy to put our own needs to the side. But it's very important to take care of our bodies. Take time to exercise and get outdoors; both of these activities can be so refreshing. It's also a perfect opportunity to spend time with your extroverted children, who thrive on activity and togetherness.

Connect with friends – introverts aren't completely anti-social – we do like people! Instead of a constant need for socializing, we are more prone to have deep relationships with a smaller group of friends. When creating time for yourself, include time with your close friends, if possible. Don't isolate yourself. As a homeschool mom, it is so easy to stay home every day with your kids and interact with no other adults except your husband. As much as you need alone time, introverts also need the deep companionship of a few close people

Last of all, pray. Sometimes you are in a season of life when things are just plain difficult. Lots of little ones with no older kids to pitch in can be an especially difficult time for a homeschooling mom. It really will pass and the kids will get older. Do what you can when you can. Teach them that it's important for you and for them to have those daily quiet times. Realize when you've had enough – watch for those times when your temper starts to flare and take a few minutes of quiet (even if it's in the bathroom!). A few moments can help refresh and recharge.

Being an introvert is OK

There is absolutely nothing wrong with being an introvert. It is OK to want that time alone or to not be the life of every party (and even dislike going to them!). The world needs our quiet introspection. If you'd like to read more about the power of your introverted nature, I highly recommend Susan Cain's book "Quiet."

When You're Feeling Behind
Michelle Cannon

If you've ever found yourself feeling behind in your homeschool, know that you are not alone. As a homeschool consultant, I've spoken with many moms who feel the same way. As a homeschool mom, I've felt that way more often than I'd care to admit.

The idea that you're behind creates a vicious cycle. First you feel behind. Then you feel anxious and unmotivated, so you do little, which, in turn, leaves you feeling behind. I know. I've been there. So what can we do to get ourselves back on track?

The first step to resolving the problem is to determine why you feel that way. When someone calls me to say they feel behind, the first thing I ask is, "Behind what or whom?" In posing this question, I am able to find out what "being behind" means to that individual. Also, it helps me find out where the problem really lies. Is the parent comparing herself to the school system? Other homeschool families? Or is she behind her own self-imposed schedule?

The comparison game

As parents, we want to know we're doing what's best for our children. Often that leads us to look at what others are doing. There's a reason parenting books and blogs abound. Parents want to see what others are doing.

Unfortunately, this can be a downfall in some ways. When we start comparing what others are doing to what we are doing, we can feel not good enough. This is especially true with homeschooling. Looking at what the kids are doing in public school, or what your homeschool friends are doing, can make you feel not good enough, too.

I often tell people, "If you could peek into the homes of two million homeschool families, you would find two million different ways to homeschool." It is important to realize your homeschool will be as individual as your family. For your homeschool to work, you will combine all the factors – your teaching style, your child's learning style, the schedule that works for you, and any specific skills, interests, or needs – to create a homeschool that is unique to your family. Embrace the individuality of your homeschool.

Your homeschool workload

Another thing to consider is your workload. Is your curriculum really working for you? If it leaves you feeling behind, you may need to cut back or completely change what you're doing. You do not have to finish what you're doing. You can make changes as you go, even mid-year. Also, don't feel pressured to finish something because your end-of-year is approaching. You don't have to finish.

Try to view your homeschool as a constant progression rather than beginnings and ends of the school year. Rather than creating starting and stopping points, view any stopping point as a break from which you will pick up and move forward, at your child's pace. Learning is gradual and constant. There's no need to pressure yourself to finish something by some arbitrary date. Just keep pressing forward.

Here's a helpful tip: If you purchased a curriculum that came with a schedule, you can adjust that schedule to work for you. It's true! No one dictates how your homeschool should work except you! This may mean homeschooling Monday through Friday for 2 hours per day for little ones. Maybe your have teens putting in six-hour days for four days each week. Maybe your kids have circadian rhythm issues, so you homeschool at night. Whatever works for your family is what you should be doing.

Perhaps your homeschooling style or method isn't working. Maybe it would work if you made some adjustments. Then again, you may need to change it completely. I did. Unschooling did allow my kids to learn, but the entire family felt it wasn't serving us well. My kids felt they weren't being adequately educated, and I felt I wasn't doing enough. While unschooling works for many people, I strongly believe if any part of the family is uncomfortable with something, that something needs to change.

Are you experiencing life challenges?

In my 16 years of homeschooling, I've experienced challenges or changes that slowed us down. A new baby, the death of a loved one, a heavy workload outside the home; all of these left me feeling behind. Perhaps you're experiencing similar circumstances.

During those times, it's OK to cut back the workload, focusing only on core subjects. You even put lessons aside for a break. It's OK. I promise. Most states require something from homeschoolers. In my state, Florida, we must attend school 180 days per year. There are 365 days in the year. That's exactly how I've learned to view it. I have 365 days to meet the 180-day requirement. Not too difficult, right?

Whatever your state requirements are, I'm sure that a break or a slow-down period to get through the inevitable events life throws your way is fine. Taking care of yourself and your family is a part of being a homeschool parent. It's no different from any other part of parenting. You will have unexpected interruptions, and times when you just need to de-stress. Take those moments to get through the challenge and then return to the normal schedule.

These are some of the most common reasons parents feel behind in their homeschooling. Did you notice that most of them boil down to our own view of what should be happening? Sometimes we just need to reevaluate our "should" and make some changes.

I hope this information has helped you to embrace the individuality of your own homeschool situation, work with what you have, and stop comparing to what others may be doing. What matters is your own family's comfort and continual progress.

Falling Behind on Lessons
LaToya Edwards

A few years ago, I lost an entire homeschool year. It was a rough time for us. We spent the first three months of the school year homeless and then the next three dealing with illness. By the time we were unpacked and well, I was already dreaming of summer. Add into the mix a child with special needs and learning struggles, and you have a recipe for complete burnout.

That has been our worst homeschool year so far. Honestly, when I look back, I realized that I should have just embraced the season as a time of rest instead of stressing over the unopened books. There have been other times when life happened and the lesson plans had to be put aside for a while.

I used to worry that my boys would be behind on their lessons. Watching as other families finished their curriculum made me a little nervous. One of my boys had spent the last two years on the same math book. I struggled with feeling like I was somehow failing my boys.

I've learned to adjust my expectations and also to have my own definition of success for my children. As long as we are working hard and making forward progress, I'm not worried about falling behind. Sometimes you can catch up and sometimes you just have to keep moving forward.

Along with adjusting my expectations, I've also learned the importance of building margin into your homeschool schedule. This is simply space during your year where you don't have anything planned. Having this time blocked off allows you to have time to catch up on lessons if you need to without losing time in your plans.

In our homeschool, there is one day a week that is really light, and we take a week off every six weeks. This gives me some wiggle room with our lessons. If there's a book that we didn't get to finish "on time," we can just keep reading during our off week. When we have to cut our day short because the weather is suddenly nice or an appointment runs a little long, I know that I have an extra day already built into the plans.

Sometimes you just have to get creative when you are behind and struggling to catch up. For me, I find it most helpful to cut out some of the extras. History, science and fine arts are things that are fun and important, but they can also be put aside to focus on the foundational subjects like reading and math. Summer is a great time to go back and do short history unit or a science project when this happens.

Falling behind doesn't have to be super stressful if you can plan for it and be flexible. Remember, you set the tone and the pace of your homeschool. Use it to catch up when you need to.

Because You Work at Home
Brenda Priddy

Many homeschooling parents are also work-at-home parents. I know many homeschooling families who give music lessons, develop programs, design websites, run blogs, provide coaching services, have sales-based businesses, run catering companies, and have dozens of other jobs right from their homes.

Some homeschooling families have both parents working from home, while others may have just one. Some families may work part-time at home, and others may work full-time.

Working at home, or working at all, is not a reason to stop homeschooling. There are ways to combine work and homeschooling beautifully, and many of you do it well.

But regardless of how well you homeschool and work at the same time, there are Those Days.

We all have them. Those are the days when the children are sick, deadlines are looming, and every customer calls at once. Those are the days when you have errands, company dropping by, unexpected projects, and a spouse suddenly called out of town. Those are the days when your eldest has a recital, your co-op demands you teach a class, your youngest has to deliver a working diorama of the body's respiratory system, and you find you are selected for an IRS audit. Those are the days your children burst in on every call, the baby screams for three hours straight, and your middle child declares a school strike.

Those days are not easy. On those days, it is easy to wonder why we bother homeschooling at all. Public school is pretty good, right? Children excel there every day. Maybe if you work a bit extra, you can afford private school. It's crazy to try to do it all, right?

Is it crazy to work and homeschool?

Working while homeschooling is hard. Homeschooling is hard enough, but when you add in work on top of school, it can get overwhelming fast. Sometimes I feel like an electrocuted chicken running through my house trying to do everything at once. I dash from thing to thing, never feeling like I complete anything and like I'm always behind one big step. Sometimes it doesn't seem worth it.

To work and homeschool successfully, you absolutely must know why you are doing it.
For me, being able to homeschool my children is my greatest treasure.

I was homeschooled as a child. Even though my childhood was not perfect, I believe it had elements of perfect that many school children today do not get. As a child, I had the true freedom that only comes with the presence of boredom. So much of my childhood was spent creating, inventing, playing, and exploring. Today, my siblings are my best friends.

I don't think I would be as close to my siblings as I am today if I did not have that time with them.

I want my children to have the same experiences. I also want to spend as much time as I can with them. I enjoy my children and I love seeing them grow and learn. I don't want to give that up unless I absolutely have to.

But, I must also work. There are few families in the world today that can exist on one income. I feel it is my responsibility to my family to provide for them as much as I can. I am honored to be able to care for them from home.

Tips for fighting work/school frustration

As much as I love working at home and having this time with my children, balancing work when they are right with me every second of every day is a challenge.

Some days, it is all I can do not to yell at them for getting in the way of work, and some days, I do not even manage that much. Sometimes my children get upset that I am spending time working and not with them. Sometimes I miss a work deadline because a child is sick or really needs my attention that day.

As a work-at-home homeschooling parent, I find it easy to feel frustrated. My day is a constant stream of demands from one source or another. I wake up to demands, live through demands, and go to bed thinking of tomorrow's demands. I often work until midnight or later trying to get through all of my responsibilities.

Over the years, I've found a few different strategies for dealing with the frustration that balancing work and homeschooling can bring. These have really helped me get through those frustrating days and face each new day with fresh eyes and a happy heart.

Have set office hours

I don't always get to do this, but it really helps when I can manage it. Right now, I have morning for work, afternoons for school, early evening for cleaning and maybe a work task or two, and a lot of work after the children go to bed. I find my children are happier if they know when I am working and when they can approach me with questions or requests.

Don't work weekends

I do not always get to do this, but I try really hard to protect my weekends. Weekends are one of the few times that I get to be just Mom, rather than Teacher Mom or Working Mom. It makes an amazing difference in my personal attitude (less crankies from Mom) when I have the weekend to relax and just enjoy my family (which usually includes some laundry and a bathroom cleaning or two).

Hold on to your reason for homeschooling

On particularly frustrating days, I have to cling tightly to why I homeschool. If you do not have a solid reason for homeschooling, you may not have the motivation to stick to it when times are tough. I am not a person who believes that all traditional schooling is evil, but I would rather homeschool my children. I think that for now, it is what is best for them and best for me.

Acknowledge what you are giving up, but also what you gain

I get a lot of comments about how "lucky" I am to be at home with my children, and of course I am. I feel incredibly lucky and blessed to spend my entire days with them. But after a while, it can get frustrating that no one acknowledges what I've given up to stay at home with my children.

As at-home, homeschooling and working parents, we have given up a lot, including:

- The ability to leave the house with ease
- The ability to be just a parent
- The ability to pursue our dream careers (mine is pretty close, but still isn't what I thought I would be doing with my life)
- Respect from others (half of the people I talk to have no idea how much time and energy it takes to work from home and homeschool, and the other half just think I am crazy for doing so)
- Being just a stay-at-home parent
- Separation of home and work
- The ability to "clock out" from work

Sometimes as work-at-home homeschooling parents, we don't allow ourselves to think about what we are giving up, because we are also gaining a lot. But no matter what life choices you make, you always give up on something else. It is OK to acknowledge and allow sorrow about what we have had to give up to be work-at-home homeschooling parents.

However, just focusing on what you give up probably won't help you feel any better about your decisions. It is even more important to think about how working at home and homeschooling has a positive effect on your life, such as:

- Extra income for savings, retirement, or doing more fun things as a family
- The ability to be with your family as much as you want
- The joy of seeing your children learn and grow
- The ability to provide "stay-at-home" services to your children, such as taking them to doctor's appointments, music lessons, and play dates

- Giving your children a visible example of a responsible work ethic
- The ability to be there for your kids for whatever they need

Make a schedule

I find an established routine is essential at our house. Days when I don't follow our normal routine are days that quickly cause us to get behind in work and school. We cannot go more than two days without a schedule before we quickly have to return to our scheduled ways.

How do you make a routine that works for you? A routine is simply a structured format for how you organize your day. I like to make specific blocks of time for specific activities, such as work, chores and school. We also like to schedule our "relaxing" time, where we just get to be a family together. Recently, we've used this time to watch movies together or read books.

What your schedule looks like isn't as important as following a structure of some sort. However, the structure you use should be up to you and will meet the unique needs of your work-at-home homeschooling family.

Address attitude problems quickly

At our house, sometimes the children get a bit jealous of my work. They would rather see me spend all day with them, which, while understandable, is impossible. In extreme cases, this leads to acting out and poor attitudes during school or regular chores.

If I let the bad attitudes go on for days (and I have in the past), it becomes problematic for not only the child, but also for me. Bad attitudes are catching, and I find myself becoming more frustrated with everything if a child has a bad attitude.

We use a few set strategies for helping our children re-set their attitudes. First, we address any heart issues (Is the child feeling neglected? How can we make that child feel included or loved again?), then move on to other correction steps. I usually find, that for my kids, they usually need more one-on-one time, they need to mix it up a bit in school, or they just need more sleep. It's pretty simple, but I know if I don't get my sleep and feel bored, I get cranky, too!

Eat and sleep better

You know what makes me have a hard time? Not enough sleep! I need my sleep and I need nutritious food. If I don't have the recharging fuel that I need, I am cranky, unhappy, and feel terrible.

It may be the solution to your frustrations is to sleep more and eat better. Try eating more vegetables and less fried foods and desserts (which is difficult for me, I love my desserts). Try to sleep for at least eight, preferably nine hours a day. It can make a huge difference.

Exercise, too, is extremely important for the work-at-home homeschooling parent. We get little day-to-day activity, which makes exercise even more important for maintaining health. I struggle sometimes, to find time to exercise, but I am always much happier when I do.

Is it time to quit?

If you feel frustrated or overwhelmed by either work or school and have felt that way for a long time, even after trying every other possible solution, it may be time to think of quitting.

Do I think quitting is for everyone? Of course not! I believe it is possible for everyone who wants to, to both work and homeschool.

But, if you are truly unhappy and feel depressed, it might be time to consider quitting either homeschooling or working at home temporarily. Discuss the issue with both your spouse and your doctor to determine if you should cut back for a while.

Personally, I know if I had another baby right now, I would have to cut back at work. I would not be able to raise a newborn and work the same amount that I do right now.

Knowing your limits is an important part of finding the right balance between work and homeschooling.

Working is hard, but it's all worth it

You may feel frustrated at times, or often, while working at home and trying to homeschool, but it is worth it. We get to be right here with our children as they grow and learn and discover the world around them. We get to give our children the ideal childhood that allows them to become the people they were always meant to be. If that means that I have to work a little extra harder or sacrifice a bit more, then so be it.

Aren't our children worth the struggle?

Making Homeschooling and Working From Home...Work

Kara S. Anderson

My day starts before the sun peeks over the trees outside my bedroom window. It's just me and a white-and-buff cat named George, who follows me around until I feed him. He scarfs down a can of cat food and then sits quietly, observing. It will be just the two of us for 2 or 3 hours, until the house wakes all at once – my husband, two children and a dog who likes to stick his feet in my teacup.

Unlike George, our dog Champion makes work a little more challenging, and so when he appears yawning and stretching, that's usually my cue to wrap up my morning work.

I'll be back at my desk (or more likely my dining room table) later, but for now, it's time to switch gears.

That's because I work at home, but I'm also a homeschooling mama. My kids are 11 and 8 years old, and we love learning together. I love the opportunity to work from home. And the two are forever intertwined, because what I do early mornings, for an hour or two most afternoons, one night a week and all day Saturday helps us afford all those Amazon boxes that come to our door, the field trips and the lessons, the co-op classes and the art supplies.

I try to remember that on the days when it isn't easy –
when deadlines are looming or one of my kids asks why I
have to work. I try to remember when a new friend at co-op
questions how I "do it all."

I don't. I really don't. And I sometimes feel as if I am failing
in all areas.

Sometimes, I even feel like quitting either homeschooling
or working from home. (Or on really bad days, maybe
both?)

So can you work and homeschool?

I used to think the answer to that question was yes.
Probably. Maybe you – but definitely not me. Up until last
year I've had times when I've worked a lot, and times when
I've worked a little.

When I worked primarily as a freelance writer, I often
didn't have control of my workload – I could say no and
risk losing a client, so I never said no.

What that's taught me is that the times when I am working
too much are much too hard on everyone. It trickles down
– the stress. Things go undone. We eat too much pizza.
And those are the time I feel like throwing my MacBook
out the window, moving to a cabin in the woods and
studying wildflowers all day; definitely calling it quits on
this work business.

So I've worked to change what I do. I've worked to make
my schedule more consistent and less reliant on other
people answering the phone and wanting to talk to me at
length about sheet metal processing.

I've worked to find work I love – still writing some, but
primarily working as a virtual assistant. I've worked to

create a job that works WITH homeschooling – that allows me to prioritize it.

I enjoy my work – I love what I do, and I've come to realize that it's OK if it's hard sometimes, because most of the time, it isn't.

Besides, the truth is, time would not suddenly multiply if I stepped away from my job or homeschooling. Because that isn't really how it works.

The truth about time

When I tell people that I homeschool and work from home, they assume that my schedule is full.

They also assume that I am really organized. One of those is right.

So in my doubtful moments, I ask myself if giving up homeschooling would free up my time – if I would find peace in turning over my children's education to others. Sometimes, when I am feeling very low, I can trick myself into thinking that sending my kids to school would be the best move.

You've heard the advice to never quit at your lowest moment? Well in my lowest moments, I've learned to not think about public school at all. Because I am not thinking clearly.

Because let's be honest. If I sent my kids to school:

- Our schedule would be dictated by someone else – from the times we woke up and went to bed, to the times we could take family trips.
- Mornings would be a hectic rush to get lunches and backpacks packed and breakfast eaten. Instead of

looking my kids in the eyes, I would be searching their rooms for missing shoes and homework assignments.

- And let's talk about homework: Most of the public school moms I know spend hours working with their kids on homework – often the time is comparable to a homeschooling mom. And they don't have the opportunity to switch to a different way of teaching something if their child is struggling.

- There would be mid-day parties to attend, concerts, book fairs. There would be afterschool activities and PTA meetings. There would be skating nights and "Muffins with Mom" and a million other things to add to our calendar because I would want to be involved.

- There would be a lot less freedom and a lot more demands, and I really, really hate demands.

- There would perhaps be less control over how we choose to allot our money, and I could easily see myself getting drawn back into full-time work. I mean, my kids are in school, right?

So let's not make this quitting thing about time, I try to remind myself. And with all that action to add to our world, let's not make it about peace either. But still, there can be guilt. Piles of it.

Guilt's a killer, man

Pretty much every homeschool mama I know is carrying around a big ol' bag of guilt.

About something.

I find that a lot of my guilt comes from feeling divided. I find it happens when my son wants me to play a game with him, when my daughter wants me to help her with her knitting project.

What does it say to them if I don't jump up this second to help them? That's what I ask myself.

When I am not working too much, when I am feeling a good work-life balance, I can see past the guilt-cloud and remember that my kids are learning from watching me balance work and school and life:

- Working models responsibility.
- It shows them that I am using skills I learned in college.
- It reminds them of one of the ways I help to support our family.
- It demonstrates lifelong learning. (True story: A couple of years ago, I did a grown-up, unpaid "internship" that led to a wonderful job!)

But when everything feels off and messy and I am doubting myself, I can only feel guilt:

If I don't, at this moment, close my laptop and make eye contact and show my kids that they are the most important thing in the world to me, well, then I better learn how to bake a file into a cake and buy two mini prison jumpsuits, because that's where all this is headed.

The secret to working and homeschooling

And so, I try really hard to come to terms with being a working homeschooling mama, and what that actually looks like in this season.

And I've discovered the absolute secret is just realizing that if I am going to do this, I can't try to be a not-working homeschooling mama.

Let me explain:

I have worked a lot and I've worked very little. And when I am working less, I have more time for other stuff. Period. Quality time with my kids is non-negotiable, no matter how much I am working.

And I can acknowledge that if that starts to suffer, it is a clear indication that either A) I am on deadline and it is a VERY temporary situation or B) something is off.

So I sometimes have to give up OTHER things.

Things like:

- Baking all our own bread instead of buying it
- Growing a huge vegetable garden
- Canning
- Knitting complex projects
- Making all of our cleaning supplies and personal care products
- Cooking every meal from scratch using kind of elaborate methods
- Creating really complex unit studies
- Doing more art projects
- Teaching co-op classes
- Facilitating our co-op
- Handling most household chores on my own

Now here's the thing — those are all things I like doing.
But I don't like them more than I like being a sane and calm mama. So during busy work seasons, I need to let stuff like that go a bit.

I have seen these cycles play out again and again, and I have learned that it all comes down to expectations and releasing guilt.

If you are a working homeschooling mama, you need to embrace that contribution you are making to your family, and you need to get OK with letting some stuff go, at least for a little while.

It might literally be one thing. It might be a lot of things.

It definitely has to include the guilt, though, about what you aren't doing. Because that's the key, I think, to being a happy, homeschooling, working mom.

As homeschooling mamas, we are ALWAYS working for our families. That work may look different on different days or in different seasons.

And whatever we do for our families is important and valuable. But so is our own peace. We can't do it all. We can do what we can well, and let the rest go for now.

How?

Making it all work

My husband took a day off so I could work on my chapters for this book. Even 18 months ago, that would have seemed crazy to us. It's taken time for us to figure out how to balance everything – for my work to feel real and not just something to squeeze into nooks and crannies.

So as I sit here at Panera reflecting on how we got to this point, it occurs to me that although it isn't perfect, I think we're figuring out a way to make my work... work as part of our homeschooling life.

This is not to say that we don't have hard days. Yesterday, lunch was French fries. But most of the time now, I feel like we manage pretty well.

Here's what I can recommend if you are a working homeschooling parent, or if you are considering becoming one.

Homeschooling

- Create a schedule. We don't do super structured homeschooling here, but we have a basic plan for each day and for the week.

- Do school early. First thing if it works for you. If not, set a time to start and do not push it back unless it's an emergency.

- Manage your resources — classes, co-ops, programs, etc. You don't have to do it all on your own.

- Choose the right curricula. Make sure the books and programs you use are working well for your family. Are you spending hours each week planning? Could you be using that time differently?

- Encourage some "independent study." This is easier with older children, but try a math program like Teaching Textbooks, or help your kids choose books to read on their own.

Work

- Find a job you actually like. I know. If only it was that easy, right? But I've tried a lot of things in the past few years, and only one has really worked. Is it a coincidence that it's the only one I've really enjoyed?

- Think about working from home. One of the things that keeps me going is the flexibility of my current job.

- Even better, see if you can be your own boss. If not, see if you can find an accommodating boss who will grant you autonomy.

- Create a schedule. I try to stick to my weekly schedule. Sometimes that's tricky — sometimes people I need to coordinate with are only available at certain times. But having a schedule is a lifesaver when it comes to finding balance and switching gears.

Parenting

- Talk to your kids about work. Explain what you do and why.

- Set expectations. "When Mom is on the phone, I need you to be quiet and keep the dog from eating the cat."

- Stick to your schedule. When you say you'll be done with work for the day, try to be done. Learn to walk away from the undone.

- Don't drag work around all the time. Smartphones can make work easier — we can send emails from the park, and check texts 24/7. In my experience, this is a great-terrible thing.

- Get your spouse on board. You need support to make this work.

- Consider outside help. Even three hours a month can make a difference.

- WAIT. I know. This is terrible advice. But I have found that as my kids get older, working from home is SO MUCH easier. I never could have done what I do now even 2 years ago.

Putting it all together

- Single-task. Whatever you're doing, be present and do it.

- Decide what's your priority. For me, it goes relationships, school, work. Homeschooling is important to me, but even more important is being a mom to my kids.

- Be realistic. Decide how much you can work without losing your mind. Don't push yourself to that limit every week.

- Take care of yourself. The moms I know who work and homeschool say their biggest struggle is having zero alone time. Schedule it if you have to. Showers should be a non-negotiable.

- Take care of your marriage. I think all parents struggle with this whether homeschooling and work are involved or not.

- Be kind to yourself. Don't expect to be able to stretch in five directions. Order a pizza. Leave the laundry and watch a movie.

Finally, know that it's never going to be perfect. So don't try to make it perfect. Keep in mind that you're setting an up-close example for your kids of how to be flexible, how to prioritize and how to do your best, even when it's hard.

Being a working homeschool parent can provide its own unique lessons. And remember, bad days happen, but that's what's wonderful about homeschooling — we can always begin again tomorrow.

The Overwhelmed Highway
Kristi Clover

I've recently been taking a ride on the "Overwhelmed Highway." My world feels like it's spinning, and I am prone to motion sickness. Not a good combination.

It's so hard for me to admit when I'm feeling overwhelmed. I like to put on a good face and encourage everyone else. I feel like admitting that I have days that feel crazy might discourage someone from wanting a large family or from homeschooling. That is usually the first conclusion that people jump to anyway:

"Oh, you're feeling overwhelmed, you should think about putting your kids in public school."

"You poor thing. I hope you aren't thinking about having more kids. Five is too many. You know, there are things you can do to prevent 'that.'"

Comments like that don't really help. They usually lead me to hide in my pantry to cry, spoon in hand, with my open container of mint chip ice cream.

Everyone gets overwhelmed, right? I felt overwhelmed at times even before having kids! Back when I had baby #1, I felt overwhelmed, too. The year and eight weeks I had my kids in public school, I had moments where I felt overwhelmed.

I know it's a season right now. Recovering from the 6 to 8 weeks of practically no sleep doesn't help things either. But like it or not, I have to get through this season. (I should note that our 2-month-old is a great sleeper and my easiest baby, but still a new baby).

I feel like, overall, I've been managing things pretty well. But it just takes so little to knock me out of sorts and suddenly I lose control of the order, and then chaos ensues.

Where is this all coming from? Well, having lots of kids, homeschooling, and running a household! But lately so many other things have me spinning.

- **My house:** I'm an organized person, but right now my house doesn't reflect that. Right now, well, it looks more like we are studying World War II in our home – a reenactment. And as silly as it might sound, I also feel like my cleaner only complicates my life. Yes, I have a cleaner who comes every other week. Yet, since the house doesn't stay clean for two weeks, I'm still cleaning it. Plus, I have to clean up all the clutter and mess before she gets here (ironic, isn't it?). Cleaning is the easy part once all the clutter is picked up. Plus, she comes early in the morning which makes for really crazy mornings. We have to strip beds, wash the sheets and get tidy, oh, and start school and all our other normal morning things.

- **Hosting friends and family:** I love entertaining, and I love family and friends. It's really not a burden at all to have people come and stay with us. But I do try to let things go (errands, emails, calls, etc.) while we have friends and family over, and that tends to get me behind on things that need to get done.

- **Kids:** We have some discipline issues that need to get addressed. This is pretty normal when a new baby comes home. Everyone is so excited, but confused as to how their roles change and gets redefined. My 2-year-old is no longer the baby. We tried to prep her for being a big sister, but until baby comes, it's not fully understood. All in all, we've let things slide and it's time to get on top of it. This, of course, requires time and patience and a ton of consistency. Discipling (not just disciplining) takes time.

- **Homeschooling:** Homeschooling is SO hard at this stage – toddler and newborn plus homeschooling kindergarten and fourth and fifth grades is tricky. Everyone needs help, and it seems they all need it at the same time. Mainly, it's my sweet 2-year-old who makes things a bit complicated. That's why I own almost every homeschool conference CD on getting things done with toddlers.

- **Eating:** I've quite the belly right now. Yes, I know it's because I just had a baby, but my post-partum body is driving me crazy. I still look pregnant. I'm still nursing, so I can't go too overboard with my diet. But I can start eating with more moderation and not downing a third of a bag of Double-Stuf Oreos. I know that's not helping. I'm justifying the Oreos being in the house, because we are studying M for Moon. Nothing illustrates moon phases better than Oreos. :) Plus, I have added guilt about how others are eating. My friend has gone gluten-free, not for weight loss or celiac disease, but because our wheat is all contaminated with all the genetically modified chemicals. So, I thought to myself, "Am I poisoning my kids by giving them whole grain bread? Maybe I should go and get organic wheat berries. That way I can grind it and make our own bread." You know, with all the extra time I have on my hands.

- **Exercise** (or lack thereof: I need to find time to walk or do something, too. It's so good for my body, but also my overall mental health. Getting outside and moving always helps. But when time is short and my hubby's schedule is crazy (meaning I have no childcare), it's hard to squeeze it in.

All that, and throw in a building project in my backyard, and my sweet puppy of 12 years dying last week, and you have the perfect storm for being overwhelmed.

So, where do I go from here?

Well, right now I'm clinging to the Lord for strength and to His truth. He promises that He is strong in our weakness (2 Corinthians 12:9 and 10).

People often misquote 1 Corinthians 10:13 when they say, "Oh, the Lord will never give you more than you can handle." The truth is that He does give us more than we can handle! He specializes in that! He wants us to reach the end of our strength so we have to rely on His strength.

So, today I'm just telling myself these four things:

1. Take things one step at a time. I'm living moment by moment. God gives us what we need for each day — for each step — nothing more. So, I'm trusting in His Word and His strength for the day. My daily bread!

2. Ask for help (and prayer) when I need it. I'm trying to do a better job of asking for help and accepting help when people offer. It's okay to admit that I'm not a supermom.

3. Try to find the humor when the day throws a few wrenches into my schedule. Learning to laugh when life gets crazy helps me to keep things in perspective. Perspective is important. I'm really quite blessed. My problems are first-world problems.

4. Pray, pray, pray! His plan for the day, not mine! His strength, not mine! The more my knees stay dirty, the more I can find joy in the chaos.

I'm really just trying to remind myself that this is a season. Yes, it seems to be a season that I find myself in a lot, but it is really just for a little bit. My kids are growing — faster than I'd like. Someday my house will be quiet and really easy to keep clean. So, for today, I'm trying to find the joy and blessing in the craziness.

"We are hard pressed on every side, but not crushed; perplexed, but not in despair; persecuted, but not abandoned; struck down, but not destroyed."
2 Corinthians 4:8 and 9

"For our light and momentary troubles are achieving for us an eternal glory that far outweighs them all. So we fix our eyes not one what is seen, but on what is unseen. For what is seen is temporary, but what is unseen is eternal."
2 Corinthians 4:17

(I think Paul was really tired when he wrote 2 Corinthians. So many great passages for me to glean from in this season.)

Mary Poppins' Advice For Homeschooling Little Ones

Michelle Morrow

"Precision and order, that's what children need." - Mr Banks

I'm sure you realize now that everyone has an opinion on how you can homeschool better when you have small children. You've probably had lots of practical tips about: establishing a better routine, cutting out all socialization with friends (aka fun), putting things away, eating a better diet and being firmer with the children. And I agree all this precision and order will help. Unfortunately, at the end of the day, it is all brimstone and treacle advice when you're drained of energy and your heart isn't in these Mr. Banks solutions.

Homeschooling with little ones is exhausting. And let me say outright: It is difficult! Everyone talks about all the glories of homeschooling and how to actually get it done, but in the first years with young ones, it does take a great deal of effort to make it happen. In my early days of homeschooling I kept a journal of all my struggles and victories along the way. Here's an entry:

> "I feel completely overwhelmed with my task... to be perfectly honest I feel like I can't

do it. God I know homeschooling is a great thing but in practice it doesn't seem workable." 2002.

As I write this chapter, it is exactly 13 years ago since I made that entry into my journal. I was completely worn out and bedraggled. I lacked sleep and felt overburdened and anxious. While I had a good set of friends, none of them were homeschooling and so I had no one to talk to who understood. My family was not close by and my husband was wonderful and helped when he could, but he wasn't there during the day.

"A spoonful of sugar helps the medicine go down." - Mary Poppins

My, how things have changed since then! As I look back on the past 14 years of homeschooling, I can see some spoonfuls of sugar that helped me get through those tiring days. Please take my remedies as kindly meant and be generous with yourself during the years you are homeschooling with babies and toddlers.

Enjoy some sweet slumber. Find time for a sleep during the day if possible. I slept in the afternoon for the first few years of homeschooling. When the baby went for a nap, I went for a nap also. (Don't use this time as a time to rush around and do things.) All my kids were trained to have an afternoon rest time. It was not a TV time, but rather a time in their rooms with books or LEGO. They were not allowed out for at least half an hour. When they came out, they had to play quietly. I was usually dead to the world as soon as my head hit the pillow. It was a big sanity-saver for me.

Kindly excuse yourself from external activities. This can seem hard to do, especially when people depend on your help. It is a transition to start homeschooling, and

I found that I needed to reduce my other commitments. That may mean not attending morning Bible studies or giving up activities that are not working for all the kids. Plan to be home so that you can establish a good routine. Later on, when your kids are more settled, you may be able to start introducing extra activities again.

Relax about the housework. Homeschooling can be a messy business, and for the meticulously clean, this can be a great source of anxiety. Neat homeschool moms tell me that good routines for housework are your best friend. Get a cleaner if you can (it's cheaper than private school). I also used the dryer whenever I needed to, and washed in big batches so that I had a few wash-free days. I know if you are a "cleany" you will think "But a cleaner won't do it properly!" My advice would be give them something they can do, like vacuum, iron or wash the floors. You can then have more time to do the other things.

Treat yourself to some private thoughts. Keep a journal to reflect and capture your ideas. When you feel isolated and lonely, when you want to tell someone who cares (and you can't find anyone), tell the pages of your journal.

Let's go fly a kite with Michael Banks

Slow down; this is a marathon, not a sprint. I have seen so many new homeschooling mothers beat themselves over the head for not doing "enough schoolwork." Interruptions happen. You do not need to do more than one hour per day when they are 5 and 6. Work out what you want to achieve daily in school lessons with your child and put all the resources in that box. Be realistic. If you have some writing activity and a little bit of a math game, put it all there. The rest of the day can be family-oriented activities, reading books and conversational learning. If you only manage to do sit-down academic work three or four days a week, that's OK. I left one day per week for my first eight years of homeschooling as my day off; a day to fly kites, socialize and/or do some errands.

Choose family-friendly curriculum. By this I mean something that is going to work for your family. Here is another journal entry:

> "My heart's desire is to homeschool and I need to call on God for more ideas... I am close to giving up if this Charlotte Mason method does not work. But I hope that this will be my breakthrough and that I will see this as a turning point and that I will continue to homeschool all my kids even through high school. I love the ideas. Help me Lord I pray."

When I changed my method to a more eclectic style based around the ideas of Charlotte Mason, we were all a lot happier. The days were now filled with short lessons, lots of books, nature study and art, and it was much more enjoyable than textbooks. A literature-based method was the turning point in my homeschool.

Changing from a traditional approach to more gentle style induces a considerable amount of fear. How will I know if I'm covering everything? Don't just take my word for it. Read about the countless number of homeschoolers who have successfully home educated without using the traditional school method. I'm not playing a cruel joke on you — it really does work. Reading aloud (and curriculums based around that) are very family-friendly as everyone can be included. I have read many books with a boomerang pillow around my waist breastfeeding a baby.

Homeschooling is not a fantasy

Stop feeling guilty. We are not perfect and when your homeschool doesn't look like a fictional family in a storybook – that's OK! Unrealistic expectations make it too easy to get caught up in our imaginary homeschooling ideals and miss the delightfulness of being with our young children. Unfortunately we shift our focus from being loving parents to task-driven, stressed out – dare I say it – crank pots. To your kids it is far more important that you give your family love than get a worksheet done or keep a spit spot home.

Our kids are not perfect either; they fight, they whine, they cling, they cry. Mommy is the most popular person around. Everyone, including Daddy, wants her full attention. Mommy feels torn every which way. When Mommy gives attention to one child exclusively, this often makes the other children a little jealous. We often interpret this jealousy as us failing to meet our child's need (and sometimes it may well be), but often we need to teach the child not to be selfish and help them understand that it's not all about them. This takes some time with immature little souls.

But it is supercalifragilisticexpialidocious

So there you have it – my spoonfuls of sugar. I know homeschooling with little ones is a very taxing experience, but it's also an incredibly rewarding time. Enjoy it as best you can. Have lots of cuddles and fun and remember it will be over before you know it! Now that I have no little children any more life seems so much easier. I'm still very busy but I no longer feel chronically tired and I get far more time to think about what I want to do next rather than being pushed from one needy child to the other.

All of these remedies will help but ultimately I found that my greatest strength for coping during these times was realizing God was helping me. Here's another journal entry;

"All this uncertainty and confusion I am experiencing is because I haven't been in worship much. I've been neglecting my quiet times. Today I saw I needed more of You... I see I need to get more passion for homeschool from You."

There is light at the end of the tunnel. Look to the Lord for strength. He knows it is tough work when you have young children and that you need a little extra tender loving care.

"The Lord God will tend his flock like a shepherd; He will gather the lambs in his arms;
He will carry them in his bosom, and gently lead those that are with young."
Isaiah 40:11

Remember with each year of homeschooling, your children get a little older, and you become a little wiser. Now my two eldest children are at university and my two youngest are in their last few years of homeschool. In four years, my homeschool journey will be over. Instead of feeling like I can't make it, I'm wishing it would never end.

"Trust in the Lord with all of your heart, And lean not on your own understanding:
In all of your ways acknowledge Him, And He will make your paths straight. "
Proverbs 3:5-6

When You're an Exhausted Mom of Many Littles

Ann Karako

Boy, do I remember the days when there were lots of littles in our home. We had five kids in an 8½-year span, so not only did I get exhausted just from running around after them all, there was the inherent exhaustion caused by that fact that my body was being used as either a home or a bottle pretty constantly for most of a decade. That is draining, y'all. As I'm sure you can relate to, if you're reading this chapter. :-)

Being that tired and just weary of it all can sure make one rethink the decision to homeschool. It is very easy to be tempted by the idea that it would be easier all around, and the kids would get a better education, if they were sent to school outside the home. But I'm here to ask you not to give up just yet. I've been through it and come out the other side, and I have lots to share about making it through this season when having so many small children can be so exhausting. First I'll give some tips and tricks I learned over the years; then I'd like to take a moment to think about what it would really be like if you sent your kids to school.

Below are my top three tips for homeschooling with littles.

1. Set a schedule

Probably the biggest thing that helped me when my children were all small was developing a schedule for our days. Now, don't discount this idea without giving me time to explain myself! Schedules may not be for everyone, but having one was a lifesaver for me.

I remember distinctly when my oldest was 17 months old and started to walk. (Yes, she really was that old. I confess I didn't exactly encourage it earlier than that... why make more work for myself?) All at once my life went from fairly sedentary to very mobile. I was no longer proactive but reactive, as I followed my little mess-maker darling around while she "explored" everything. I rapidly decided this was not working for me and called an older lady friend, who gave me some great advice: Make a schedule for your toddler.

What a difference that made. #1's day was planned, from meals to naps to activities — playpen time at 10 a.m., book time at 4 p.m., etc. — and the resulting peace, and the feeling of being somewhat in control of life again, made me a believer in schedules. So it should be no surprise that when we started homeschooling, making and following a schedule was a priority for me.

By then I had been introduced to the book Managers of Their Homes, written by Teri Maxwell. Teri is the mother of a very large brood, and she developed a system for scheduling every member of the family, with activities changing for everyone every 30 minutes. The book comes with a kit including slips of different-colored paper; you write an activity on a piece of paper, color-coded to each individual, and move it around on a grid until you are able to design the best routine for everyone. You can plan for mom to work on math with Jimmy at 10 a.m. and then with Jane at 10:30 a.m., while big sister does spelling and baby takes a nap. Then later the older children can be scheduled with something they can do quietly and independently while Mom nurses the baby (something I always preferred to do in peace and privacy.) The book is a wealth of information and good ideas.

I still have my schedule from 2002, when I had kids in second grade and kindergarten, and a 4- and 2-year-old, and was pregnant with #5. (That must've been the first year I made a spreadsheet on the computer, rather than playing around with colored slips of paper.)

There was some variation within each time unit, but mostly it was pretty tightly configured. The afternoon was similarly scheduled, and there was little to no "free" time overall. (More on that shortly.)

I forget how many times it actually happened the way it was planned out on paper. I'm guessing not many. :-) There's no way to predict teething and fevers and doctor visits and temper tantrums and phone calls from long-winded relatives. But it gave me something to aim for.

Each year, before the school year started, I would make a new schedule similar to the one above. At the time, it was what I needed to do to keep my sanity and the young children from constantly coming into conflict with one another and the house relatively picked up. I'm guessing if I had it all to do over again, I'd still do something similar. I don't do chaotic well, even today.

Although, for the record, I TRIED living without a schedule sometimes, I really did – I think it was in the name of feeling like I deserved a break. And what invariably happened was that we all got cranky. When the kids got to decide what they wanted to do all day, they would actually complain more. They'd get into more arguments, they wouldn't take good naps, the chores would not get done – and I would be stressed. The "break" was actually more irksome than the schedule.

You see, one of the reasons that having a schedule is so helpful during these years is that it keeps the children from making too many decisions for themselves throughout the day. Yes, you did read that right. In my opinion, small children are too young to be able to handle the power that comes from too much self-determination. As they decide more and more things for themselves, such as what they will do all day every day, it seems that they also begin to feel that whether or not they will obey Mommy is something they can decide for themselves. Giving small children a schedule to follow is one very practical way to teach them the habit of obedience. And when we don't have to deal as frequently with obedience issues, all of life becomes less exhausting!

Let me just point out an example of what I'm saying. On the schedule above, you'll see that in the morning, the children are scheduled for "sleeping/books on bed." In our house, when the children awoke, they were not allowed to get out of bed right away. We showed them what 7:30 looked like on the clock, and until that time, they were to "read" books on their beds. This meant that the house stayed quiet for those who were still sleeping, and I was not required to be in full combat mode (in a manner of speaking) until a specified time each day. It was much less stressful to know that the beginning of my day was determined by me and not by my children.

Yes, it takes time and thought to make a schedule, and it often needs to be tweaked and re-tweaked; but it gave me a place to start. It gave a greater sense of order to our day, rather than randomness. It gave the kids a routine to follow so there would not be "discussions" about everything we did. I would recommend making a schedule to any mom who is feeling overwhelmed or exhausted.

2. Create quiet time

Probably the second biggest sanity-saver for me was our daily habit (without fail) of having quiet time in the afternoon. This was a time when everyone spent at least an hour (and very likely, two hours) on their beds or in their rooms (depending on their age) during the time that was the younger children's naptime. The children who were too old for naps played quietly or read books, but everyone was required to stay in their rooms for the appointed time.

This gave me a much-needed break. If I was physically exhausted, I could stretch out on my own bed for a while. Or I could spend some time in my Bible and prayer. Or I could start dinner, or pick up the house, or even just sit and read a book.

And believe it or not, it also gave the kids a break. Their own emotions and bodies and personalities benefitted from time alone, when they were not expected to do anything (other than be quiet) or talk to anyone. I made certain they were all in separate places; those that shared a room took turns either being in the bedroom or on the sofa. With creativity, you can find a spot for everyone. We all came back together after the afternoon quiet time with a better ability to get along and be productive and cheerful.

3. Stay in

This one is in third place only by a very small margin: I did not schedule us for very many activities outside the home. I can't stress this enough. Young children do not need the structured activities outside the home that today's advertisement-based culture says they do. Children need time and space to be creative and imaginative, and they can do that in the comfort of their own homes. They need love and rest and healthy food, all of which is best found at home.

Not to mention that it is exhausting for mom to have to get everyone dressed in clothing and shoes that are acceptable for public display, then into and out of car seats multiple times, refereeing squabbles from behind the wheel and being sure to bring enough snacks and drinks for all to stay happy while away from the house. Trips into public restrooms with multiple children are enough to raise any mom's blood pressure. If you're anything like I was, then the children see Cranky Mommy much more often while doing these supposedly beneficial activities than they do when everyone stays home.

We did go to our homeschool co-op once per week (when everyone was healthy), and church, but other than that, we stayed home. I gave up women's Bible studies and other activities for myself, too, because doing them often meant carting the kids with me to put them into nursery yet another time. Why does today's culture consider that for me to sacrifice my own activities for my kids' best interests is a bad thing? When the kids grew older, I was able to add some of these things back into my life. But when they were small, even I was happier to stay home.

More ideas to lighten the load

There are also a few other things that come to mind that helped make things run more smoothly when our house was full of littles. These are in no particular order.

When it comes to homeschooling small children, be sure you know the laws of your state. You might find them easier to live with than your own preconceptions about what school for these years should look like. For instance, in my own state of Missouri, the child does not have to be officially schooling until the year they have turned age 7 before September 1. This was huge for me. That meant no recordkeeping, no lesson plans, and no grades, until my son was starting third grade (he has a late September birthday). This really lightened the work load for me for several years. Maybe your state is similar. Why do more work than you have to? :-)

Early elementary children do not need to have instruction in all of the subjects that older children do. I concentrated mostly on reading and math for those years, with the other subjects being very lightweight. Many times we did not have any formal curriculum for history or science; we just read books that included them, or we drew pictures about them, or we watched The Magic School Bus and other videos. When there are lots of littles around, it helps to do as many "group" subjects as possible. Read-alouds are great for that.

It is never too early to start your older children down the path of independent learning. Once a child can read, he can begin to do some of his schoolwork on his own, even if only for a little time each day. For instance, those elementary math lessons are often not too difficult to understand; your typical second-grader can read them and complete the exercises with only occasional help from you. This frees you up to do whatever else you need to do.

Another really neat thing is to have the older siblings work with the younger ones. An older child can read stories to the younger ones, or play with them for awhile, or even help them with their schoolwork. This is something we built into our schedule.

Kids as young as 2 years old can help with chores. I remember one of mine at that age using the Dustbuster under the kitchen table after meals. Keeping the house clean is one of those things that can exhaust us; but many hands make light work – so use them all! But don't expect it to be truly clean.

Speaking of which, overly high expectations can drain the energy out of anyone. Young children are not going to be stellar at anything. Don't expect your kids to be even remotely close to perfect in their schoolwork, or their behavior, or their noise level, or their ability to go to sleep. Remember that life is messy. Not expecting it to be otherwise prevents a lot of heartache. :-)

I would almost put this one in the top three as far as saving myself from exhaustion goes: When there are lots of little kids around, it makes a huge difference to limit the quantity of their possessions. We lived in a small house then, so I was forced to pay close attention to the accumulation of stuff. And little kids can sure accumulate some! My final solution was to allow each child one under-bed box in which to keep what they loved. Papers, Happy Meal toys, umpteen birthday cards from relatives they didn't even know but couldn't bear to part with anyway, candy, crayons, coloring books, marbles, bouncy balls, etc., etc., all had to fit in that box or be gotten rid of. Their bigger toys like dolls and games were all strictly rationed.

Sometimes I pulled out a cardboard box and piled a bunch of playthings in it, then stuck it in a closet for several months. When it came out again, the stuff inside was greeted like it was brand new – and other stuff went into the box in its place. A decluttered home has always equated to a less-stressed brain for me.

Would putting them in school really solve the problem?

Personally, I don't believe that putting the kids into school will help solve the exhaustion problem. By putting them into school, you are setting yourself up for the need to get everyone up early in the morning, dressed, fed, lunch packed, and ready to leave – before the sun is even over the horizon. You are now driving them every day to their school (or schools, depending on their ages). Then you still have the younger ones to care for at home – and right in the middle of naptime, you have to go pick up the older ones to bring them back. Then there are all of the school activities – band and choir concerts, sporting events, etc., to be fit in betweentimes, with younger children in tow. That all sounds even more exhausting to me; especially because it is a commitment that I cannot change or get out of at my own discretion. At least with homeschooling, the daily schedule can be adapted to fit the needs of the entire family.

But maybe it's not the exhaustion itself that is the concern; maybe it's the seeming results of the exhaustion: the kids aren't being schooled well because Mom just can't keep up and is perpetually tired. I get that; I really do; but I think this is when we need to remember some of the non-obvious results of putting the kids in school. For instance, your children are now surrounded all day long by peers who may actually present examples of disobedience and disrespect. Your children are now being taught in a classroom with at least 20 other children, so individual attention is at a minimum. Your children are now being indoctrinated by government programs such as Common Core and sex education (at younger and younger ages, it seems).

For us, this was always the crux of the matter. I did not want my children's character development to be negatively affected by putting them into a school outside the home. I felt that even with all my inadequacies as an exhausted mom, home was a better place for them to be. Just the thought of all the wrong thinking and behavior obtained at school, which I would have to correct in the very few hours they would be home, was enough to make me think that homeschooling while chasing littles was a walk in the park by comparison.

Let me leave you with just one more piece of encouragement: I've been there. I know how difficult it is. I know the meltdowns, and the messy house, and the wishing things could be easier, and the incredibly desperate longing for the opportunity to just go pee by myself without someone knocking on the door or starting to cry somewhere down the hall. But with all of that, I can also say that I made it through – and if I could, then you can, too! – and I am so glad I persevered with homeschooling. They say motherhood is the hardest and best thing you will ever do. I'd have to say that homeschooling is a very close second in both categories. It is hard; but it is worth it. Hang in there.

It's true what they say, that you'll blink and your kids will be older. Be sure that who they are when they are older is someone you want to see after the blink.

How to Cope When Homeschooling Means Isolation for Mom

Sara Jordan Panning

"Sara? Sara?"

I was waiting at the doctor's office for my appointment, one of the rare occasions that my kids weren't with me. It took me a few seconds to realize that the nurse was calling my name. You see, I usually go by "Mama" at home. It had been so long since I'd heard someone call me by name that I'd almost forgotten what it was!

Has this ever happened to you? As a homeschool mom, it can be all too easy to lose our individual identity and forget what it's like to interact with our own set of friends, rather than just our kids. If you're an introvert who has just moved to a new state and you don't know anyone in the area, it's even worse!

I knew we would be heading into lonely territory when we moved. Living rurally with three kids age 10 and under in combination with my own chronic illness issues and my daughter's autism is a recipe for isolation. I had to develop some coping strategies very quickly to maintain some balance in my life.

5 Ways to Cope When You're on Your Own

Focus on the positive. The truth of the matter is, sometimes life is just plain hard. We end up in less than ideal situations. It's during those times that we need to give ourselves a pep talk (yes, you're allowed to talk to yourself!) and remember that "this too shall pass." Children grow so quickly. Circumstances change. You will find friends, or at least peace in the waiting. It won't always be this way.

Keep a journal (or blog). When you have no one else to talk to, put your thoughts and feelings into the written word. It doesn't have to be public like a blog, but just a simple journal for yourself. Use this time alone to get to know yourself. It can help you work through your fears and doubts and gain confidence in your own abilities when you see your strength shining through your written words. It might one day become a keepsake for your children as you record this time. Or it might just be an outlet with the freedom to be completely honest without ever showing it to anyone. Maybe you can even turn it into a best-selling book to help other homeschool moms one day!

Find online support. Sometimes getting out just isn't an option, so you have to improvise. I've been blessed to meet many fellow homeschool moms over the years through online resources. In the beginning, it was through Yahoo groups. Now I belong to Facebook groups and forums. Even if you never meet in person, you can form friendships that last for years. (I have been able to eventually meet some of my online friends in person and it was great fun.) You might feel like a pioneer all alone in the homeschooling wilderness, but the Internet really does make it a small world. Reach out and connect online!

Think outside the box. Homeschoolers are good at that! If you are able to get out, but there are no homeschool groups in your area, try starting your own. Check out the story hour at your local library. You're likely to find other moms there who would enjoy some social interaction. You can also look for like-minded moms at MOPS meetings (Moms of Preschoolers) or AWANA or even local scouting groups. If you really want to talk to other moms, don't limit yourself to just homeschool moms or those with kids your own age.

Pray. I can't make a list about anything without including this one. If you lack the opportunities for adult conversation right now, you can turn to the One who is always listening. Use the solitary time to deepen your faith. Even if things are chaotic, you can still talk to God. He can hear you above the sounds of children crying or being rambunctious. He can hear your heart even when you don't know what to say.

Are you lacking adult conversation time right now? Do you feel alone on this journey? Don't be afraid to reach out and ask for help!

A Lonely (but not so lonely) Homeschool Journey
Monica Lynn

The decision to stay-at-home with our son and newborn twin babies came easily after daily regret of leaving our little boy every day for the previous two-and-a-half years as I headed off to work. I eagerly anticipated the adventure of spending each day with our three children and knew it would be exciting. Since it was uncharted territory for me I anticipated some difficulties, however I wasn't prepared for the loneliness that accompanied the journey.

Shortly into my new role as stay-at-home mom I cried tears of distress as sleep and adult company became a thing of the past. I didn't regret my decision to be home with our sweet little babes as I cuddled, loved and delighted in them. Yet, it was turning out to be a very challenging time of transition.

For the previous 16 years I woke up every day, got ready for work, and headed off to complete something meaningful alongside my colleagues and peers. I welcomed the feeling of reward as I completed a project, provided a service, developed a program or offered someone a new career opportunity.

Not every day was necessarily exciting but I developed relationships with men and women as we worked towards the same goals. There was unity, a feeling of togetherness, with many of whom I would call "friend".

And then one day that abruptly ended. Gone were the days of team projects, No longer was I recognized for good work, given a pat on the back for a job well done, gaining a "win" when I found the perfect candidate for our organization or paid for many long hours of work.

Instead, I was up to my eyeballs in laundry and poo, with seemingly no opportunity to see friends and colleagues, and a husband gone working two jobs. In my frazzled state, it seemed like the only "win" I got was when I actually got to take a shower that day or maybe got a few hours of sleep the night before. And the only pay I could think of was what I received in the form of a dirty diaper.

I did my best to get together with people who I could have a meaningful conversation with but the sheer demand of mothering and coping with the transition (did I mention we had just moved two weeks before the twins were born?) kept me from fully experiencing relationships with other adults in a way I wanted and needed. Yet our three children kept me busy enough that I didn't have much time to think about it.

Fast forward a couple of years to 2012 when we made the decision to homeschool our oldest at four-and-half-years-old. This bright little guy had already been reading for a year and a half, was soaking up information like a sponge and was eager to consume more. We felt that homeschooling would be the best option for him, allowing him to learn at his own, very rapid, pace.

I knew walking down this unpopular path would be difficult and although at that point I was much more comfortable in my role as stay-at-home mom, I still experienced challenging days. Yet even with all my doubt and hesitancy I knew that's where God was leading us and I couldn't ignore what He was asking us to do. I was apprehensive, yet excited, about this new adventure and what the future would hold.

That year turned out to be one of the hardest. I was trying to figure out homeschooling, potty train two very busy two-year-olds who got into everything, keep up with a very inquisitive and eager learner and not getting a whole lot of sleep in the process. And at that point, not only was I lacking regular adult contact but I also didn't personally know anyone else who was homeschooling their children.

All the local homeschool groups, at least the ones I knew about, began when a child was five-years-old or in kindergarten. Even though our oldest was working on kindergarten work and beyond, age-wise he wasn't old enough for us to join. Reading homeschool blogs was my saving grace as I saw that women online were successfully homeschooling their children. They proved to me that I wasn't alone even though I often felt like I was.

The following year I began to build confidence in our decision to homeschool as I built relationships with other homeschool moms through a homeschool group we became a part of. By the end of the school year I had made some connections and didn't feel nearly as alone. And now, a couple of years later, I have developed and strengthened even more friendships.

Earlier this year, my local community of homeschoolers was nearly disbanded when the church decided to eliminate the program. Many of the moms were devastated by the news, myself included, because this was where our children saw their friends and where we saw our friends. During this trying time, as we waited to see what would happen, I realized how important this homeschool community has become to me and how truly critical it is for our homeschool success.

Thankfully, two fellow homeschool moms were so determined to keep the community together that they were willing to spend hours upon hours to create a new parent-run program that mirrors the previous program. They saved it because that is how important community is to them. Those of us still involved have been willing to volunteer our time to keep the program going and the community together.

Community is what provides a feeling of belonging and a sense of togetherness. Before I found a community of homeschoolers, I knew it was important, longed for it and prayed for it. Yet, it wasn't until I found it that I realized how critical it was for our homeschool success, for building friendships and for my mental well-being.

Maybe your experience is similar or maybe you are in the midst of searching for other women you can connect with as you walk through this journey of homeschooling. Either way, I'm guessing you'll agree that community is important.

But what exactly are the benefits of joining a homeschool community?

- Developing friendships
- Sharing stories
- Making connections
- Discussing curriculum
- Brainstorming solutions for issues that arise
- Spending time together

If you are interested in finding a local homeschool community, you can search online for local homeschooling groups or check with your church.

Although developing in-person relationships is wonderful, you might not have a local homeschool community available to you. If that isn't an option for you, then there are some wonderful online communities that you can become a part of. I am not familiar with all the communities that are out there, but here are some that I am a part of:

- iHomeschool Network - You can link up with other homeschoolers via social media platforms such as Twitter, Google+ and Instagram.
- Confessions of a Homeschooler (COAH) Community
- Facebook communities for individual curriculum choices.
- Homeschool Scopes Periscope Facebook Community

You can make connections and spend time together with fellow adults in many other ways too.

- Join a Bible study or other group
- Become more involved in your church
- Become active on social media - I did not take full advantage of this in the early years and I know it would have been helpful to me. Social media can be a time sucker and if abused can take time away from your family. On the flip side, if you use it responsibly you can develop connections with others as you become part of an online community.
- Get together with friends for field trips - with full schedules it can be difficult to coordinate this but keep communication open and remain flexible. Getting together with other homeschool families can be refreshing for both you and your children.
- Get together with friends on the weekends
- Hire a babysitter and go out on a date with your husband

Even with a homeschool community and other friends and connections, there are still days when I struggle with loneliness, sadness and frustration. Many days I love what we are doing and why we are doing it but other days are incredibly challenging. When those days come, I know I need to take positive action, even when I don't feel like it.

As a Christian, the most worthwhile and effective solution for me is reading God's Word and spending time in prayer. Stepping away and going to my room (or the bathroom where I can lock the door) and sharing my heart with the Lord, pouring out my burdens and frustrations to the only One who can calm my soul is beyond compare. However, I often follow up prayer with a simple, practical action because combined it can completely transform my day.

Here are some other ways you can put joy back in your day when you are feeling alone or frustrated (these are my favorites):

- Get out of the house and take the kids to the library or book store
- End the school day early and go to the park or the zoo
- Listen to music
- Open the windows
- Call a friend
- Complete a fun activity with the kids
- Sit on the couch, snuggle with the children and read books together
- Write in a gratitude journal

It is my hope and prayer that you have a community of people, whether in-person or online, that can support you through this homeschooling journey. We are built for community and living life together so that when the tough seasons come we will have others there to support us and we can do the same for them. Especially when we are choosing the path less traveled. The one that is filled with obstacles such as loneliness, doubt, insecurity and criticism. But when we put our trust in the Lord and our arms around each other we can do this wild and wonderful thing called homeschooling.

**Note: There are times when loneliness and sadness cannot be helped by a simple, practical solution. Many physical and psychological causes can affect a women and should never be ignored if they last for longer than two weeks or cause someone to feel utterly hopeless. In those cases, contacting a professional is the most appropriate action.

Fighting Fears with Faith
Sara Jordan Panning

Today I found lost toys. I made art projects. I cooked meals. I answered questions and homeschooled my kids with a thankful heart and a passion to raise up the next generation in truth and knowledge. I gave hugs and kisses. I smiled and encouraged and reassured. I did it all with true joy in my heart. It was a good day.

I can slay giants. At least my daughters think so.

But tonight, when the house is finally quiet for the first time in almost 18 hours, and I am utterly exhausted as I lay down to sleep, the fears and doubts creep in.

- Did I do enough?
- Am I able to meet the challenge of not only raising, but educating, my children?
- Am I missing something?
- Am I enough?

That's because I can clearly remember the days that I faced giants that I couldn't tackle: the giants of second-guessing my decisions, of losing my patience, of feeling worn-out and inadequate to the task. I can name each instance of failure, sometimes with much more accuracy than I can acknowledge and name the successes.

Deep down, I believe that in the end, with the perspective of time, those feelings evaporate in the light of the overall accomplishment of a life well-lived. But how do I fight those feelings of inadequacy in the day-to-day of it all while I'm slogging through it?

I pick up the five smooth stones of faith with which to slay the giant of inadequacy.

What do those five smooth stones represent? Truth. Hope. Wisdom. Love. Joy. I've found these verses from Philippians to be a constant source of encouragement:

Truth

I know what it is to be in need, and I know what it is to have plenty. I have learned the secret of being content in any and every situation, whether well fed or hungry, whether living in plenty or in want. I can do all this through him who gives me strength.
~ Philippians 4:13

Hope

Not that I have already obtained all this, or have already arrived at my goal, but I press on to take hold of that for which Christ Jesus took hold of me. Brothers and sisters, I do not consider myself yet to have taken hold of it. But one thing I do: Forgetting what is behind and straining toward what is ahead, I press on toward the goal to win the prize for which God has called me heavenward in Christ Jesus.
~ Philippians 3:12-14

Wisdom

Finally, brothers and sisters, whatever is true, whatever is noble, whatever is right, whatever is pure, whatever is lovely, whatever is admirable — if anything is excellent or praiseworthy — think about such things. Whatever you

have learned or received or heard from me, or seen in me
— put it into practice. And the God of peace will be with
you.
~ Philippians 4:8

Love

Therefore if you have any encouragement from being
united with Christ, if any comfort from his love, if any
common sharing in the Spirit, if any tenderness and
compassion, then make my joy complete by being like-
minded, having the same love, being one in spirit and of
one mind. Do nothing out of selfish ambition or vain
conceit. Rather, in humility value others above
yourselves, not looking to your own interests but each of
you to the interests of the others.
~ Philippians 2:1-4

Joy

Rejoice in the Lord always. I will say it again: Rejoice! Let
your gentleness be evident to all. The Lord is near. Do not
be anxious about anything, but in every situation, by prayer
and petition, with thanksgiving, present your requests to
God. And the peace of God, which transcends all
understanding, will guard your hearts and your minds in
Christ Jesus.
~ Philippians 4:4-7

I realize that not everyone shares the faith that allows me
to call out the lies of feeling inadequate, or the strength and
hope to push past the fears. I would contend, though, that
we all have a longing for a sense of transcendent truth in
our lives and that denying it leads to discontentment.
There is no peace in life without faith, hope, and love.

As I drift off to sleep tonight, I will remember that the river
of life that threatens to overflow and overwhelm me at

times is the same river that shapes and smoothes the edges on those stones that help me to defeat my fears.

I do this so that tomorrow I might pick up my five smooth stones of truth, hope, wisdom, love, and joy, and slay the giants once again.

Digging deeper

- Do you fight feelings of inadequacy in your homeschooling?
- What is the root cause of those feelings?
- Can you answer back with the truth, like a favorite Bible verse or encouraging phrase to get you through the rough spots?
- What words would you write on your five stones?
- Do you feel called to homeschool? If so, then believe that you were called for a purpose!

Feeling Inadequate to Homeschool High School

Sara Dennis

I don't know about you, but I sweated buckets the summer before my oldest son started homeschooling high school.

I researched curriculum. I made detailed plans. I purchased everything we'd need for the school year.

Then, two weeks before the start of the new school year, I tossed everything aside for a completely different high school program.

I was terrified I was going to ruin my son's life.

Are you going to ruin your child's life?

I'd toss and turn in bed that he'd never make it into college. I'd forget something essential and condemn my son to a life on the streets. He'd curse my name forever.

You know, it was just like the years when we first started homeschooling.

I'd toss and turn in bed that I'd never be able to teach my kids to read, to do their math, to write a paper. I'd forget something essential and condemn my kids to a life on the streets. They'd curse my name forever.

Nothing like that ever happened.

My kids have learned to read, to do math, to write a paper. My oldest did take the SATs and get into college. None of my worries materialized.

You can teach high school subjects

Before we go farther, write down what subjects you're good at. Are you great at English, history, or science? Those subjects shouldn't be a problem for you to teach or guide your teenager through.

Now write down what subjects you're weak in. Perhaps math or science is a weak area. You always have the option of working through the course ahead of your child.

However, the good news is you don't have to teach those subjects!

Perhaps your husband loves these subjects so you can farm them off on him! Do you have a homeschooling friend who excels at the subjects you're weak in, but is weak in your strengths? All you need to do is trade subjects with each other.

Your friend can teach English literature and history. You can teach science and math. It's a win-win situation for both you and your kids.

Other options are using a tutor, enrolling your child in an online course, or finding a self-teaching curriculum for your weak subjects.

You can even check out the virtualhomeschoolgroup.org for free online courses for your teenagers.

Design your own high school courses

One of the many perks of homeschooling is the opportunity to design courses around your child's interests. Some of these courses are offered through textbooks, online, or mail.
If you simply cannot find a course that fits your needs, design your own!

You can choose the books for your teenager to read, or you can allow your son or daughter to choose. I chose the latter.

My son came home with thick, long, and dry books on his favorite subject from the adult section of the library. He then spent many happy hours in study.

I also required several written papers as part of his course. These made wonderful additions to my son's portfolio.

While your child is reading and writing on their chosen subject, do keep a list of the books read and the hours spend studying. As a rule of thumb, 135 to 150 hours of study equates to one high school credit.

Portfolios

I love portfolios. They're easy, organized, and give you a clear record of what was studied during high school.

Choose a large 3-ring binder. Divide it by subjects. Place all assignments, tests, papers, or lab sheets into the appropriate spot. Keep a sheet in the front to write all books read over the school year. By the end of the year you'll have a satisfyingly large portfolio of work to create a transcript through.

Each summer sit down and use the portfolios to create a transcript and book list for the previous year. Believe me;

it's hard to remember everything you did three years ago while filling out applications. You'll be grateful senior year that it's already filled out.

Freshman kids versus high school seniors

You would think it would be obvious, but I'm going to let you know that ninth-grade kids are still kids. They are immature, unused to a high school work load, and more child than adult.

Don't be surprised if your ninth-grade child collapses one day in agony over the aches and pains of high school level work. Drop back and reduce the workload. Seriously, you won't ruin your child's life.

Remember, babies don't turn into toddlers overnight. Nor do our young teenage kids turn into voting adults overnight.

Eventually your child will be able to handle a heavy course load. Just give them time to grow into it.

Case in point, two years after our meltdown, the same child asked me to add more work to his day. He could handle it. You know what? He did!

Don't compare

High school teens, like babies, mature and grow at different rates. One baby walks early and talks late. Another child talks early and walks late. Yet a third walks and talks right on schedule.

Teenagers are the same. Some mature early. Some mature late. Some kids excel at math and science. Others struggle.

While looking at what your friends' teenagers are doing is great for new ideas, it's horrid on the nerves. Make your high school plans based on what is right for your teenager, not your neighbor's. Don't expect your second child to be identical to your first.

Each high school teen is unique. Do what is best for your child and ignore the rest.

Check the colleges and universities for entrance requirements

Do the colleges your child wants to apply to require 3 math and 2 science courses? Or do they require a physics course at some time during high school?

Senior year doesn't give you much time to add extra courses, or frantically try to recreate your child's reading list over the past 3 years. Plan ahead, check all the schools your child may wish to attend, and plan accordingly.

In my case, I took the most stringent requirements and went from there. In addition, check to see if there are additional requirements. One school requires testing, another school requires book lists. A friend looked at a college which required a year of physics.

Check requirements now. Plans may change, but you'll be armed with the information you need to make good decisions.

Typical course of study

A full-year course, such as ninth-grade English, is awarded 1 credit. A credit is usually around 135 hours of study or completion of 75% of a textbook.

Almost all high school teens complete at least 19 credits for graduation, with college-bound teens completing 24 or more credits.

Below is a typical college-bound distribution of credits. Again, check the colleges you and your child are interested in before making final decisions about your course of study.

- English: 4 credits
- Math: 4 credits
- Lab Science: 3-4 credits
- Social Studies: 3-4 credits
- Foreign Language: 2 credits
- Physical Education: 1 credit
- Fine Arts: ½ - 1 credit
- Electives

Transcripts and diplomas

Homeschool kids are being accepted at colleges and universities all over the country. You don't need to have accredited classes on the transcripts to be accepted.

Lee Binz at The Home Scholar specializes in transcripts. She often holds free web seminars on creating transcripts. I attended one when my oldest son was in ninth grade. It's guided me on creating transcripts and courses for all my high school kids since. In addition, Lee Binz offers professional services and books if you'd like more help creating transcripts for your children.

You are allowed to issue your child a diploma upon high school graduation. Home School Legal Defense Association has a Frequently Asked Questions guide should you have any questions about legalities.

For a free diploma to give your child upon graduation, I recommend Donna Young. She has a couple different options.

You can do it!

Homeschooling high school is intimidating as you approach and plan for it. You wonder how you can teach the subjects, whether your child will receive a diploma, and whether they will move on successfully into adult life.

I'm here to tell you, you can do it! Homeschooling high school is simply another transition in the homeschool journey.

The kids gradually become independent scholars handling most of their education themselves. They're able to attend online classes, use distance courses, or create their own classes.

Homeschooled teenagers end up with a personalized education that reflects their interests. They graduate high school and move successfully into adult life.

Homeschooling High School
Ann Karako

I have been a somewhat lonely homeschooler for the past several years. It began when we chose to homeschool high school – and most of our homeschooling friends did not. True story: Out of the 20 to 30 families we knew who homeschooled back when our children were in the early elementary grades, I can think of only a handful of them that continued homeschooling through the high school years.

I confess that this bothers me.

Of course I've wondered why this phenomenon occurs – because I don't think it's specific to just my experience. In general, it seems that most families that begin to homeschool their elementary child do not continue homeschooling through high school.

I'm sure there are several reasons for this, but I have no doubt that one of the biggest is just plain fear -- fear that homeschooling high school will be too hard, that we will be inadequate to do it well. Furthermore, I think that this general fear can be broken down into three specific sub-fears that parents are concerned about:

1. Fear that they can't provide as good an education as the public school.
2. Fear of the more difficult subject matter — I mean, chemistry and calculus, yikes!

3. Fear that they will shortchange their child somehow so that he won't be prepared for college.

And I get these; I really do. The idea of homeschooling high school can be very intimidating, even for those who have homeschooled through all of the elementary years. But you know what? I can truthfully say that it doesn't have to be that hard. There is no reason to quit homeschooling when your child reaches the high school years.

In this chapter I'd like to look at each of the fears mentioned above and see if I can alleviate them somewhat. Having graduated three daughters from our homeschool, I think I have some encouragement to share. After that, I'm going to finish the chapter by explaining the 10 reasons I have LOVED homeschooling high school. I think that if you stick with me to the end of the chapter, you'll see that homeschooling high school is a very doable and wonderful thing. :-)

Fear 1: Not being able to do what the public school does.

So many people think they have to do high school at home the same way that the public schools do. Well, they are in for a pleasant surprise, because the homeschool high school experience does NOT – I repeat: NOT – have to replicate the public or private high school experience. In fact, this is one of the advantages of homeschooling high school. The state does NOT decide the specifics of what your homeschool looks like; you do. Obviously you will follow the requirements of your state's laws, but usually they provide a lot of leeway with regard to things like these:

You decide what high school courses are required for your student to graduate. You do not have to follow your local school district's requirements. You can graduate your child whenever your own requirements have been met. This is a very freeing thing. For instance, if your child has no intention of majoring in anything technical at college and does not want to take math every year, then you don't have to make them take it. And I didn't. And guess what — they got accepted to college anyway!

You decide what to give credit for. If your child is a violinist and you want to give them 3 credits per year for violin because they practice three hours a day, you are free to do so. (And I did.) If your child is spending a bunch of time learning to drive, you can give credit for that (and I did). Homeschooling high school means your child's interests and activities can be counted as part of the school curriculum, rather than in addition to it. This means you don't have to fit in as many academic credits or try to come up with a bunch of electives just to fill the schedule. See how much easier this is beginning to sound?

You decide how quickly your child must complete a given course. There is no need to rush through to be done by the end of the semester, unless this works better for you. If your child needs to spend an extra week reviewing a particularly difficult chapter, you have the flexibility to take that time. You can continue working into the summer, if need be. This is another case where you are not shortchanging your child but actually creating a better learning environment. And knowing you can take as long as your child needs, because you are the decision-maker, definitely decreases the stress level.

Guess what? No homework. Because it's all already been done during the school day. And no getting up early, either, if you don't want to. It doesn't get much easier than that! Now listen, I know what you're thinking, but just because these things seem simplistic doesn't make them any less true. And these are the type of thing that make the difference between a difficult day and a not-so-difficult one.

There are more resources now for making a success of homeschooling high school than ever before, especially because of the internet. There are online courses and online tutors, and Google is your friend to help find elusive answers. Homeschool co-ops abound; then there are conferences, LOTS of high school curricula, blogs — in short, there are plenty of ways to find support when you need a helping hand. Knowing you are not alone in this thing goes a long way towards relieving those fears of messing up or being inadequate.

Fear 2: More difficult coursework.

Yes, high school courses are more difficult than those for the earlier years. But don't forget that your students are also commensurately more able to handle the tougher stuff.

In fact, by the time they reach high school, your children will most likely have the ability to learn most things independently. That means that they will be the ones teaching themselves chemistry (or any other "too hard for me to teach" subject), not you, especially if you are careful to pick curriculum that fosters the child working on their own.

And lest you see this as shirking your responsibility, I would say that by forcing them to figure it out for themselves, you are actually doing them a valuable service. Education should be a continuous process; it does not end after high school or college. You want your child to develop the habit of processing information, occasionally working through something that may be more difficult, and coming to a place of understanding, by utilizing their own effort. It is by this process that they will be prepared to continue learning through college, during continuing education at the workplace, and later in life.

Of course, if something is just plain too much for your student to figure out, you might need to seek out someone who knows more about the subject than you do. That's really not much different than finding a doctor when your child is sick or a piano teacher when they want to learn how to play music. There's probably someone in your church, or on your street or at your hubby's work who would be willing to answer a question or two over the phone every now and again. And you'd be surprised how many questions can be answered just by Googling them. I do that a lot.

If it will help, I do have some curriculum suggestions for the subjects that most parents are most concerned about: writing, math, science, literature and foreign language.

Writing: I have come to the conclusion that high school writing doesn't have to be that hard. The big thing is just to get the student to write and to play with language. Help them to not be afraid of writing by giving them many opportunities to put their thoughts on paper. Also, make sure they have access to lots of great books, so they are exposed to great writing all. the. time. It does rub off, believe it or not.

I will also say for the record that I think thorough and fairly demanding grammar instruction – yes, into the high school years – is definitely in order. No one can be a great writer who cannot handle grammar and spelling.

And when it comes to grading the writing, it doesn't have to get super-specific. These days I just assign a number of total points for a given assignment and deduct as I see things that are not working – such as poor grammar/spelling, a flimsy introduction or conclusion, not supporting their opinion, poor transitions, etc. But mostly I am fairly generous; in fact, I have been known to add points for a particularly effective turn of phrase or creative spin.

So here are some of the homeschool high school writing curricula we've used successfully:

- **Bravewriter – Help for High School.** This course is specifically geared toward homeschool high school students and has been a big help for us. Help for High School teaches the student how to write an expository essay. What's so neat is the way it's done. The first several chapters are called "Preparation for Essay Writing," and they are filled with ideas and exercises designed to get your child to just start writing. Topics are ones the kid is familiar with, such as his own life experiences, and these chapters guide the student in getting something on paper that has creative words and sentence structures. The student also learns to look at different sides of an argument. And one of the neatest things is that they learn to look at their own writing and communicate about it.

  The second and larger section of the book gives them the tools they need to craft an expository essay. They learn how to choose a topic and analyze it, how to write a thesis statement, how to design and execute supporting paragraphs, and how to write an effective introduction and conclusion.

  The entire course is written to the student, so it is suitable for independent learning – although the parent will need to give feedback on writing samples on a regular basis.

- **Rod & Staff 9 and 10 (Communicating Effectively Books 1 and 2).** These are primarily a grammar curriculum. As I said, I think grammar is über-important, even at this age. However, these books do also include writing. There are several chapters (alternating with chapters that focus on grammar) that deal with different types of writing —

persuasive, descriptive, etc. These contain thorough instructions about how to write in each genre. What I really like is that they provide a detailed grading scale for the teacher and the student. So the teacher knows exactly what to look for, and the student knows what to work toward.

- **Lightning Literature.** I'll share more on this curriculum when I talk about the subject of literature later in the chapter, but suffice it to say here that any of the LL courses are a great way to bring more writing into your child's high school curriculum. They don't focus on writing, but most of the assignments given require some type of writing. What I like is how creative they get with their assignments. They might ask the student to write a poem about a theme in the book, or describe the setting in their own words, or write a scene from a different character's perspective. In this way the student is not bored, so they tend to write more creatively and spontaneously.

Math: There is a wide range of comfort levels when it comes to high school math. If you are less comfortable, then take advantage of all the extras that can come with a curriculum – solutions manuals, videos, online coaching, etc. Just remember: You don't have to be your child's math teacher. Consider yourself the guidance counselor who can point your student to where they need to go to find the answers they need. Here's what we used:

- **Grade 8 or 9: Elementary Algebra, by Harold R. Jacobs.** This is an engaging book with explanations that kids can follow, which means it works great for independent learning. My kids loved the comics at the front of many of the lessons (whatever it takes, right?). This is a solid Algebra I textbook. It is not cheap, but if you are going to use it for multiple children over the years, it is fairly reasonable. I have no doubt that it is no more expensive than other math curricula that are not as thorough nor understandable. Besides, unless you agree with Common Core curriculum or the "new" math – which I don't – there is no need to require yourself to buy a new or recent textbook. Math has been the same for centuries, so you can buy the book that was published in the 1970s and still know that your child is getting a good math education. Probably better, in fact.

- **Grade 9 or 10: Geometry, by Harold R. Jacobs.** Why mess with a good thing? The Jacobs Geometry is just as great a textbook as the Algebra one. Again, the kids used this mostly independently; they asked me when they had a question or couldn't understand something. But that did not happen very often, which tells me that these two textbooks did their job. I don't have the time to sit with my kids and learn every lesson with them. Buying a textbook like this means that I don't have to.

- **Grade 10 or 11: Intermediate Algebra, by Lial, Hornsby, and McGinnis.** This textbook was written to be used at community colleges. Hence it is written to the student, with thorough explanations, practice problems, and even tests built in. This textbook is down-to-earth and easy to understand. Do not buy a recent edition – no need to waste your money. Find the cheapest older one (in decent condition) that you can get. The math is still the same! As the homeschool mom, you determine what is required in your math courses. No need to bow to the pressure of having to be "current."

- **Grade 11 or 12: Precalculus, by Lial, Hornsby, and Schneider.** We had such success with the Lial Algebra 2 that we used her textbook for precalc also.

As the student reads the explanation for each lesson, there are guided problems to solve. Then a full exercise set for independent practice. My kids worked through everything independently; then I graded their tests. We also purchased the Student's Solutions Manual so they hardly ever had to ask me much of anything. Pretty handy! Again, get an older edition that fits your budget.

None of my kids has made it to calculus in high school. I did find a copy of Saxon's Calculus at a curriculum sale for not much money, so I snatched it up. My son might get there; we'll see.

Science: We use Apologia for every science course, from physical science through biology, chemistry and physics. I can't say enough good about the Apologia courses. They have all been very readable for the kids and seem to be a thorough treatment of the subject. We always buy the study guides (not sold by Apologia; I got ours at Rainbow Resource) so that lesson planning has already been done for me. These courses not only teach the subject but force the student to learn how to study for tests. I like that.

You may be wondering about labs. You know what? They don't have to be a big deal. And you don't have to do them for every level. Chemistry is the one lab course we do for the high school years; it's the easiest one to implement a lab for, in my opinion. (And you may be getting the picture now that I am all about easy!) The labs in the Apologia books are all simple to follow. You can look online for sample lab reports and use those as guidelines for your kids to write theirs. Or not. It's your call!

Literature: Yes, it's important for high-schoolers to read good literature and learn how to analyze it, but this does not have to be intimidating. Good curriculum takes much of the scariness out of it.

- **We start off with Windows to the World** (from the Institute for Excellence in Writing), which is a great introduction to literary analysis. Students read several short stories and learn about character arcs, plot graphs, etc. We follow this course with at least two from Lightning Literature, which I mentioned in the writing section. Here is a review I wrote awhile back about one of LL courses:

- **Lightning Literature: Shakespeare Comedies.** Everybody needs some Shakespeare in their education! Our eldest also did Shakespeare Tragedies, but it turns out that that course is very similar to this except for which plays are read. Each covers Shakespeare's biography, Elizabethan Theater, and other historical information. Also well dealt with are the usual subjects in literature and plays in particular, such as characterization, blank verse, irony, soliloquies, stage direction, et al. And the comedies are a great way to go for those afraid of iambic pentameter — somehow it's easier to keep track of what is happening when you are amused! One time I heard #2 actually laughing out loud while reading A Midsummer Night's Dream — now that was a homeschooling moment!

Foreign language: We did try using textbooks for some of our foreign language coursework, supplemented with computer software – but I can't say that doing it that way gives you the full audio experience you're looking for when studying a foreign language. So if you're looking for a course that the student does completely on their own yet is also closest to being in a classroom (without actually being in one), then I would recommend German 1 with Oklahoma State University. The OK State people have done a WONDERFUL job with their online high school German courses. They offer German 1 through German 4 and then AP German. The price for homeschoolers is very reasonable, considering what other online courses cost. All instruction is on the computer, but there are worksheets to fill out by hand as you watch; and all quizzes, tests, and writing assignments are done online. There are also occasional speaking tests (done over the phone or Skype), and perhaps the neatest thing is the weekly individual tutoring session (also done via phone/Skype). My son did German 1 in eight grade – so it is definitely doable. SO worth the money.

Fear 3: I will miss a requirement and my kid won't get into college

This is actually a fairly simple fear to put to rest, although you might not think so. And that's not surprising; many of the posts I read about homeschooling high school are very daunting. They make it appear that if my child hasn't read all of these 500 books or volunteered for umpteen service organizations or learned how to write a 20-page research paper, that he will never graduate from high school or be accepted to college. I get so frustrated reading this type of post, because I know it does not have to be that way. No wonder so many homeschooling families put their kids into public or private school once they hit ninth grade. If I believed even half of those posts, I would, too.

But the fact is that there is no special formula. We don't need a huge list of must-do's, the thought of which bows us down with dread, wondering how we will ever accomplish it. We can get the information we need about high school curriculum requirements for college acceptance by completing a very easy exercise that can be done for the most part online.

The best way to know what colleges expect is to just look it up. Almost every college/university has an online catalog these days. And inside that online catalog, usually at the beginning, is a section on admissions – specifically on admissions requirements. And there is where it will say how many credits of high school English the college requires, how many credits of math, of history, etc. It will even sometimes list specific courses that the admissions department would like to see the applicant to have taken in high school, like American History or British Literature. (This information is often not found in the general admissions section of a college website; it is usually only in the catalog.)

It is neither difficult nor time-consuming to pick several colleges and look up this information on their websites. You might want to check out the local community college, and then maybe a state school, a couple of private colleges, your own alma mater, even an Ivy League, if that's where your child might be headed. The idea is to get a cross-section of colleges and universities that your child might be interested in attending. If you're the organized type, you can make a chart depicting which colleges require which credits and classes. And what you will learn is that they all have different requirements.

Let me repeat that: Each and every college or university has its own requirements for what it expects to see from its applicants. There are no state laws about this, because every school draws students from many different states. Schools know that a child from one state's public school system may have been required to have so many credits of history in high school, but a child from another state may not have been required to have that many. So the colleges determine their own requirements, which may or may not match those of the state they are in.

This is very freeing! Once you understand that requirements vary by college, then you begin to realize that there is no one right way to do this high school thing. You discover how flexible a high school curriculum can be — and then the task becomes a whole lot easier.

Most eighth-grade and younger students do not know where they want to go to college, so right now this is just a data-gathering exercise. If you do happen to know that your child will be going to XYZ College, then by all means look up those requirements and plan that child's high school curriculum to meet them.

But if your child is still unsure of their college or career goals (and most are at this point), you can still get an idea of what will generally be required by most colleges and what your child needs to do to meet those requirements. You can use this information to make an overall plan of classes that will fulfill the requirements for most places.

Another interesting thing to notice, too, is that many colleges do not require a minimum number of credits even close to what the states require for high school graduation. This can also be very relieving. Frankly, I don't know why we even care about state requirements for high school graduation. I mean, they're fine to use as a reference or starting point, but it seems to me that when planning high school we tend to forget one of the great perks of homeschooling — the fact that we are in charge.

This bears repeating, even though we discussed it earlier in the chapter: We can decide how many credits our child needs to graduate and what courses he is required to take. We don't have to follow what the public school does in any regard, much less this one. Let's not make it more complicated than it needs to be. (Obviously, we do need to follow the homeschool laws in our state, but these are usually much different from public school requirements, as was also mentioned earlier.)

I believe doing this little bit of research will ease some of the fear about homeschooling high school. When we know what colleges expect, we can plan to achieve that. It is not something we need to go into blind. Colleges do not have some magical hidden process by which they decide on the fitness of their applicants. It's all there in black and white, written in their catalogs.

And it goes without saying, that if I can homeschool high school, anyone can. I am by no means an intellectual or a go-getter. I am just little ol' average me. I was afraid, too, at the beginning; but as time went on, I realized I didn't have to be.

In fact, homeschooling our kids through the high school years has been one of the highlights of our homeschool journey. I am so thankful that we committed to that goal long ago and have not departed from it since. Here are 10 reasons why.

10 great reasons to homeschool high school

1. **Our kids learn to work independently.** I've written earlier in the chapter about how I love independent learning, that I think it is one of the most important things to teach our children. Well, the high school years are when this occurs. Students that are homeschooled through high school learn to take ownership of their own schooling, doing almost everything for themselves — reading the lesson, answering the questions or working through the problems, checking their work, studying for the test, etc. This is key, because it prepares them for college, where they must take full responsibility for making sure they understand everything and keep up with the syllabus. No one will hold their hand there, or even really notice if they fall behind. Even if they don't go to college, the independent learning they practice during the high school years will instill in them a lifelong learning habit. This is a good thing.

2. **Character development remains a crucial focus.** For us, one of the biggest reasons we chose to homeschool in the first place was the character and demeanor of the high school kids around us. We were impressed with those who were being homeschooled — not so much with those who were not. My own opinion is that too many parents give up working with their child's character too early. When our kids are home for high school, we are able to see first-hand who they are becoming and help guide them to make wise choices on a daily basis. They have no opportunity to hide aspects of their character from us. We are not dependent on their teachers to tell us about their behavior; we see for ourselves and can respond accordingly. At a time in their lives when character is being solidified, this is key.

3. **Our children are not exposed to peer pressure — or at least, not as much.** This is directly related to point 2. Our homeschooled teens are able to develop their own individuality without concerns about fitting in or being popular. They can pursue things that interest them without being artificially grouped. Their innocence is protected for just a little longer. I want my kids to feel confident in who they are before they have to stand firm in an often-harsh world. And we all know that the public (and possibly private) high school can be one of the harshest places out there.

4. **Our kids have the time and opportunity to really focus on what interests them.** They can try multiple things or specialize in just one or two. Because they are homeschooled through high school, their schedule is more open for really digging into a hobby or career path. For instance, my daughter was able to practice her violin for three or more hours a day — and we could count it as high

school credit. A homeschooled teen can pursue an internship at a local employer (and work during school hours), or spend time concocting culinary masterpieces, or even start a business. Going to a school would not provide them opportunity for such focused effort.

5. **There is time to talk.** The teen years are a wonderful opportunity to talk with our children. They are thinking through so many issues at this age, and having them at home means we are there to listen and discuss when they are of a mind to share. This helps cement the relationship between child and parent, so the child knows they have a safe place to come for help. And it helps us to see their heart. This is invaluable.

6. **Sibling relationships remain important.** Having our kids home through high school meant that they had no opportunity to separate themselves from younger siblings — though they sometimes wanted to! Being together all day every day means conflict resolution gets practiced often; it is true. But it also means there is greater opportunity for doing things together and just having fun with one another. The high schoolers learn to serve the younger siblings. The younger ones don't feel left behind, and they have more opportunity to watch their older siblings' example. There is a sweetness in watching siblings interact that doesn't happen if they get sent off their separate ways every morning.

7. **There is time for reading.** If you've read my blog for any length of time, you know that I am a reader. And my kids are readers. Being home through high school means my kids have more opportunity to read for reading's sake. Of course they have assigned literature for school, but they also have more time to just pick up a book and enter another world for a

while. This is still crucial for language development, writing skill, formation of goals and ideals, and just plain entertainment. I'd rather have my kids reading than participating in gossip or other unhealthy conversation at the local school. I'd rather have them reading than doing a lot of things, in fact.

8. **We can be spontaneous.** I love this aspect of homeschooling through high school. If we want to postpone school and head to the local theme park for a couple hours, we can do it (and the lines are SHORT!). If my husband needs help hauling wood, we can all put our books down and go pitch in. If someone comes across a hilarious Jimmy Fallon clip on YouTube, we can watch it together, for a little break. Of course we try to stick to our homeschool schedule for the most part, but the schedule is not our taskmaster. Even more important for our family is the fact that we can adapt to my husband's travel for work – when he is gone we can work harder, so that when he is home we are more able to spend time with him. If my kids went away from home for school, they would not see him nearly as much.

9. **Our kids can get the rest their bodies need at this age.** There is a reason teens are known for sleeping in – because their bodies are changing and growing so much and so quickly that they need A LOT of rest. Our kids don't have to get up super early in the morning to catch the bus or be in class. If they are caught up in their work, they can even sleep in on a weekday! If their body needs sleep, they don't have to deny it and run the risk of getting sick – nor of being cranky or emotional. Teens are predisposed toward drama anyway; no need to exacerbate that due to exhaustion!

10. **Mom gets hugs throughout the day.** Don't underestimate the power of this one! My teens are

the best at seeing when I am frazzled and giving me encouragement via a hug or rubbing my back or even making lunch. And there is something about a hug from your teenager – knowing that they are choosing to show you love rather than the disrespect or rebellion that one can tend to expect from that age – it's just wonderful. Give me all the opportunities for those that I can get!

Making the choice to homeschool high school can be scary, but it is SO worth it. It is, to my mind, the best opportunity to develop a relationship with our teens that will last into adulthood. I hope this chapter has alleviated some fears and provided reasons why it can be one of the best seasons of a family's homeschooling career.

When You Feel That Public School Would Be Better

Selena Robinson

A year ago, I got to the lowest point I've ever been in my homeschooling journey. I had four young children: a toddler, a kindergartener, a first-grader and a fourth-grader. We had homeschooled from birth, but this was the first time I was attempting to teach my three oldest while working and attending college full-time myself. It was a circus.

I felt that homeschooling could not possibly be done joyfully with everything I was trying to manage, so I gave up and put my children in public school for the remainder of the school year. I thought, "Public school has GOT to be better than the kids having to deal with me like this." I was wrong.

While I'm glad I tried public school with my kids, I did learn that, for us, public school was absolutely NOT better than homeschooling, even frazzled homeschooling. If you ever feel that public school would be better for your kids, please read on to see what the public school experience was like for our family.

Public school is inflexible

It's true that spending every day with your kids can be a challenge, especially if you don't have a lot of family support. But if you think that homeschooling presents a tough schedule, I can tell you that public school is far more inflexible.

Once we started public school, all of my children had to wake up at 6:15 a.m. and be at the school by 7:05. For me, that meant waking all of them, even my toddler, and rushing around to get everyone up, dressed, and out of the door in 40 minutes. It was terrible. I found myself thinking, "This was supposed to be easier. This is definitely not easier."

Public school is a LOT of work

At our kids' school, the faculty requested that the children wear uniforms. So I suddenly found myself up to my ears in laundry that had to be washed, folded, and ironed a couple of times a week. For a mom who was used to teaching kids in their pajamas, that was a lot of additional work.

Another unexpected shift was how much effort I'd have to expend helping the kids with their homework. Instead of being able to teach all three kids together, I now had to help each child with different homework. Often, they barely remembered what was covered in class, so I had to teach the material again and then help them with the assignment. I was homeschooling even though my kids were in public school!

Public school is a huge adjustment

My children had been homeschooled from birth, so they'd never attended a daycare, a preschool, or any other kind of structured educational setting. Entering fourth grade was a real challenge for my oldest daughter, who found herself being bullied for the first time ever in life. And while bullying is, unfortunately, not uncommon these days, it was heartbreaking to see it happen to my child.

I also found that my children were starving when they got home from school. After a couple of weeks, I learned that my two oldest children were scheduled to eat lunch at 10:10 a.m. That's 10:10 in the morning. No wonder they were ravenous at 2:15 in the afternoon!

We also had almost no time together in the evenings. By the time the kids finished their homework, it was time to make dinner. Then we'd eat and it would be time to get the children ready for bed. Our normal family time in the evenings became a thing of the past. And I think we all missed it.

Why I feel that homeschooling is still better

After weighing all of the pros and cons, I decided to bring our kids back home and homeschool them again. And I'm so glad I did. They're excited about what they're learning again and I'm enjoying teaching them again.

Instead of rushing to wake everyone up at the break of day, we can relax and begin our days gradually. We still cover the same amount of work as the kids did in school, but without the stress of homework and weekly tests. My home is much more peaceful and relaxed, and the kids can spend time with their dad in the evenings without rushing off to finish their assignments.

To try or not to try?

Ultimately, whether you decide to try public school or not is completely your decision. Trying it was a good thing for me, because it finally helped me do away with all of my doubts about homeschooling. And in some cases, parents face circumstances that make homeschooling impossible. If you truly feel that homeschooling is beyond your ability right now, don't feel guilty about sending your kids to public school.

But if you're feeling like public school would be a better experience for your children, take heart. You're more than capable of providing a quality education with less stress for you and your kids by sticking with homeschooling.

By the way, if you'd like to read more about my personal experience with sending my kids to public school, see the series "The Great Homeschool Public School Experiment" at Look! We're Learning!

Feeling Under-Appreciated as a Homeschool Mom

Karyn Tripp

There are days when it seems no matter what you do, the kids are still unhappy. You take them on a big, fun field trip to the aquarium and they cry all the way to the parking lot because you did not buy them the turtle toy in the gift shop. Spend half of the day doing a big experiment with them, and they cry when asked to help clean up after it.

I sometimes wish they had even the smallest inkling of how much a mother does for her children in one day. I sometimes wish I could trade places with them for a day and be served all day long!

As moms we give up our whole lives to be parents. When we choose to homeschool those kids we lovingly brought into the world, we add another layer of self-sacrifice to the mix. We are literally giving up our chance of free time for teaching them all day. We have made this choice to better their lives, yet they don't seem to realize it or appreciate it at all!

How do we as moms deal with this frustration and not let it get to us? How do we not wallow in self-pity over this fact? We have to change our own attitudes first. We were all once children and all most likely acted the same way. I remember my own mother making remarks about us not appreciating all she did for us. I never got it, until I was a mother myself. In fact, I remember so many times thinking of my mother in awe after becoming a mother and wondering how she did all that she did! One day, our children will grow up, become parents, and look back at their lives and wonder the same things. Until then, we have to learn to deal with the here and now.

Lower your expectations

I asked my mother how she dealt with it. She told me that she had to lower her expectations for everyone around her. This made me laugh a little at first. But when you think about it, you really can only expect the most out of yourself. When we set expectations for everyone we surround ourselves with, we are almost always going to be let down. Most of the time expectations are set in our own minds without telling anyone else what they are. When we do this, we expect others to live up to something they know nothing about! How can anyone do that? Set expectations for yourself and do your best to meet them. Maybe one of those expectations could be to lose your temper a little less often with the kids. (Or maybe that is just me!)

Now, I am not saying we should not expect things from our family. Children have many things they should be required to do. We expect them to clean their room. We expect them to clear their dishes. These expectations are clear and well-known. Respect and kindness should also be something that is expected. Recognizing a mother's level of greatness and the amount of work she does in a day is not an expectation a child can realistically live up to! This is something that is learned over time. This is something they gradually begin to understand as they age and take on more responsibilities in their own lives.

Look within yourself

I think it is important for you to look within yourself. Ask yourself why you are not feeling appreciated. What areas in your life are lacking support or appreciation? Is it something you can repair on your own, or is it something that can be taught to others? Do you feel like you are of value? Sometimes when I am at my lowest points it is because I am not feeling like I am of great worth. Feelings of self-worth can come from many areas in your own life. For me, I turn to my faith. When I am grounded in my faith, I am my best self emotionally. Find what makes you feel of most worth and turn to that when you are feeling under-appreciated.

Think of parenting and homeschooling the same way as service or giving a gift to a friend. You do it because you want to. You do it because you love somebody. You do not expect anything in return. Are you homeschooling your kids so you can feel like a better person? Are you doing it for appreciation or obligation? No! You are doing it out of love.

If you feel your own needs are not being met, take some time for yourself. Maybe you and your husband can take some time away together. Or maybe it is as simple as a night out with some friends. Do what you need to heal yourself. It is so important to be whole so you can best serve your family.

Teach kids respect and hard work

Respect is such an important thing for kids to learn. I remember my dad getting so mad at my brother when he said something unkind to my mom. He said we were NEVER to talk to our mother in that way. I am not sure I had ever seen my dad so upset before. It made me realize how much he loved and respected her. Never allow your children to treat you poorly. Do not stand for it! Parents are to be valued and respected. If your children are not treating you with respect, start with that lesson first and foremost.

Kids need to be taught to value what others do for them. When you are a child, so much is done for you. You may not understand that it could be any different. Begin by teaching them to thank others. Teach them to use respectful words to those they love.

Give kids opportunities to serve others so they understand what it feels like. Giving and serving others is the best way to learn appreciation. Also, teach them to do hard work! When kids are working hard, they learn that your work is hard, too. The more often they work hard, the more they will understand it.

Find like-minded friends

Sometimes the best solution is just having friends who are in the same situation. When you have a support group, it does SO much for your emotional well-being. My homeschool friends have taught me so much and healed me in so many ways. If you do not have a group of friends to support you, find some! You may have to find an online support group to help you if you have no local groups available. Online support groups can be tremendously helpful, too. My homeschool friends are there for me to bounce ideas off of, but also they relate to the things I am going through. It is so nice to have people who are there doing the exact same things and feeling the exact same way. Even if none of you has the answer, you feel better knowing you are not alone in this!

Show them how good they have it

One last piece of advice: If nothing is working and you have tried everything, take a break and let them see how much you do for them by doing nothing for a while. Make them step in and take on your responsibilities and see how they feel. Trade places for a day. Put them in charge and you be the kid!

You are valued!

You are doing your best and you are appreciated, whether you feel it or not! You are valued and you are loved. What you are doing for your family is giving them so much more for their lives and their future. Be proud of yourself for being strong enough to make the decision to homeschool. Nobody ever said it would be easy, but it is definitely worth it.

Homeschooling When You Feel Unappreciated
Shannen Espelien

Homeschooling can be a lot of work. A lot. That work doesn't only come in the form of lesson planning and teaching, but also the emotional support and guidance for daily life.

We put our whole hearts into homeschooling, so it hurts when we feel under-appreciated.

I love my husband with all of my heart, but giving compliments doesn't come easily for him, and kids don't really understand the work that moms do until they become parents themselves.

Especially during the young years, when you are changing diapers, potty-training, and feeding a baby alongside schoolwork, the days and months can drag on with very little in the way of thanks.

The big picture

What's our goal with homeschooling? Why are we putting in all this work? What's our long-term objective?

For most of us, the big picture keeps us going. We want our children to become intelligent, resilient adults with strong morals and values. If we just wanted them to love us more than anyone else in the world, we'd probably choose something other than being their bossy teacher all day!

To keep the big picture in mind, make sure you write out your mission statement, and even better, if you can, keep it posted in a place you see often. Have a hard time getting your thoughts into a fluid statement? Write out a bulleted list of your top long-term goals instead.

In the end, working toward those big goals with your children is such a gift. You know that you are starting them on a strong foundation of knowledge, values, and family love.

Who are you trying to please?

It's a bonus to please the people around us while we are homeschooling, but ultimately most homeschoolers are trying to please their creator when teaching their children at home. If your husband doesn't verbally give thanks for your hard work, does that change how God views your efforts? When the kids complain about their math assignments, does that change how God is blessing your homeschool with guidance and light?

If God is the reason you homeschool, then He is the one who will show His mercy on you and your work.

Birds of a feather

Who knows the work of homeschooling better than other homeschooling moms? When I'm really feeling like no one recognizes the work and sacrifice I put in to our homeschool, my fellow homeschool mom friends are the perfect pick-me-up.

Other homeschool moms recognize that it's not just about the lesson plans and picking out curriculum. The amount of emotional energy we use when we are building a learning environment for the next generation is sometimes greater than the intellectual energy we use to pick out the perfect history book, or decoding the various math curriculum options.

I would even suggest that if you find a tribe of like-minded homeschooling moms, hold them close. They will be the ones to pull you through that tough month (or year!) and help you see there is hope on the other side. They will share their struggles with you, and listen to your struggles without judgment. To find such a group is such a gift, and I can say I've been blessed enough to find such a great group of women, and one summer when all of us were very busy and we didn't meet often, I felt the very real difference in my confidence as a homeschool mom.

Take a vacation day

Just because we are home all day, and may or may not change out of our pajamas every day, doesn't mean we aren't working. Schedule in your own vacation days! For some families this is easier than others, but when there's a will, there's a way. For a single mom, that could mean setting up a play date for your child with a friend so you can get a latte all by yourself for a couple hours, or it could mean a movie night for the kids so you can veg out and knit for a couple hours.

As moms, we tend to fill our vacation days with doing stuff for the kids, whether that's heading to Goodwill and getting something fun or taking the day to plan curriculum. If that rejuvenates you, then go for it! If not, then try one of these ideas:

- Go to a movie
- Take a full-day class or seminar

- Enjoy a day outside with a favorite book or craft project
- Get a massage
- Get one night at a B&B
- Head to an amusement park (it's not just for kids!)
- Find a new book at the library and sit down and start reading it
- Find a study circle or craft circle that interests you and attend (Don't know of any? Try meetup.com)

Keep a journal

I don't mean to keep a "Dear Diary"-type journal, though if that is therapeutic for you, then have at it! What I mean is to journal what you do in your homeschool. The idea is to focus on your accomplishments, and what the children have accomplished through your hard work. Even when you are having a hard week and feel like not much is getting done, you can usually find some areas of success to focus on. Write down when they had success with a previously challenging math problem, or when they found interest in certain historical figures.

You are facilitating a learning environment for your children, so note additions and changes you make to that environment also. Did you hang up a world map in your home this week? Did you move your reading area to a spot with more natural light? Did you get some fun beanbags for the kids to sit in for read-aloud time? Write that down!

Read between the lines

Many of us have heard the following story (author unknown):

A man came home from work and found his three children outside, still in their pajamas, playing in the mud, with empty food boxes and wrappers strewn all around the front yard.

The door of his wife's car was open, as was the front door to the house, and there was no sign of the dog.

Proceeding into the entry, he found an even bigger mess. A lamp had been knocked over, and the throw rug was wadded against one wall.

In the front room the TV was loudly blaring a cartoon channel, and the family room was strewn with toys and various items of clothing.

In the kitchen, dishes filled the sink, breakfast food was spilled on the counter, the fridge door was open wide, dog food was spilled on the floor, a broken glass lay under the table, and a small pile of sand was spread by the back door.

He quickly headed up the stairs, stepping over toys and more piles of clothes, looking for his wife. He was worried she might be ill, or that something serious had happened.

He was met with a small trickle of water as it made its way out the bathroom door.

As he peered inside he found wet towels, scummy soap, and more toys strewn over the floor. Miles of toilet paper lay in a heap and toothpaste had been smeared over the mirror and walls.

As he rushed to the bedroom, he found his wife still curled up in the bed in her pajamas, reading a novel.

She looked up at him, smiled, and asked how his day went. He looked at her bewildered and asked:

"What happened here today?'"

She again smiled and answered, "You know every day when you come home from work and you ask me what in the world I do all day?"

"Yes," was his incredulous reply.

She answered, '"Well, today I didn't do it."

Most family members don't know what it takes to keep the house in running order, especially when almost everyone is home all day.

Sometimes we have to read their silence as appreciation, because honestly, most people will complain rather than give compliments. If we aren't hearing complaints, then all may be well.

Also, listen to how your family talks about homeschooling to others. So often I hear wives say their husbands will seem uneasy about homeschooling, but then when they are around others, they'll proudly state that their children are homeschooled. Maybe he shows his concern to you, but is overall pleased with the bigger picture of homeschooling.

In the idea of reading between the lines, please assume the best. We should always assume the best of others, and especially our husbands. If you are concerned about something, talk about it.

Say what you mean and mean what you say.

Do you show appreciation?

When was the last time you told your husband you appreciated him going out to work every day for the family? When was the last time you told your parents you appreciate them, in how they raised you, or the help they've provided in your adult life, or maybe how they show love to your children? How often do you tell your friends you appreciate them being a support in your life?

We've become a culture so involved with making sure people know what we want, what we need, and what our rights are, that we forget there are others who are asking the same thing.

What if we took another path and made sure that others had their rights, needs, and wants met before we were asked?

I'm not talking about giving and never receiving, putting yourself last. What I am talking about is setting the stage of appreciation and being the one to give first. You can set the example of how to show appreciation to others, and even if your adult family members do not pick up the habit, we can pray that our children do, and show us appreciation as they get older.

Thanking ourselves

Not being appreciated for your hard work is hard, and it sometimes it can make you want to quit, or just give less to your homeschool, but doing less won't make you feel better about yourself.

Sometimes a "thank you" comes years and year later. In my years as a supervisor, I very rarely got any thanks while I was anyone's direct boss, but they would come to me later and express that my leadership helped them grow to be a better employee, and ready themselves for growth in the professional world.

You may not hear much for thanks until you have grandchildren and your children can live for themselves what it was like to be in your shoes. Even if it takes that long, your goals are still the same. In fact, as much as I hate to admit it, others giving thanks doesn't positively affect your homeschool one bit.

So, let's thank ourselves, and pray that our creator is pleased with what we are doing. That's the point anyway, right?

Homeschooling with a Traveling Husband

Kristi Clover

From time to time I'll have a girlfriend call me when her hubby is out of town on a business trip for a night or two. I usually hear, "How do you do this? This is so hard!" You see, I'm the "go-to-girl" for my friends when it comes to traveling husbands, since for years I've been a traveling salesman's wife.

The thing is, my husband started traveling before we had kids, so it was never a complete shock to my system like it would be to other moms who experience it less frequently than we do. We kind of had our own groove. We were used to it. It didn't mean that there weren't times when I wanted to pull my hair out, but we managed.

The hardest time in our lives was when we only had two kids and weren't even homeschooling yet. My husband was not only traveling, but he worked from a downtown office and would often have to get to work early and stay late. It was a bit crazy to say the least! Luckily, it didn't last more than a few years. We were able to go back to our "normal" routine of having him work from home when he wasn't on the road. It was nice, although it made homeschooling a bit harder since he needed a quiet place in the house during some of his important business calls.

Let me say for the record that my hat is off to single moms and military families! I was raised by a single, working mom. I know it's hard work! My husband's longest time away from us has only been eight days. So, juggling things when your spouse is out of town periodically is one thing, but managing a household and homeschool long-term on your own is quite another.

All that said, having a traveling husband makes life with kids and homeschooling a bit of a juggling act.

Let's face it, one of the things that is the hardest about a husband who is not at home regularly is that we need help! Whether your husband is traveling or not, the days are really long and we need a break somewhere in our day!

So, what are my secrets to making a crazy travel schedule work for our family? How did we manage homeschooling and the added stress of an on-again-off-again one-parent home environment? Planning! Lots and lots of planning — okay, and a bit of flying by the seat of my pants. We can't have it all together all the time.

Survival tips for when your husband is away

1. Conquer bedtime!

The best bit of advice I can give any mom who is handling an evening alone is to get on top of bedtime! Having a good bedtime routine is the most important part of surviving when my hubby is traveling or working late.

We start bedtimes really early! Nothing will bring you to the brink of insanity faster than trying to get tired kids ready for bed. Even just going a few minutes past bedtime can make the whole night harder. If our nights start going long, then I start going crazy. I'm tired and ready for the house to be calm and quiet. I'm ready for some "me time." So, I plan ahead.

I've found that when I get my kids completely ready early, then it's easy to just put them to bed if they start melting down. We skip the power struggle that'd we normally have. Once your kids are overly tired, it's a losing battle. I actually move our entire evening schedule up. We have an early dinner, early bath, early PJs, and early teeth-brushing. Sometimes we'll do Bible and prayer early as well.

I will never forget calling my friend at 3 p.m. when my boys were little and asking if she thought it was too early to put my kids to bed. I was so tired and ready for my day to be done.

2. Schedule downtime for yourself!

I cannot stress the importance of finding time for yourself throughout the day. This is not an easy task when you are homeschooling. One of the top questions I get when people find out that we homeschool is, "How do you find time for yourself?" If I told them my husband traveled, too, they'd really be floored.

Society seems to think that everyone needs "me" time. We do to a certain extent. I believe there is an element of surrender involved in parenting when it comes to "our" time. However, it is important to reboot your system with some moments alone. Call it "me" time if you must.

When you are a homeschooling mom (or even a stay-at-home mom with only littles in the house), it's really important to find some point in your day to get a little break — especially when your husband works crazy hours or is away from the house for extended times.

My break has always been during our scheduled quiet time. Quiet time in our house is from about 2 to 4 p.m. I try to coordinate it with the littles' naps. I have my older kids either read or play quietly in their rooms, play outside, or get more schoolwork done upstairs.

Not every day is perfect. I don't always get my whole two hours. Naps don't always align. Basketball practice for the older boys sometimes interrupts our nap schedule. Plus there are days when we didn't get as far with our schoolwork and need to continue working into naptime. But I really do try to get a break.

3. Get help!

I've learned that it's OK to ask for help, and absolutely necessary to accept it when it's offered. There is no cape you will be awarded for trying to be a supermom! Don't be afraid to reach out and ask.

I've swapped childcare with friends to get a break from time to time. I've also hired a babysitter to come to the house so I can get away for a while, either to run errands kidless or just get that "me" time we just talked about. Me, coffee, and a good book are a good thing.

Another way to get support is homegrown. I've found my kids are highly capable of not only helping with housework but also with meal prep. We've taught our kids to make several basic meals. Often at the end of a long day I have my older kids take care of part or all of dinner. It's fun to work together — and it's free!

4. Plan ahead!

I've found that having a basic flow for our days helps our days run smoother. I work really hard during the summer planning out our homeschool year. I set up organizational systems for my older kids so they are able to do a majority of their work independently.

However, having a plan for our meals when daddy is out of town saves the day. Now, I'll be very real with you here! When my husband isn't home, I get VERY lazy with meals. Only in the last several years as my boys got bigger (as did their appetites) did I start making "real" meals for dinners. Before then we'd keep it fairly simple while my husband was away: smoothies with mini pizzas, breakfast for dinner, pasta with jarred marinara, burritos and more. Anything easy!

Even when I was serving up basic meals, I still had a basic meal plan. Recently, I created a handy-dandy meal planner and grocery list. I find it really helps me to have an overview of what we will be eating for the week.

Make it fun, homeschool style!

Having a husband who travels makes life a bit more challenging when you add homeschooling to the mix. But, you know what? There is blessing in it too. On the hard days when I start getting frustrated with busy travel schedules I'm reminded of the blessing of work! Having a job and providing for a family is a very important role for a man. My husband is blessed to have work that he really enjoys doing and that utilizes his talents. The way the economy has been these last several years, just staying employed has not been easy, so we have a lot to be grateful for. Work is a blessing! So, we make the travel aspect of work a blessing, too. We really try to view it as an adventure and make it fun.

Map It! (Geography and More)
Our adventure starts by tracking him on a map! We get excited to see what cities he will be going to, what the weather is supposed to be like there, how far the trip will be and what time zone he's in, and what fun things there is to

do there. It's really fun when there is extreme weather in the region he's going to and beautiful weather where we live. (OK, probably not as fun for him.)

Chart It! (Math)

When my boys were little, I'd create charts for them so they could get a visual of when he'd be coming home. We'd move a little cut-out airplane from one Velcro dot to the next to let them see when he'd be back. I just created a one-week calendar with the days of the week on top of each square. I had a little family picture (or you could use a simple star) to represent what day he would be home. It was a lot of fun to watch them get excited about tracking how many days until he'd return.

Love Notes! (Writing and Art)

Over the years we've had fun sneaking notes into his suitcase or making signs for him to come home to. If my kids are really inspired while he's away, they will draw a picture for him.

FaceTime and Skype (Computer Science)

Technology has improved so much since we first started having kids. It is so nice for the kids to get to "see" their dad when he's not home. My youngest son loves having my husband give him a tour of his hotel room. A fun little thing my husband sometimes does on his trips is to take along a couple of the kids' toys with him. He texts pictures of the toy with him wherever he is (on his pillow, on the plane, at dinner, and other fun locations). The kids get excited picking out which toy they want him take. Often times the toys are in the background as we FaceTime.

Reading Aloud Together (Language Arts)

Sometimes my husband will take along one of our read-aloud books when he's out of town. Our evening phone calls or FaceTimes then become a nice reading time with dad.

The best part about homeschooling and having a spouse who travels

Homeschooling is actually a huge blessing for families with husbands who travel. My husband's travel schedule was one of the many reasons why we started homeschooling! When my husband is home, we are home. We can take breaks when he can take breaks. We can grab a snack with him in between his business calls. We try to eat lunch with him when he has a break in his schedule. (OK, many days I'm tiptoeing into his office with a meal in hand while he's on the phone.) The kids love making smoothies and treats to take into him while he's working from the house.

It's important to embrace the fun that you can have when flying solo while your husband travels. It's all about perspective and choosing to see the positive aspects of this lifestyle. You'll find that joy follows when you focus on the blessings.

Flying Solo When Dad Travels or Works Late

Jennifer A. Janes

My first experience with my husband being away from home for a more than a night or two occurred when my children were 2 and 4 years old. I was busy during this time, to be sure, but I thought I was handling everything pretty well until Wednesday night, when someone at church said, "Jennifer, you look exhausted. Are you OK? Is there anything I can do to help?" I was at the beginning of our homeschooling journey, and I was trying to juggle doing some pre-K lessons with my eager-to-learn older daughter, managing my constantly crying younger daughter who had some health issues going on, keeping food on the table, dishes and laundry washed, and getting time for myself, which is a necessity for my introverted personality. I figured sleep needed to factor in somewhere, too, but it was hard to come by.

We're in our ninth year of homeschooling now, and my husband has had jobs with long hours or lots of travel (or both) for most of our marriage. Regardless of the reason you're flying solo, life is more challenging for Mom when Dad's not home much. Having Dad away means you're short a vehicle to help transfer kids to and from activities and appointments, a pair of hands to help with household chores, chat time to brainstorm solutions to household and parenting problems, and opportunities to get away from it all briefly while your spouse watches the kids. Feeling like everything rests on your shoulders, plus homeschooling, can be overwhelming and make you feel like you want to quit.

Fortunately, there are steps you can take to preserve your sanity and keep your homeschool going strong, even when your spouse is away from home.

Enlist help

Asking for help is hard for me. I am the one others turn to for help, so to have the tables turned and need assistance from others takes some getting used to. One of the easiest places to find help, if they're old enough, is your children. As my children have gotten older, I have admitted to being unable to handle everything alone and have begun to teach them what it takes to run a household. As a result, I now have two efficient and capable helpers at home, and they usually ask me what they can do to help when they see I have a lot going on. Having my kids help means that household chores get finished sooner, I can start writing earlier and get finished faster, and then we can have some fun together.

Even if your kids are younger, they can still help. There are lots of online resources that list age-appropriate household chores for all age groups. Start training your kids to help out. Yes, it's draining at first and things take longer, but it's worth it!

There are things that your children can't help with, though. Until they reach driving age, or if you don't have an extra vehicle, you may need help getting the kids to activities and appointments, especially when you're supposed to be in two places at once. See if family, neighbors, or friends with children in the same activities can help run errands or get your children where they need to go. They're often more than willing if you'll just ask!

Asking for help is good for you and for the people you ask. Many times people have agreed to help me and then thanked me for asking. They wanted to help but didn't know what to do.

Even with lots of help, though, sometimes it's just not possible to do everything.

Keep it simple

When you find it impossible to keep up, focus on simplicity. Taking care of everyone's basic needs and getting some lessons done each day is a lot of work. Lower your expectations. You need to determine your family's priorities and focus on those when you're overwhelmed and stretched too thin.

Decide what your minimum standards are for your home. Each family's priorities differ. I can tolerate some dust on the furniture but really can't stand dirty floors or bathrooms. I don't handle piled-up laundry or dishes well, either. When I can't get to everything I would like to do, knowing this about myself helps me to focus my time and energy in ways that enable me to feel productive while preserving my sanity.

Keeping things simple in the kitchen is a critical factor for me too. We deal with food allergies, and convenience foods are expensive. I have to prepare a lot of our allergy-friendly foods and snacks from scratch, but I can take other steps to keep my life in the kitchen simple. (See the chapter I wrote about spending so much time in the kitchen if you want to learn more.) When I need to streamline my life, I sometimes turn to plastic silverware and paper plates. I know it's not great for the environment, but it sure does make my life easier for short periods of time.

Helping each of your children finish a lesson in every subject may not be realistic every day either. Decide what your priorities are for your homeschool too, and go easy on yourself for the rest when your husband is away. In our household, math, reading, and language arts are the non-negotiables. On days when there's not enough of me to go around, I call it a successful day if we get those done. Most days we manage to do other subjects too, but knowing that my husband and I have decided that these are the critical lessons helps take the pressure off.

Be flexible

When you're parenting solo for a period of time, it's important to be flexible. You may have planned out each day for minimum stress on your part, but life happens. A child or pet may get sick and require medical treatment or a storm may knock out your electricity (and derail your online curriculum plans). These changes to your routine will be easier for you and your children to deal with if you can quickly come up with a Plan B.

A child gets sick? Resting on the couch with Netflix documentaries related to science concepts you've been studying or movies about time periods you've covered in history is in order.

The dog needs a trip to the vet? Turn it into a field trip. The kids can learn more about taking care of their pet responsibly, and the vet or assistant will usually answer questions about what it's like to work in a veterinary office and what education is required. He may even share about some interesting cases that have recently come into the office.

You have no electricity or internet to power your curriculum? Spend the day working jigsaw puzzles, reading books, doing craft projects, listening to music, and playing board games together. There's a wealth of educational value in those activities too.

Everyone is just out of sorts because Dad's gone? Mix things up with an unplanned field trip, change up your schedule for the day by schooling in the afternoon and using the morning for a nature walk, or move schooling outside or to the park and have a picnic lunch while you're at it.

While keeping up a routine is important, flexibility and a change of pace might be just what you and your kids need occasionally to keep going while dad's away.

Evaluate

Make sure you take time periodically to see what's working for your family and what isn't. Sometimes you have to revisit those priorities you set and make adjustments based on what you're learning about yourself and your kids and how you function when dad's away.

Do you need to buy a new cookbook with simple recipes the kids can help prepare? Look at your curriculum choices. Do you need to find resources that are less teacher-driven and will allow for your kids to do more independent work? Sign your kids up for online programs or classes? Subscribe to a video-streaming or audiobook service that would allow your kids more variety in their learning while still meeting educational goals?

Taking stock periodically will help you to make small changes over time that will make your household function better both when your husband is away and when he's home.

Take care of yourself

Finally, be sure you take care of yourself. While paying a babysitter and getting away for some "me" time may not be feasible in your situation, make sure you're getting plenty of rest, healthy foods, and exercise. When most of the responsibility for your household falls on you in your husband's absence, your family needs for you to be healthy and functioning well.

Try to take time for yourself every day too. Do something you enjoy, if only for a few minutes, whether it's reading a book, knitting, taking an online class in something you've always wanted to learn about, watching a movie, or writing in a journal. (My only caution is that you not stay up too late trying to get this time for yourself. I really struggle with this and end up too tired as a result until I can rein myself in.)

Whether your husband is away for long days and is home every night, travels often, or is away for extended periods of time, you can keep homeschooling and survive this season!

When Mom Has Meltdowns
Ann Karako

I haven't yet decided whether or not it is a compliment that the iHN team chose me to write a chapter about wanting to quit homeschooling because of having meltdowns in front of the kids. It's one of those areas that you might not want to be considered an expert in, you know? :-) But in reality it's an honor to be selected for this part of the book, because emotions are such an integral part of being a woman. They affect everything we do, including homeschooling. I'm hoping that some of what I share in this chapter can help in many other areas of life. And I'm grateful to have the opportunity to make an impact beyond just the subject of homeschool.

Let me start out by saying that yes, meltdowns are real; and no, we don't really want to make a habit of having them. I have been an emotional person my entire life, and I have pitched some doozies, y'all. But I am always trying to learn how to better control my emotions and behavior. The Bible talks about self-control as a fruit of the Spirit. So I am not here to excuse meltdowns – just to bring them into proper perspective.

The truth of the matter is that if we are prone to having meltdowns, we'll have them whether we're homeschooling or not. The kids will see them at some point or other in our lives. Homeschooling can exacerbate some of the factors leading up to them, but it's not going to create a meltdown where the potential for one did not exist in the first place.

As an old friend once said, "What is in the well is going to come up in the bucket, no matter who (or what) is pulling on the chain." So to decide to quit homeschooling because of our own emotions is just putting off the inevitable. And as I will share later in this chapter, there can even be good that comes from our weakness.

But since this is a book about homeschooling, let's first look at some of the things about teaching our kids at home that may prove to be catalysts for difficulty with our emotions, and what we can do about them.

Five homeschool scenarios that can create a meltdown

1. Having to be a task-master all day. This is otherwise known as trying to keep the daily schedule intact. Wow, there are times when I feel like the kids have no desire to move any faster than molasses. And if one kid gets behind, everything snowballs – including my plans for my time. So I start nagging... and the more I nag, the more I get wound up about staying on schedule – and the more unglued I become.

2. Discipline issues. Aargh. I really prefer to avoid child training, don't you? But we know that if we avoid it, it'll come back to bite us later. I've heard it called credit-card parenting: You put off dealing with an issue, but eventually you'll be forced to – and then you'll pay interest. I'd laugh except it's so painfully true! The crazy thing is that having to discipline our kids can often tempt us to exhibit behavior that is just as bad as theirs. Disciplining in anger is not unheard of in my house... been there, done that. Yesterday, in fact. :-(

3. Children not learning as quickly or as well as I think they should. Don't you get impatient sometimes, wondering why your kid just doesn't "get it?" I know I do. Some of this has to do with personalities – after all, they're our kids, so they will know how to drive us crazy – and some of it is that we adults, who have more knowledge, forget to have patience with someone who of course isn't going to know as much. What seems obvious to us is not going to be so obvious to them.

4. Having to clean and cook and teach and serve all day every day with no break to even go to the bathroom without being trailed by someone who needs something. So that we feel like we are constantly giving and not receiving. Which is wearing to our emotions, and gives us a martyr syndrome – and then we need to let everyone know about it. (Don't ask how I'm able to just lay that out there in all its gory detail without even pausing to think about it.)

5. Guilt that I'm doing it all wrong. Like, all of it. The schooling, the character training, the cooking and cleaning – we can get to feeling extremely inadequate. Which can often lead to a sort of paralysis, where we don't feel like attempting anything, because we just KNOW it won't go right. Tell me I'm not the only one who gets there sometimes!

So what's a girl to do?

Giving into these issues by screaming and yelling or kicking holes in walls (don't ask – but yes, the plural is intentional. Who knew drywall was so thin? Sigh...)? Anyway, this is obviously not the solution. The way I see it, the road to dealing with our emotions as we homeschool is a two-fold process. On the one side, we need to address our heart issues. But also, we need to amend the logistics of the situations themselves.

Let's look at each of the above scenarios again, this time with solutions in mind. I'd love to go into greater detail for all of these, but for now I'm just going to provide food for thought. It won't be difficult for each of us to ponder these and find our own ways to apply them.

Task-Master Mom. In our hearts we need to recognize the sovereignty of God in our day-to-day moments. The milk that gets spilled that needs to be cleaned up that makes us late getting started in the morning is not a surprise to Him. We also need to see the bigger picture – God's purposes are more important than our agenda. One thing that would help logistically is to make room for margin in our schedules. Build in time between tasks. Take some tasks off the list altogether.

Angry Disciplinarian Mom. I think we often get angry at our kids for misbehaving because we see it as a reflection of ourselves. How dare they act that way? I never taught them to do that! We are personally offended, even though the actual offense was not against us. Or we are just SO disappointed that the child made that choice, because we know it is not in their best interest. We need to learn to recognize that our child's sin is not about us. "The wrath of man does not achieve the righteousness of God" (James 1:20). Rather, it is God's kindness that leads us to repentance (Romans 2:4) – and the same will be true for our children. This does not mean no consequences. In fact, that is part of the practical solution. Set up consequences for behavior and be consistent to stick to them. When consequences are decided in the rational moments, then during the conflict it's easier to stay calm. I must confess I am STILL working on this one, though my kids are almost all teenagers and above.

Impatient Teacher Mom. Practically speaking, educating ourselves about learning styles is crucial as homeschool moms. I did not pay as much attention to this as I should have. It's actually quite fascinating, and it's fun to discover where family members fit. Now that my kids are older, I am better able to see which ones learn like their father and which ones learn like me. I wish I'd figured it out sooner. It becomes a lot easier to be patient when we are willing to accept that the child learns differently than we do. And on a more spiritual level, who are we to be impatient about our child butchering the multiplication tables, when there are lessons God has been trying to teach us for YEARS that we are still struggling to grasp?

Poor Me Mom. This is one is easy to fall into. It happens when we take our eyes off of our calling and focus on our own wants. The fact is that we were bought with a price, and Jesus did not come to be served, but to serve. But... there is also such a thing as self-care. We do need to build time into our day for rest, exercise, and a little bit of "me" time. This is not selfish – I liken it to the idea of putting my oxygen mask on first ("In the event of a loss of cabin pressurization..."), so that I can help my child with theirs. I need to take care of myself so that I can be a better wife and mom and servant.

Inadequate Mom. I think there is a bit of pride involved here, at least for me. I want to be REALLY good at everything – at least I want everyone to THINK I'm really good at it. But the fact is I'm not, and I won't be. But I am always reassured by the idea that God gave me to these children as their mother and their teacher, because He thought I would be best for THEM. He wants ME in their lives. And in my weakness, He is strong. It's not about me; it's about Him working in me and through me. But it's hard for me to remember this if I am not in His Word. Spending time in the Bible is crucial towards maintaining a right mindset about who I am and who He is.

So often when we get emotional, it's because we have lost sight of our big God and are dwelling on our circumstances. In each of these five scenarios I can remember that I don't want to be THAT mom. I can think on the truth as it's found in God's Word, while at the same time taking some practical steps to help alleviate the situation.

When you are heading toward a meltdown or have already had one

What about when you wake up one morning and just KNOW you can't handle the day? Maybe you've done all the right things and had all the right attitudes, but life has snuck up on you and you're exhausted. Or maybe your hormones are raging – they can turn any one of us into someone we don't recognize! Or maybe you've already become overloaded and "lost it," and now you're trying to pick up the pieces.

The wonderful thing about being homeschool moms is that we do have options. We can adapt our day to either prevent a crash and burn situation – or to recover from one. Here are some recommendations for either of these cases, all of which are tried and true in my own life.

Re-evaluate the plan for the day. Can I change my to-do list to put off the things that are more strenuous, whether emotionally or physically? Or substitute other things that need to be done but seem more appealing? Yes, I realize this is essentially giving a big "you go, girl" to the idea of procrastination. And sometimes that just makes things worse later, so this step must be taken with care. But you might be surprised how much a small change in the plan can affect the emotional outlook. And as far as the homeschool day goes, there are several possibilities for re-arranging the agenda. We can:

Take the day off. Sometimes it's better to just ditch the books and do something fun. This is called making a better memory for the children than sitting under scary mommy's tutelage all day.

Assign some independent learning for an hour or two or the whole day. This can look like assigning books to read or math lessons to do ("just skip the ones you don't

174

understand and we'll get to them later"); another option is to have them write a story or a journal entry. Or draw pictures. Or create a rocket ship with Legos. Or design a maze on graph paper. Assigning something the children can do completely on their own gives you some breathing space to pull yourself together, while still comforting you that something school-like is being accomplished.

Find a LOOOOONG educational video for the kids to watch. Or several short ones strung together. Guess what? This happens at the public school all. the. time. You are not short-changing your children; you are providing them with "research" from outside sources. You are using multimedia to vary your lesson presentation. :-) You're not going to do this every day, but in an emotional emergency situation, this is a better option than pushing yourself over the edge by thinking you must stick to the lesson plan and be the hands-on teacher when you can barely function yourself.

Room time. This was a staple in my house when the kids were young, and I still pull it out of my hip pocket occasionally, even with teenagers. Room time is when everyone goes to their own room and spends an hour or two (or some specific amount of time initially pre-determined by Mommy but subject to change without notice) without coming out. It means the house doesn't become a wreck, and the kids don't have as much opportunity for creating conflict with one another. It gives Mommy a breather, or time to pick up some clutter (an uncluttered house always helps me feel better), or a chance to start dinner without being interrupted, or to read a book (what a concept!).

Remember your purposes for homeschooling – and they are rarely to push through the curriculum at all costs. Many of us are homeschooling with the character development of our children in mind; it would hardly be beneficial to this goal to force ourselves and our children to keep working when Mommy is severely struggling to keep it together. If a meltdown is imminent (or has already occurred), then discretion becomes the better part of valor. Step back and take a break. Leave your kids as emotionally whole as possible.

Pay extra attention to self-care. We mentioned this earlier; there are definitely things we should be doing every day to take care of ourselves, such as eating right, getting enough sleep, exercising regularly, etc. These give us the strength and stamina to do our job well. But on a more difficult day, give extra effort to doing those things for yourself that make you feel emotionally stable and/or physically attractive and healthy. Take your vitamins. Eat meals in a timely fashion (for me, hunger alone can put me close to the emotional edge). Get dressed in clothes that make you feel good. Paint your toenails. Ignoring this type of thing is NOT being a good Mommy; it is setting ourselves up for failure. Pampering ourselves when we feel emotional goes a long way toward making us want to be productive human beings again.

Admit to your family that you are feeling weak, or apologize if you have already behaved badly. This may be hard to do, but I believe it is crucial. It is my opinion that these times provide a unique opportunity to actually strengthen our relationship with our kids. Why do I say this? It's because I think being transparent with my kids is a key parenting reality. Allowing them to see when I am struggling binds us together more closely than if I always present myself as bigger and better than they are, and as never having problems. It shows my kids respect when I am willing to admit my failings to them.

Also, I think my kids need to know that I know I am fallible. They need to hear me apologize regularly when I mess up. They need to know that I acknowledge my errors and my sin and my stupidity. Being transparent with them about my fears and failures (in an age-appropriate way, of course) forges bonds of forgiveness and trust.

Furthermore, when I admit to my weakness, my kids see that it is very normal not to be perfect. This is healthy, because then they realize that they don't have to feel badly that they are not perfect. They don't need to be afraid that their imperfection makes them less valuable. They see that we all love one another through (and in spite of) our imperfections and weaknesses and poor behavior, and they find a place of security. There is definitely something to be said for us all knowing the worst about each other and still holding fast to one another.

And so, believe it or not, our emotionalism, while not ideal, is not without positive ramifications.

Remember you are not indispensable. This is a biggie for me. I tend to think that whatever it is won't get done unless I do it. Nobody else will do it right. (Can you say "controlling"?) On difficult days, I need to remember that other people, including my kids, can do most things just fine. I need to delegate tasks to them and lighten my load. And then I need to shower them with thanks and praise, even if it's not done the way I would do it. You know what they say about skinning a cat (although one does wonder why they would want to do that or even talk about it). The same thing applies to laundry and dishes and cleaning the kitchen floor and giving a spelling test and checking a math problem and (insert many other tasks here).

This is actually a great way for our children to learn how to help and serve. They feel important when they can do something for Mommy, especially during a time when "Mommy isn't feeling well." Our kids know very well that they need us; I think it is also important that they know that we need them. A family is a mutually-supportive entity. We should all be able to rely on one another in times of weakness. Kids learn to step up to the plate only as they are called upon to do so. And they often surpass our expectations when we lean on them for support and help.

I think to a certain extent we can try to protect our kids TOO much. Striving to be always cheerful and always "with it" in front of them is not only an exercise in futility; it is also not conducive to family unity. Yes, they are children, so no, we don't want to overload them; but in age-appropriate way, we need to let them know they are necessary for the logistical and emotional well-being of the family.

So here again, our weakness can actually foster positive results. This doesn't give us an excuse to "lose it," but it does provide hope that when we do, God's grace brings good even out of the rough stuff.

Pray, and then give it all over to the One who can handle it all without my help. This should actually probably be #1 on the list! What happens often for me is that the load becomes burdensome because I try to do it all, and/or I think my plan is the one that has to happen. I forget the bigger agenda, which is based on eternal realities that I know nothing about. So I need to pray sincerely to be reminded of the TRUTH, and then I need to LET. IT. ALL. GO. I need to decide to look ahead with joy at what God will do, not with foreboding that it won't turn out the way I want it to. Truly giving it all to God can prevent a meltdown from happening in the first place, or it can rebuild our souls after we've fallen to the temptation of having one. He knows us intimately and will meet us right where we are.

What's the big picture about meltdowns?

In conclusion, I have a few "big picture" thoughts. Let's take a step back from the nitty-gritty and put meltdowns in perspective. Personally, I don't think being emotional and/or having meltdowns is any worse for our kids than any of the other wrong things we do in front of them. Can you say that you are perfect in every other way except for the meltdowns? I certainly cannot. We are women; we have emotions. Giving into them occasionally is not the end of the world, though at the time we may feel like it is.

And as a mom of three high school (homeschool) graduates and two teens left at home, I know for a certain and undeniable fact that I have indeed warped my kids. Just like I was warped by my mom, and she by her mom. It's part of parenting! We would like to think that our children will only remember the positive about us and that we have only done good in their lives, but that would be far from reality.

The hard truth about parenting is that in the end we really are not responsible for how our children turn out. God is. He will perform His purpose in their lives basically no matter what we do. This was difficult for me to see when my kids were younger and I had so much control over them; now, as my kids are older and are making their own decisions, I am very aware how much it is God's work in their hearts that makes the difference and not how great or poor a parent I am.

That doesn't mean I can just ignore the need to parent well, or give into every temptation to melt down that comes my way. My parenting affects my relationship with God. It is about whether I am obeying Him or not. In truth, how I parent determines how I turn out.

So I encourage us all to learn the best ways to develop self-control, some of which I hope you have found in this chapter. But I don't see having meltdowns as a reason to quit homeschooling. That would be like throwing the baby out with the bathwater. The reasons we homeschool go far beyond our own inadequacies – or we would never even consider homeschooling in the first place. Because in our heart-of-hearts, we all know how inadequate we are in so many other ways beyond meltdowns! But we can trust God to be strong when we are weak, that He will fill in the gaps in our parenting and our homeschooling. He is faithful that way; let's trust Him through all of it.

When the Bottom Falls Out
Marlene Griffith

Motherhood is a season of life that, once begun, never ends. Once a mom, always a mom.

From the moment they are born and you look into those beautiful little eyes, you become overwhelmed with love and instinctual protection. You want to give them the best. With motherhood comes a sense of responsibility, a sense of need to protect, a sense of need to create the perfect world for our children. We want to create a safe world, one where they can grow, live, explore, and achieve the greatness they are meant to.

We're joyful, sometimes forcedly, but nonetheless, we try and greet them moment after moment with joy and excitement. We protect them and shelter them from our world, a world filled with realities we don't want to burden them with. We daily attempt to shake off anything that could taint their cute little world. Arguments with your husband, loneliness from the lack of friends, the stress caused by your strained family relationships, making ends meet with the little money you have, worry about your sick relative. Whichever of this it may be, or whichever other it may be, we keep these things bottled up inside when we're around our kids.

We create a blissfully engaging environment around our children, as best we can. And rightfully so. They are young little humans with many things to do, learn, and discover!

We should create an environment in which they can do this without worry. And then one day, the bottom falls out. And you feel like everything you built crumbles.

You're topped off with the overwhelming amount of things going on in your life. You're home all the time raising these precious children of yours. If you're not home, you're sure to be with them wherever you go. You're devoting your time, your mind and your energy to them sacrificially and willingly. You would do it all over again, too! But it's draining, demanding, and leaves little time for you to even process your own thoughts.

Then that day comes when you lose your cool. You have a meltdown. This meltdown, it doesn't happen in private, of course. It happens right in front of them. When someone spills the milk for the thousandth time, or they throw a tantrum because you won't let them have cake for breakfast.

The meltdown is heightened by the fear that you're screwing your kids up, making you feel twice as terrible: once for the meltdown and over again for the guilt. You feel like a failure; you feel like a hypocrite for not being patient, for not maintaining control of yourself. And you're scared. It's messy now.

This fear, this meltdown, this guilt: We've all felt it. We all just don't talk about it. It's a closely guarded secret that most of us refuse to associate with. It's as if we fear defiling the myth of maternal bliss, floating around as these perfect beings smiling day in and day out. Maybe we'll admit to the "stress" of the messy room, or running late on dinner, but we never admit to those moments when we feel and fear we have royally messed up our kids.

This ruse has more to do with fooling ourselves than hiding from everyone else. Have you ever locked yourself in the bathroom to cry? Have you jumped in the car as soon as your husband walks in the door, only to drive around crying so hard you lose your breath?

I want you to know something. You have nothing to be ashamed of. Your humanness – it's OK if your kids see that. They need to see mom being a real person.

They need to see you work through those emotions and get to the other side, where you are collected and take responsibility for your actions and behavior. We spend so much time loading them up with information on how to do this or how to do that. But we forget that the best teaching moments in motherhood are letting our children see us live out life.

Your children will forgive you; it's just part of their beautifully God-given nature. They are forgiving little people, eager to love, and you are their main love.

There comes a day when your kids reach an age when they notice when mom is falling apart. If we pretend like it's not happening, we begin to demonstrate an unhealthy approach to dealing with internal (and external) issues. When you're falling apart in front of your kids, or have already fallen apart in front of them, you need to address it.

So, what do you do when you have a meltdown in front of your kids?

Step back for a moment, gather yourself, and breathe. You are not messing them up; that's the first think you need to tell yourself. The next thing is, you can work through this. And finally, open up to them, as realistically as possible.

If you lashed out at them, apologize. Don't justify (i.e. I'm sorry I snapped at you, but you were...). Simply apologize and ask for forgiveness. Use this as a teaching moment and a humbling moment for you, too. In doing this, you're teaching your children that even Mom messes up. But you're also showing them that when you mess up, you need to deal with it properly.

If you fell apart in front of them due to something that had nothing to do with them, you can't just let that go either. For the purpose of an example, let's say you just hung up the phone with someone who got your really upset. They might have heard you talking or maybe you became super expressive once you hung up the phone. Then you quickly become short with them and impatient. Your frustration with the caller begins to reflect in the way your respond to your children.

The same method applies: Step back, gather yourself, and breathe. This is another great teaching moment. Our children learn from how we respond in our everyday lives. Is it OK for you to allow the emotions you're feeling toward that caller to pour over onto them? No. But it's not the end of the world that you did this; you're not a bad mom; and you're not ruining your kids either. Open up to them and apologize for being unfair and pouring those emotions on them.

You never want to apologize abruptly. Meaning, you want it to be sincere. Fleeting and empty apologies are not wise, and set a poor example of owning up to something. A simple "I'm sorry I lashed out at you" or "I'm sorry I was acted that way in front of you" isn't enough. You need to explain in detail the "why" of the apology.

When we have unaddressed meltdowns in front of our kids, we are just teaching them that it's OK to do this. That is why it's so important to sit down and talk with them about it. Some of us feel as if we are more prone to falling apart in front of our kids, or falling apart period, and we have no idea how to stop it. Approaching these things head-on is key to minimizing them and moving past them in a healthy manner.

Looking ahead

Should you make it up to them? I don't think so. At least not in the way most would consider "making it up to them" to mean. You don't need to go buy them a new toy as an apology and you don't need to take them to their favorite restaurant either.

The urge to do those things come from the guilt in our hearts. It's a terrible feeling to have meltdowns in front of your kids, even if it is not directed at them. But there is no need to make things up to them; you all have these meltdowns. There is no need to hide from these realities of life, realities they'll once day face themselves. Doing so will do them a disservice.

You are the mother our beautiful Creator chose for these little people. You will live out a life meant for them to see, for whatever purpose it may be. We might not get that, we might not want those moments to happen because we feel terrible during them, but they are opportunities and moments given to us to help us and our families grow.

The most valuable things you can offer them in those moments, and after, are your heartfelt words of repentance; your heartfelt apology and honest pursuit of forgiveness. It's not a tangible object, it's a moment of raw emotion that will heal the mess and draw you all closer to one another.

It's OK if your children see your humanness, your realness. Just take responsibility for your actions and apologize. It's what we are teaching our kids to do too, right?

Running Errands with Little Helpers
Crystal Wagner

"The days are long, but the years are short."
Gretchen Rubin, The Happiness Project

I received many stares while running errands with my children when they were young. Some of the stares communicated sympathy — times such as when my daughter threw a tantrum because she didn't get her way. Some communicated understanding — times such as when I was trying to hurriedly pay so I could nurse the crying infant. Some communicated envy — times such as when I walked into Hobby Lobby on a beautiful spring day with a princess, dressed complete with tiara, and stopped to smell the purple and yellow pansies.

Running errands with little helpers can be a stressful experience, but there are strategies you can employ to make errands more enjoyable and train your children so they are helpful.

Set realistic expectations

Running errands with children of any age will take longer than going by yourself. Plan that into your schedule and you will be less frustrated. This may mean not accomplishing as many tasks. You might need to split the list of errands into multiple days. The times I have tried to push the limit and go to "just one more store" were usually disastrous. The girls were tired and complained the whole way through the store, and we were all frustrated and grumpy by the end of the trip. If I had saved that last errand for another day, we would have gone home happy.

Communicate expectations

I found it particularly helpful to communicate my expectations before entering a store. When the girls were younger, I turned around in my seat before ever unbuckling anyone and reminded them of how I expected them to behave while in the store. I also communicated that we would leave the store and they would not be allowed to go shopping with me again for a while if they did not behave. Be prepared to follow through on that promise.

I distinctly remember an embarrassing time we almost left the store. I was six months pregnant and my daughter was 2½ years old. In the middle of Target, I told her she couldn't have the toy she saw. She started screaming so loudly I think people parking their cars could hear her. I picked her up and gently, but firmly, placed her in the shopping cart and kept walking. I knew she was out of control and the only way to calm her was to leave the store or ignore the cries while staying close. My cheeks were red with embarrassment. In my mind, I was one of "those mothers" that day — the one with the screaming child. Others were probably thinking I had no control over my child, and why didn't I give her the toy, or why couldn't I make her be quiet. It was a difficult shopping trip, but it did improve. She calmed down and we were able to finish our shopping, but I was prepared to walk out of the store if necessary.

Take advantage of the opportunity to train in life skills

View running errands as training in life skills. One day, your children will need to do the exact same thing as you. Keeping in mind your child's age and developmental ability, find a way for him to help with the errands.

Young children still sitting in the shopping cart can place nonbreakable items into the cart's basket.

Children old enough to walk alongside the cart can learn to walk beside the cart. This was particularly challenging for one of my daughters. She danced everywhere. That's lovely and a joy to watch when we are home, but it can be disastrous in a busy grocery store. It required a lot of patience and training to help her understand that she had to stay close to the cart and could not twirl and swing her arms or she might hit someone or knock something off the shelf.

Once children can see over the shopping cart, allow them to push it through the store. Help them learn to watch where they are walking and how to steer the cart around corners. When we first started allowing our daughters to push the cart, we kept one hand on the side of the cart. Eventually, we were able to trust them and only help in tight spaces.

Children can also be responsible for getting items off the shelf and placing them in the cart. This helps them learn where items are located and which brands you prefer. As they get older, you can help them understand how to compare ingredients and prices.

After your children have proven you can trust them and know where to locate items in the store, allow them to get an item while you continue working through your shopping list. I allow my daughters to do this in the grocery store when they will be only an aisle or two away. For example, while I wait in line at the meat counter, they might get juice. After each item, they come straight back, place the item in the cart, and ask for their next assignment. This also helps them build confidence and independence.

Be prepared

Plan for errands like you would any trip away from home. Think about what you might need to make the trip more pleasant for everyone. If you have a small child, make sure the diaper bag is packed and include a board book, a special lovey, or a toy to keep your child occupied while waiting in line.

Always take a snack and a drink. Even elementary-aged children will behave better with full tummies. Make sure everyone is wearing clothes and appropriate shoes. I'm serious! I allow dress-up clothes out of the house and have been known to go shopping with a princess and a Laura Ingalls Wilder lookalike, but I require appropriate clothing and shoes. Occasionally we have left the house and I didn't realize they were still in dress-up clothes that were way too big to be safe, or they had on heels from their pretend play. I've learned to check before leaving the house to make sure everyone is wearing clothing and shoes that are safe and appropriate. I've known friends that keep extra shoes in the car because their children often left the house without any.

Alternatives to running errands with kids

Sometimes you need to run errands alone. Whether it is because your children lost the privilege of going with you, it's one of "those" appointments, or you just need a few minutes alone to recapture your sanity by walking the aisles of Target with a Starbucks drink in hand, there will be times you need to go alone. Here are a few options that have worked well for me.

- Trade kid-sitting responsibilities with a friend. You can plan to have days where you trade kid-sitting duties so the other can shop, or it can be unstructured and scheduled as needed.

- Go when your husband can be home with the kids. Better yet, send him with the kids.

- Order online

Before you know it, the kids grow up, and you will send them on the errands because they think it is cool to drive. Little do they know you are sitting home with your feet up, drinking a cup of coffee. Well, maybe that dream won't actually come true, but there will come a day when you are no longer wrangling little children's feet out of shopping-cart seats. There will be a day when you no longer need to hold a little hand while walking through the parking lot to keep them safe. Cherish the time you have to run errands with your little helpers.

When Your Kids Are Intense
Brenda Priddy

My daughter, Monkey, is an intense child. She has always been intense. As a baby, she would cry for hours, regardless of whether you were holding her or not. As a toddler, she would scream for something as simple as the sun being in her eyes. And when it came time for school, she sometimes responded – and responds – in extreme ways with extreme emotional responses.

Some days, teaching her is a breeze. She loves learning and is crazy-smart, on her own terms. But catch her on a bad day, and I feel like I am trying to teach a monkey how to write Shakespeare (there is a reason her nickname is Monkey!) or a dolphin how to divide fractions.

When I first started homeschooling Monkey, I didn't know that she had ADHD, and possibly some undiagnosed learning differences as well. In those early days, I felt like a homeschooling parent failure. I didn't understand why I wasn't able to provide her with the happy, carefree education I always envisioned. Many days, I've thought about quitting.

One of the most important homeschooling lessons I've ever learned is this:

Homeschooling does not look like a magazine photo shoot.

Kids get upset. They have days when they do not want to do school. Sometimes there is shouting. Sometimes there are tears. Sometimes there is a struggle to get your child to sound out a single letter or to add two simple numbers together. Sometimes it feels like more trouble than it is worth.

All of these problems are magnified if your child is "spirited," "intense," or any of the even less flattering names given to children with special needs or learning differences.

For better or worse, homeschooling an intense child is not the same as homeschooling a child who has a different learning style. Homeschooling the intense child will never be as easy as homeschooling a child who believes learning is as exciting as Christmas morning (I have never met such a child, but I'm sure at least one exists somewhere).

I don't want to underplay how emotionally and physically draining it can be to homeschool a child with special needs or a child who has learning differences that are vastly different from your own. Homeschooling any child is difficult, but homeschooling the intense child can be even more difficult. Over the years, I've come up with a few coping strategies that have really helped all of us keep our emotions in check while homeschooling with intense children in the house.

These tips work both for children who tend to be intense often, as well as for children who have moments of intensity (most children have at least a few periods of intensity).

Temper expectations

For us, the biggest help has been tempering our expectations. Before I had my own children, I thought I would be the parent who could do it all. We'd always have a clean house, children would always obey, and school would always be fun for the children and for me. Of course, that did not happen at all. From the first day that Monkey took over an hour to read the word "it," I knew that my expectations had to be in a much different place.

Today, I expect Monkey to do what she can do in a day, but I don't expect anything else. I know she struggles with sitting still or focusing when there are other distractions around. I try to keep our environment calm and allow her the freedom to move. I've made these concessions on my part to make it easier for her to learn. I also work to make sure that I am not asking too much of her, which brings us to my next point.

Understand your child's limits

If you have an intense child, you know that when their limits are reached, all hell can break loose. At our house, that typically manifests in explosions of anger and frustration (I typically react this way too, when my limits are reached). It has taken a few years, but I now know how to recognize the signs that Monkey displays when she is reaching her limits. Typically, she will clinch her hands or teeth together, fidget a lot more, or breathe faster. In some cases, we can work through these moments together and move beyond them, but I know when she starts acting this way, it is time to pull back, move to something else, or quit for the day.

This year, I've been following her cues a lot better, which has made this year our best school year yet.

Acknowledge the struggle

When it comes to homeschooling, we like to focus only on positives that reinforce our choice to teach our children at home. But only focusing on positives tends to make people feel that struggles are abnormal. If everyone only talks about the positive experiences, struggling parents feel left out and as if they are doing something wrong.

This feeling is even worse when your child is typically labeled the "bad" child, because she acts up at co-op, has trouble focusing in class, or ignores other adults or children when they speak to her. Your experiences will differ depending on your specific situation and needs, but the sentiment is still there. Homeschooling a child who isn't a poster child for the "ideal" homeschooling child is even more challenging than homeschooling the average child.

If you have an intense child and are struggling to homeschool, it's easy to blame yourself, particularly when everyone else does as well. I feel like most of the "dear mom who is doing everything wrong" articles are directed at me. However, you have to realize that in the case of an intense child or special-needs child, it really isn't you. The struggle is real, but it is not caused by you.

I felt such a sense of relief when I stopped blaming myself for every homeschool roadblock we've faced. You are not a bad parent or teacher if your child does not react like most other children.

Provide the right tools

Do you know what excites your intense child? One of the biggest benefits to having a hyper, intense, and unusual child is how excited they get about things they love. For Monkey, everything is an intense high or an intense low. When I am able to bring in as many of those things that she sees as positive and happy things into school, our day goes much, much better.

Part of the reason we're focusing so much on STEM right now is because that is what makes her happy. She loves exploring the world and finding out how things work. This week, she had to write an expository paper, and she was delighted to write a long paper talking all about cheetahs and what makes them special.

Everyone prefers to learn about things they are interested it, and as homeschoolers, we have the unique ability to be able to make that happen much more efficiently than in other educational venues. If you know your child loves hands-on activities, try to provide as many of those as possible. We find that switching between subjects that are enjoyable and subjects that are not quite as fun helps keep interest up and extreme emotions in check.

As a general rule, try to find lessons that can:

- Teach using the style in which your child learns best (a lot of hands-on activities if they are a tactile learner, for example)
- Provide information on topics your child is interested in
- Teach core subjects in an enjoyable manner (nothing too dry or boring)
- Be short enough to keep the child engaged

Find the right motivation techniques

Sometimes, children with intense tendencies are difficult to motivate. For example, I cannot get Monkey to learn anything through a song. She has decided that educational songs are silly, and she will not have anything to do with any educational thought delivered through song.

Because I know this, I know not to try and motivate her through music. However, she does respond well to progress charts. She loves earning physical prizes and working toward a listed goal. Charts where a car races to the finish line, for example, are highly motivational for her. She loves earning progress badges and small prizes on her way to greater victory.

This is one reason why we enrolled her in Girl Scouts this year, because she loves earning the badges, which encourages her to go beyond just the basics of every lesson.

What motivates your child may be different, but once you find it, use that motivation technique to your advantage. Common motivations include:

- Competition
- Progress tracking
- Rewards
- Completion

Consult with experts

In some cases, a child who seems overly intense may have a medical condition. Monkey has ADHD, and we are in the process of checking for any other possible medical reasons for her intensity. If you feel that something is different about your child, definitely have a medical expert examine your child. There could be bigger issues going on than you realize.

In addition to consulting with medical experts, consult with other homeschooling parents of children who have intensity issues or special needs like yours. Maybe your child is dyslexic and another homeschooling family in your group also has a child or two with dyslexia. If your child has autism, perhaps there is another family who has an autistic child in your homeschool group. Ask the advice of other homeschooling parents who have children with similar struggles as yours. They may have advice on how to best approach the education of your child.

Make learning fun

Dry education is boring. I thought I hated science until I went to college, because my science textbooks had always been so boring. I had never experienced the fun of scientific discovery in a hands-on way.

Try to bring some fun into your lessons. We like to make our lessons fun by doing some of the following:

- Going on field trips
- Speaking to an expert on that topic (sometimes this can be combined with a field trip)
- Turning school into a game
- Learning something completely different
- Watching educational videos
- Making fun projects
- Doing a life-skills class
- Putting on a play

Explore scheduling options

Monkey thrives on structure and does not respond well when that structure is interrupted. She is thrown off by schedule changes and "off" days. For this reason, we have to follow a fairly structured scheduled each day. When she was younger, we could get away with just having the correct order of tasks, but now that she can read the clock, we have to stick to her schedule. She likes to start school at a specific time and complete her other responsibilities in order.

We've come up with a schedule that works for the both of us, and I encourage you to involve your children in your schedule-making if you can. They will appreciate being able to help determine their daily fate.

Take necessary breaks

If your child gets overwhelmed easily, perhaps a long block of school each day is not the best approach. Instead, try taking a mini-break after each subject. I let Monkey have a break after her most intense subjects before moving on. For some of the less intense subjects, I have her complete several in a row. My ultimate goal is to help her ease into longer blocks of work, because eventually, she will have to deal with long school or work days in high school, college, and when she eventually has a job.

However, we allow her to take the breaks she needs to recharge and reset her brain between subjects.

Refuel as a parent

Homeschooling an intense child can be hard on the parent as well as the student. It is draining always working as referee and buffer for learning differences and mood swings. It is important to take time for yourself both to be just a parent and to have time alone or with just other adults.

If you can only manage to take off once a month, or even once a quarter, that is fine, just make sure you refuel as much as possible. I like to watch dumb TV shows at night when I can, read books, or take a relaxing bath. These simple measures help me get rid of extra stress and face the next day with a clean slate and a happy attitude.

Don't neglect yourself in your attempt to help your child become the best person she or he can be.

Homeschooling the intense child is difficult, but rewarding

As a homeschooling parent of an intense child, I know that it can be hard. I know there are struggles that some other parents may not have to deal with. But in the end, although you may feel like quitting sometimes, I believe that the parent is often the best teacher for a child with higher-than-average needs. This kind of child benefits the most from the one-on-one learning environment that homeschooling brings. I remind myself of this fact on days when I feel like quitting. It usually helps and I feel much better about the educational path I have chosen for my children.

Homeschooling An Intense Child

Nicole Walter

Over the last 17 years of raising children, we have gone through the struggles of raising two intense children. We have one who is an intense teenager now, and he keeps us laughing regularly. The other intense child is a very, very intense child. There are so many challenges that we have overcome along the way of parenting them, and hopefully I can share some of our tricks and resources we have used throughout the years that will be helpful to anyone on the road of teaching an intense child.

About 15% to 20% of children are born with a highly aware and quick-to-react nervous system. This makes those children have very intense emotions and overexcitability in daily situations. These are the children who can emotionally go from 0 to 100 in a second; it is something that to this day still amazes me how fast it can happen.

All kids do go through a stage of these behaviors, but the other 80% of kids outgrow it in a short period. Sometimes the children who do not outgrow this can be called or are described as being emotionally immature, emotionally intense, spirited, difficult, challenging, high-need, etc.

When our intense boys were younger, people told me that one of my boys had ADHD, and that the other had to have autism. There was just something different about them that didn't quite fit either of those diagnoses completely. We finally brought them both in to see one of the only neuropsychologists in our state for some testing to get answers. I needed to know what was exactly going on with them to know how to best help them.

Those tests showed that our son who was diagnosed with ADHD was also found to be highly visually gifted; he also suffered from anxiety. To this day, he is a little silly and needs to follow a list to get things done properly, but almost all of the ADHD symptoms are gone. The other one, who was only 3½ years old at the time of the evaluation, had the IQ of Einstein along with major sensory issues, age regressions, and possibly autism if his executive functioning didn't get better in the next couple years.

It often makes me wonder how many kids are diagnosed with ADHD, autism, Asperger's or sensory dysfunction when the big problem is the fact that they have a hard time managing their intense emotions because they are gifted. I wonder if they have struggles in mainstream schools because they need to be challenged at a level above what schools can offer them.

When I started doing research into gifted children, I quickly noticed that these children will excel in certain areas, but lack in other areas (quite often the emotional area). This is the part of having a gifted child that many never see! These kids feel everything around them so much more than other kids. They are not trying to be naughty; they just don't know how to deal with the intense emotions they have. Raising two intense children has taught me so very much about being a parent. But the most important thing I have learned is that you have to really pick and choose your battles! If something won't matter years from now, it's really not worth making a big deal about.

These children will quite often push us as parents to the limits and leave us feeling like we are failures. I am just glad my very intense child was my fifth and I knew the other kids were nothing like this. If he had been my first child, I would have thought I failed miserably as a parent. I would have constantly wondered if I should have done things differently.

The hardest thing is when your intense child has a breakdown out in public. All the noises, lights, smells, and commotion everywhere are so hard for them to handle. The looks you get and the things people will say to you are not nice at all. If I had a penny for every time someone came up to me and said "You just need to spank him," I would be rich. Those are the times intense prayer helped me not say to those people what my initial thought was.

What are your child's struggles?

The first step in teaching your intense child or children is to find out what it is that they struggle with. I suggest keeping a journal for the next week or two.

- Write down things that help you children when he or she has an intense moment, and try to figure out what things set him or her off in each of the situations.

- Write down what subjects they are excited about doing, as well as the ones they struggle with and dread doing.

- Make a list of the things that are working well and another list of things that aren't working well.

After making these lists, decide what you can do differently to change things around.

How to deal with intense children's struggles when teaching them

There are a lot of things we have done over the years to help my intense children while teaching them. One of my intense children really struggled in reading, and while he was great at most math things, he couldn't count to 10 without skipping numbers. We found hands-on and visual ways for him to learn these skills, and repetition was essential for him. Sitting after the first hour of school is a struggle for him as well; we also work hard to keep him as calm as we can because he learns so much better that way. Some of the things we have done over the years are:

- Prayer. First and foremost, I start my day off reading God's word, and pray regularly throughout my day. Without the strength of God and His word, I couldn't get through what I do every day, simple as that. If I am starting to get stressed out, I pray for strength and guidance on what God wants me to do, not what I feel like to think I should do. The Holy Spirit will guide me on what needs to be done. I also memorize Bible verses that will help me when these struggles come up.

- Have a fidget basket. We have a little basket full of fidgets so the kids can fidget while I am reading stories or while they are working. You can even find fidgets to put onto pencils to touch or even chew on.

- Eat a crunchy snack or snack through a straw. Since my intense child has lots of oral sensitivity issues, he will chew on clothing or fingers when he gets anxious. We will give him crunchy snacks to eat in between classes; other times I give him applesauce or pudding to suck through a straw. This gives him the much-needed oral input and dramatically decreases his chewing on things.

- Use a wiggle seat or exercise band. We put the wiggle seat on the chair, or have an exercise band around the legs of the chair, to help them stay seated during school.

- Take regular breaks to get wiggles out. Every 30 minutes to an hour, we take a quick break to run around the backyard for a few minutes, going up and down the stairs, doing push-ups and jumping jacks, using our sensory swing, etc.

- Change things up. Some days, for spelling words, instead of writing them on paper in pencil, we might write them on the marker board, spell them out in playdough, use a special pen or pencil on paper, spell them out loud, or just do something different that gets them moving and keeps their interest.

- Join a sport. Our intense kids have tried a few sports throughout the years, and as of last year we have found that getting these intense kids into intense physical sports makes a big difference. This doesn't exactly have to deal with school, but essentially it does. My intense kids have been in a three-day-a-week intensive gymnastics class doing college-level conditioning, and the improvements I have seen in the home and in school are amazing. They can sit for longer periods with fewer distractions, and are a lot calmer.

- Heavy work. Giving your intense child some heavy work to do before starting school and in between classes can make a big difference.

- Take animal walks.

- Carry a milk jug filled with rocks, beans, water, etc., around the room a certain amount of times.

- Play on a jungle gym, climb the rock wall, use the monkey bars, etc.

- Play with a medicine ball.

- Use a scooter board laying on your stomach and using your arms to push yourself around.

- Lay on your stomach reading a book while being squished between two pillows.

- Carry books, a bucket filled with toys, or buckets full of sand around.

- Dig holes in the dirt.

- Help with chores like vacuuming, scrubbing, transferring laundry from washing machine to dryer.

- Pull a wagon with people, rocks, or dirt inside.

- Go around on a hop ball.

- Do woodworking that involves sanding and nailing.

- Do push-ups.

- Use a rewards chart. Sometimes the only incentives kids need are completely visual. In our spelling and reading program, kids put a sticker over the lesson number of the printed-out chart. Picking and adding the sticker is great fun for the kids, and they look forward to it at the end of each lesson. You can find many free charts you could print for any class and put stickers on after each lesson.

- Visual chart. My very intense child struggles when he doesn't know what is going on with our daily schedule. By the evening, he is so out of whack that he couldn't even think about deciding what to do to help himself calm down. We put together our own visual schedule; every day he helps me decide what to put into the schedule for the day, including the order of his classes. As we finish a class, he will put a check under that one for the day. We also have a weekly calendar that shows upcoming outings, appointments, therapies, and more.

- Switch curriculum. While many homeschoolers don't want to switch programs because it isn't working for that child, especially in the middle of the year, sometimes it is necessary to do so. We decided to switch over to Montessori teaching for a few years when my very intense child was younger. He wanted to know how to do everything adults could do, at only 2 years old, but he struggled with fine motor skills. Now we make sure to look for programs for him that offer many different ways of learning, and they always have to include visual and hands-on learning.

- Use listening therapy. This is a concept that I only learned about 9 months ago. Where one of my sons does therapy, they have started giving the kids these special headphones with certain music that helps them stay calm, regulate emotions, get moving, and many other great skills. Because the headphones are quite expensive, they now have an app out that you can install on your tablet or phone so you can play the songs without the headphones. We will use this music before we start school, during the day when lots of energy needs to be released, before bed, while trying to calm down, etc. I would like to get the headphones in the future because the songs are longer then the app songs and the headphones have special qualities that, from what I have heard, are just what these intense kids need.

- Get them help if they need it. Because the intense children feel everything so deeply, you need to make sure this isn't causing them emotional problems. Our intense child has been going through many illnesses and surgeries during the last year. This started effecting him negatively in his behaviors around the house. We are now seeing a psychologist every week who does play therapy with him to work through the busyness that he is going through right now.

- Skip school. I know some of you will think, "Why would I let my child skip school?" The reason for this is that there are just some days that are not good days at all, and chances are, you won't get much done without big struggles anyway! Expecting your child who is struggling to complete their normal school subjects can just sometimes lead to disasters and lots of frustration. As time has gone on, I have realized it is just better to find other things to do on those days. We tend to find a calming or fun activity to do on those days. Below are some of our favorite things to do on those days.
  - Playing board/card games
  - Reading stories
  - Coloring
  - Arts and crafts
  - Playdough
  - Busy bags
  - Baking something together (cookies, muffins, bread, etc.)
  - Doing heavy work activities
  - Playing in a sensory bin
  - Using a DIY homemade light table

Now you have quite an extensive list of what to do to figure out where your intense child is struggling, as well as what to do to help your intense child while teaching them. There are many other moms who are in the same boat or have been there before, so do not feel alone.

A couple of my favorite books that give great advice and ideas for raising your intense child are listed below. You can find either of them on Amazon, both as digital and physical books.

- Parenting A Child Who Has Intense Emotions by Pat Harvey and Jeanine A. Penzo

- The Highly Sensitive Child: Helping our Children Thrive When The World Overwhelms Them by Elaine Aron

Homeschooling Outliers
Caitlin Fitzpatrick Curley

I never set out to homeschool. It's not that I had anything against homeschooling, it's just that it was never on my radar. As a product of public schools and a school psychologist, I always assumed that our children would attend public schools as my husband and I had.

Never assume, folks!

After a pretty cruddy year in kindergarten, a year that was filled with complaints about school and a mounting pile of behavioral warnings, we decided to have our oldest son, Leo, assessed by an outside psychologist. We knew there was something different about him, something the school had failed to see in him, and we assumed that if we had it on paper school would be better for him.

Once again: never assume.

Our oldest son, Leo, is an outlier among outliers: a profoundly gifted, twice-exceptional child. Results of the outside evaluation indicated that Leo's cognitive abilities were above the 99.9th percentile, and that his academic abilities were two to six years above grade level.

Once I had those test results in my hand, I saw our gifted reality, and it was messy. We had a 6-year-old child with the intellect of someone more than twice his age but the emotions of a 5- or 6-year-old and academic abilities everywhere in between.

How, on earth, would a K-3 elementary school meet the needs of a kid with that profile? From my experience as a school psychologist, I knew they couldn't do it well. My husband and I decided to homeschool our son the week that the results were in hand. It was the most impulsive decision of our lives, and it was terrifying, but we knew in our guts that it was the right choice for our son.

Homeschooling outliers

Here's the thing about giftedness: Everyone assumes that you are lucky, that your child has a leg up over his or her peers. (Never assume!) When one hears the word gifted, they tend to think of the straight-A student, the well-behaved kid at the front of class who is destined for Harvard. This is not my reality. The reality is, giftedness is messy, and it's made messier because no one really understands these kids.

Gifted children are asynchronous

Of all the definitions of giftedness that are floating around out there, my favorite is this one from the Columbus Group, because it touches upon giftedness as asynchrony:

Giftedness is asynchronous development in which advanced cognitive abilities and heightened intensity combine to create inner experiences and awareness that are qualitatively different from the norm. This asynchrony increases with higher intellectual capacity. The uniqueness of the gifted renders them particularly vulnerable and requires modifications in parenting, teaching and counseling in order for them to develop optimally. (The Columbus Group, 1991).

Asynchronous development is one of the hallmarks of giftedness. While most children develop in a relatively even manner, gifted learners are asynchronous in their development. And the more gifted the child, the more asynchronous that child may be. There can be huge differences between a gifted child's physical, intellectual, social, and emotional development. A gifted child can have the intelligence of an adult with the social-emotional development of a child. It is often said that gifted children are "many ages at once;" they are quite literally out-of-sync.

What does asynchronous development look like in a child?

- A 2-year-old who cannot sleep at night because he's afraid that humans will suddenly become extinct for some unknown reason, just as the dinosaurs had.

- A 3-year-old who, while playing with his peers, sees a garden trellis and stops to admire its beauty. Awestruck, he exclaims, "Hey guys! Look at that! Doesn't it look like a portcullis?"

- A 4-year-old who creates amazing inventions and yet cannot wait in line for more than five minutes without dissolving into a mushy mess, tantruming like a 2-year-old.

- A 5-year-old who uses the term galoshes when talking to his friends.

- A 6-year-old who loses sleep at night because he is terrified of global warming.

- A 7-year-old who loses sleep at night because he fears God will take revenge on our "too selfish society."

- A 7-year-old who cries at a family barbeque because a lobster boil is cruel.

- A 7-year-old who loses sleep at night, worrying that the sun is going to burn out.

Put simply, our son's mind houses thoughts that his emotions cannot yet handle and this can result in anxiety, inattention, and behavioral challenges.

Twice-exceptional (2E) adds a unique challenge

Do you know what complicates matters further? My son is twice-exceptional: profoundly gifted and learning disabled. He has some amazing strengths but he also has significant challenges, including sensory processing disorder, ADHD characteristics, and anxiety.

Homeschooling outliers can be challenging

Parenting and educating a gifted and twice-exceptional child can be a lonely venture for many reasons.

- **You didn't set out to homeschool.** Many homeschoolers have planned to homeschool their children all along. They planned for it and had a vision. Many gifted parents, however, are thrust into homeschooling because they feel they have no other choice. This causes them to feel overwhelmed and disconnected from the homeschool population.

- **Your child is quite different from his or her peers.** Because your child is so asynchronous, he or she may have trouble interacting with same-age peers.

- **Your child has an atypical learning profile.** If your 5-year-old is reading The Hobbit as mine was, it may be challenging to find co-op classes and other community courses that meet his needs. All too often, courses are age-based and this is challenging for gifted youth.

- **No one feels comfortable talking about giftedness.** No one wants to use the g-word because they don't want to be identified as That Parent, they fear that others will assume they hothouse and push their children to achieve. Because of this, you feel as if you are on the only person struggling with these issues.

- **Put simply: These kids are intense.** Gifted children are tough to parent and educate because they are many ages at once. Plus, many exhibit gifted overexcitabilities that can result in boundless energy, extreme sensitivity, and emotional intensity.

- **Curriculum choices are challenging** because your child's skills are so incredibly asynchronous. You cannot purchase grade-based curriculum when your child's skills are so asynchronous.

- **You worry about your child surpassing your abilities.** It can be intimidating to homeschool a profoundly gifted child. You find yourself constantly worrying about the future. What will I do when he surpasses my math skills? How will I teach him?

8 tips for homeschooling outliers, from someone in the trenches

Folks, I don't claim to be an expert on this topic. I'm right there in the trenches with you all. Still, I am happy to share what has helped us navigate our gifted homeschooling journey.

- **Research, research, research.** When we first decided to homeschool, I spent my hours reading about giftedness, 2E children, and homeschooling. It was well worth it because I not only grew to understand my son more fully, but I found a variety of resources that have proved invaluable.

- **Ignore naysayers.** We live in a fantastic town, one of those towns that folks move to for the school district. One thing that I was surprised by when we first made the decision to homeschool was how many people were offended by our choice. Our decision to homeschool is based on our experience with our child and others should respect that. If they don't, ignore them.

- **Find support.** Parenting a gifted child can be really hard. It can be lonely. You feel as if no one else truly understands the challenges. Find a community. If you cannot find one, create one. I co-founded a Facebook group called Raising Poppies with a dear friend of mine and it's amazing and refreshing to connect with parents on the same path.

- **Take care of yourself.** It can be tough to be around intense kids all day long. Be sure to take care of yourself. Find out what makes you feel good and whole and do that.

- **Find a community for your child**. Research has shown that gifted children need intellectual peers. It can be tough to find other gifted families when you first start homeschooling because no one likes to talk about it. That said, I assure you that there are gifted families out there! When we first started on this journey, there were no local NH supports. Over time, I founded Granite State Gifted, a local community of gifted families, and it has been amazing to see my son connect with peers who understand him!

- **Be creative about curriculum.** I've learned that you need to be flexible with curriculum when homeschooling a gifted learner. When I choose curriculum, I look for something that my son can use for a long time – that means something that allows for multiple grade levels or creativity. He learns so fast that he can cover entire grade levels quickly and that can get costly.

- **Ask for help when you need it.** Whether that help is from your spouse, other caregivers, gifted parents and educators, physicians, or counselors, be sure to ask for help and accept help. It takes a village!

- **Trust your gut.** There will be times when you question your decision to homeschool. You will worry and lose sleep over choices made and upcoming decisions. Trust your gut, and remember that you were your child's first teacher. You know and love your child more than anyone else on this planet and you are fully equipped to do this. Don't get in your own way!

I never set out to homeschool. It was a sudden and unexpected path for our family, but it is perhaps the best decision we have made as a family. Our son's passion for learning has been restored. His smile has returned. We have learned so much from our homeschooling journey and we look forward to what the future holds.

Homeschooling Through A Health Crisis

Nicole Walter

I think if you asked a group of people how they would define a health crisis, each individual would probably define the word differently according to the health crises they have personally been through.

Some people do not go through many health crises, for them, just getting really sick would be one. Other people have had to deal with themselves or their children's long-term health issues like cancer, arthritis, autoimmune diseases, or other diseases that affect their lives daily for quite some time.

There are different ways we handle health crises in our house, depending on who is having health problems. We homeschool our kids year-round for a couple of reasons, but the main reason is so that we can be flexible in our daily lives. Really, because of the fact that our life is always throwing us curveballs, we like to have the opportunity to just take off of school if we need to deal with a crisis without it affecting our school much.

The first six years of homeschooling our kids, we took summers off. However, due to life happening and having to take off of school unexpectedly, we would often be doing school into the summer. There was a year or two where we still had a couple of chapters left in a couple of classes because life that year was hard.

There are a few things I have learned while dealing with continual health crises.

- **Be flexible.** This one in number one because it is that important! The one tip I have learned that I wish I would have learned years ago is to be flexible in our homeschool as well as daily life. If some things don't get finished I had hoped to do, oh well, we can do it later. This is where year-round homeschool gives us tons of flexibility.

- **Pray.** When I am struggling with the craziness of our life, especially during health crises, it is usually because I am not trusting that God has my back even when I don't feel like he does. Remembering to go to Him in prayer will often change my attitude about the situation.

- **Put family first.** If you have a family member who is struggling through a health crisis, help him or her do whatever they will allow you to do, even if it's just visiting. School will still be there tomorrow; you will not be upset that you spent that time with that person. You will, however, be upset if you didn't spend that time with that person and he or she is not there tomorrow. Besides, if more parents nowadays taught their children how to care for others, this world would be a much better place!

- **Find the positive.** This is another critical piece in my opinion. Life can seem like it is crashing down around you during a health crisis; finding the positive in every single situation, no matter how hard that is, will make things so much easier. I truly believe if you think you can't, then those are the results you will get. If you think you can, you can do anything you put your mind to!

Mom health crisis

The first will be a Mom health crisis. Our family has been through this many different times with my multitude of health problems. I have walked around with a hole in my lung for two weeks; I have come down with a very serious case of pneumonia; and had toxemia after delivery. I also deal daily with the effects of many different health problems, and very strong medicines taken weekly that wipe me out for days.

We all know that when Mom is the teacher, school becomes a problem when she is sick. Usually when I am sick, the kids will just get the time off of school. I do this because I usually need the time off to just heal and not worry about school and checking things. I know that if I don't take care of myself, things are not going to go well! Usually it is enough for my husband and kids to make sure there are three meals a day, the kids are dressed, and appointments are made. Worrying about having school done and checked is just not a priority during this time.

The kids will do other activities during these times like crafts, reading, board games, coloring, researching something of interest, helping to make meals, helping with household chores, etc. If I am very sick and my husband cannot be home to help with the kids, I will snuggle with the kids and watch movies. This is the only time in our house the kids are allowed to watch above their couple hours of screen time a day, so you can imagine how much they enjoy it!

Child health crisis

As you can expect, with six children (five of them being boys), we have had our fair share of child health crises. We have had spur-of-the-moment problems, like a child bit by a dog very badly, Kawasaki Disease, a multitude of surgeries, broken bones, a few different cases of stitches, doctors freaking out because they swore one of our kids had a deadly childhood cancer (he really didn't, though), a finger getting caught in the garage door track, and many others.

We also have had long-term child health crises in our house. During the beginning of our homeschooling journey, one of my kiddos had severe asthma, and we also discovered he had severe allergies to everything around in the environment. They did not have him on a good medicine regimen, so he would get severely sick from just a common cold. Once that happened, we would end up with pneumonia with respiratory distress and be frequently visiting the hospital and doctor's office. Now we have a kiddo who gets weird health conditions that suddenly come up, like Kawasaki Disease and a weak immune system. That kiddo was also born with a cleft lip and palate, and has brain damage. This means he spends lots of time at doctor's offices, in for surgeries, and in five hours of therapies every week.

You know you have been through lots of interesting medical trials when your pediatrician says they are going to call you when they have a hard time diagnosing something. Or when the psychologist tells you, after hearing the history of just one of your children, that you should write a book.

We do what we need to do to get our school all done anyway. During surgeries, the person who is having surgery will get off of school; how intense the surgery is will determine for how long they get off. If our older kids have to babysit while we are taking the child to appointments, in for surgeries, or to the hospital, they get those days off of school. The other older kids will continue to do their independent classes on their own, and I will check it to make sure the work is done when I can. Our group classes are put on hold until life settles down.

School on the go

At this stage in our lives, because we have a couple kids who have a lot of therapies they have to attend each week. We spend about five hours in therapy a week right now for just one of our kids; that has been going on for over a year. We also have another child who has two hours of therapy to fit in between there. I will often work with a child in the waiting room while the other one is back for therapy. This works out great and gives us time to get school finished despite not being at home.

If we go into doctor's appointments for the day, we will bring our reading or something that we can work on at the office or in the car on the way there. If we visit doctors out of town, I will bring work in the car for any of the kids who go with us, which will keep them busy for a while. I will also bring other fun activities with us to keep them busy for a long car ride. The kids at home may do school or may get the day off; it just depends how many other days we have taken off for the year.

Family member health crisis

A family member health crisis could include your parents, grandparents, an aunt or uncle, etc. A couple of the family member health crises we have gone through are my sister having a baby and us babysitting our niece for a few days during our school week, and my mother going through liver failure and many health complications the last two years of her life.

We often try to do whatever we can to help someone in a health crisis. Sometimes that means making a meal for a family, driving them to appointments, or just visiting and spending some time with them. Sometimes this will mean taking a whole week off of school to help pack up a house, provide support, or whatever needs to be done. Other times we will only do morning school and take the afternoon off to do what needs to be done; still other times, we will need to take the day or a couple of days off of school. Homeschooling year-round is what gives us this flexibility without affecting our classes.

Prayer and keeping God first

During any health crisis, the only thing that gets me through it is God. Now, I know not everyone feels the same way, and that's fine; you are welcome to skip to the next section.

I don't know how I would get through health crises without God, His grace and His strength. Starting each day in prayer and reading His word, even if life is crazy and busy because of the crisis, is just essential in my opinion.

During those crises I find it good to look for stories in the Bible where God has given strength and perseverance to someone during very trying times. Other times I will go through a Bible study pertaining to a character trait I want to work on. Memorizing a verse about God giving us strength and repeating it when I am struggling is also helpful to me. One of my favorite verses to remember during a crisis is:

Be strong and courageous. Do not fear or be in dread of them, for it is the LORD your God who goes with you. He will not leave you or forsake you.
Deuteronomy 31:6

Year-round homeschool

Due to the fact that we deal with ongoing regular health crises with multiple people in our house, we have decided to homeschool our kids year-round. We have only been doing this for the last four years, but now that we have been doing it for a while I sure wish I would have done this earlier.

Our regular full school year runs from August through June, with December off of school. During our school year, our kids do all of their regular classes and participate in sports, and homeschool groups. During July, kids have a lightened school load of math, reading and Bible, as well as adding in science for the middle school and younger kids (it's too hard to do science with snow on the ground). We also spend quite a bit of time out on nature trails, at beaches and in the woods exploring our local wildlife and habitats and getting to spend time outside with friends and family.

Because we do school year-round, if we have an unexpected health crisis come up, we just take time off of school without any problems. If we didn't end up having any health crises (which we haven't yet), we would just get to take a few weeks off during the school year. Before we did year-round homeschool, we would have to take time off and make it up on the weekends, or at the end of the school year. Having more flexibility and not having this stress in our lives while a health crisis is happening has been such a blessing.

Independent work

We currently have four older kids who are able to independently complete their school with just oversight from me to check that it was finished. In order to keep them on track and make it easier for them to know what they need to do each day, we provide them with a calendar notebook at the beginning of the year. The calendar will show them what classes need to be completed each day and they just check it off. They will write the lesson or page number in the calendar each day so that when we do take off for a health crisis, the whole calendar isn't messed up.

We have two younger boys who are mostly independent in some of their classes, and they also have a couple other classes that they need my help with. The actions we take with these boys depend on the health crisis that arises. Usually we would do a lightened load of school and do a couple of classes each day; occasionally we will completely take off.

Teaching the kids to work independently was not something that happened overnight, and it surely isn't something that was very easy. Now that we are seeing the fruits of our work, I am so very happy we have done this. Besides, someday they will need to know how to independently work at their jobs and in real life, so in my opinion, it is an essential skill to learn.

Now you have a look into how we deal with health crises in our homeschool. I pray that some of these ideas will be helpful to other families going through a health crisis.

Homeschooling Through a Move

Crystal Wagner

From an old English parsonage down by the sea
There came in the twilight a message for me;
Its quaint Saxon legend, deeply engraven,
Hath, it seems to me, teaching from Heaven.
And on through the hours the quiet words ring,
Like a low inspiration: DO THE NEXT THING.

Many a questioning, many a fear,
Many a doubt, hath its quieting here.
Moment by moment let down from Heaven,
Time, opportunity, guidance, are given.
Fear not tomorrows, Child of the King,
Trust them with Jesus. DO THE NEXT THING.

Do it immediately; do it with prayer;
Do it reliantly, casting all care;
Do it with reverence, tracing His hand
Who placed it before thee with earnest command,
Stayed on Omnipotence, safe 'neath His wing,
Leave all results. DO THE NEXT THING.

Looking for Jesus, ever serener,
Working or suffering be thy demeanor.
In His dear presence, the rest of His calm,
The light of His countenance be thy psalm.
Strong in His faithfulness, praise and sing!
Then, as He beckons thee, DO THE NEXT THING.

When you move, there is so much to do. With scheduling inspections, setting up utilities, packing, and then unpacking, how do you fit in homeschooling too? We have moved three times since we began our homeschool journey, two long-distance and one across town. Each was different and had its own unique challenges. Here are some ways I have learned to cope and even thrive during a move.

View the move as an adventure

Recognize that it will take time to settle into a new routine when you move. Even after the last box is unpacked, you will have to find a new rhythm for the new house. Even a move across town demands new workflows. If you move to another state, you have additional challenges of finding your way around town and learning the best places to buy groceries. One of our moves was 12 hours away. We had to adjust to being much farther away from family, finding our way around, and learning to live in a new climate. We kept an attitude of adventure and were able to roll with the punches instead of getting frustrated or angry.

Do the next thing

There is so much to do when you move, it can be overwhelming. Instead of being overwhelmed, focus on the next thing. Make a list of what you need to accomplish. Choose the five that must be done today and get started on those.

Keep moving forward

Keep your eyes looking forward. Instead of focusing on what you are leaving behind, focus on the adventures awaiting you. You will discover new favorite restaurants and field trips. You will make new friends. Remember the Girl Scout song, "Make new friends, but keep the old. One is silver and the other gold." I now have friends all over the country because of our moves, and cherish each one.

Set realistic expectations

With the added responsibilities and stress of the move, you will not be able to maintain your normal level of academic lessons and activities. Cut back to the essentials or take a break. Your children will not be behind and will gain valuable life skills. This is a great time to listen to audiobooks while packing up the books homeschool families seem to collect faster than rabbits reproduce.

Involve the whole family

Children can contribute a lot during a move. Keep your child's developmental ability level in mind and find tasks that will allow him to contribute. Even a young child can wipe out a cabinet after the dishes have been packed. When my girls were 6 and 9 years old, they were able to help pack clothes, toys, and books, carry lighter boxes to the truck, and hold doors open as we moved heavy furniture.

Rejoice in new perspectives

Every part of the country is different. Even moving across town can have a different feel. I am thankful for the different perspectives I have from living in different states. I am able to tolerate the winters in Oklahoma because they are far milder than those in Wisconsin. When someone says, "Brr. It's cold," I can reply, "No, I can still smile and my teeth don't hurt. It's not cold yet."

Express gratitude

Keeping a gratitude journal is a great way keep your move in the proper perspective. This one simple tool helped me keep my attitude of adventure during a difficult move. Encourage everyone to share something for which they are thankful at dinner.

Extend grace

Moving involves a lot of different emotions. If you are moving to a different town, you and your children will leave behind old friends. There will be uncertainty about the new house and new town. It will take time to make new friends. Extend grace to yourself and your family as you make this transition.

Maintain habits

This is not a time to allow bad habits to creep in. It will be difficult to maintain good habits, but doing so will be a blessing in the long run.

Explore your new town

Contact your local Chamber of Commerce for a new resident packet and see what cool things your new town has to offer. Is there a farmer's market where you can get a feel for the town? Where can you take a field trip to learn about the area? Visit local parks and find your new favorite one. If you go during school hours, chances are you will meet some new homeschool families too! And don't forget to meet the librarian. She might be able to help you connect with other homeschool families and let you know what resources the library has to offer homeschoolers.

Seek support

Contact state, regional, and local homeschool support organizations. This is a great way to learn about the homeschool regulations in your state and meet new friends. Most towns have at least one support group. Getting connected quickly will allow your family to start putting down roots and feel settled.

Moving is never easy. There will be many challenges, but there will also be many blessings. Choose to find the blessings in the midst of the chaos.

Homeschooling through Job Loss or Financial Crisis

Emily Copeland

Most homeschool families know the struggles and sacrifices that come with balancing household expenses with homeschool expenses. Because that balance is often fine, even small unexpected expenses can quickly complicate the family budget. When bigger financial obstacles come along, many homeschool families are faced with questions about how and if they can continue homeschooling.

Those are the soul-searching moments: Do you really believe that all of life is a learning experience, or does it just sound like the right thing to say? Three months before our youngest child was born, my husband told me that his full-time employer decided to restructure and phase out his job. Within a month, we went from a household with one full-time income and one part-time income to a family of almost four living on a part-time income. For more than a year, we lived off of his remaining part-time salary and, while it wasn't glamourous or easy, we made it through and learned life lessons along the way. Life is a great teacher.

Homeschooling presents its own challenges under normal circumstances, but when financial stresses threaten, the feasibility of homeschooling is often the first thing questioned. The first thing to remember is that it's always

OK to take a break from the way you've always approached homeschooling and try something different for a while. You may even find that you prefer the changes.

One of the beautiful things about homeschooling is that you can adapt as needed to best suit the needs of your family. That may mean forgoing your curriculum preferences and choosing less expensive options. It may mean searching for work-at-home options and transitioning your children to self-led homeschooling. It also may mean asking friends and family to help while you work outside the home. The options may not seem ideal, but they may be necessary for a season.

Free or low-cost homeschooling

In times of financial crises, your budget simply may not allow for new curriculum, shiny new school supplies, and all of the fun things that come along with homeschooling. The good news is that homeschooling is absolutely possible even when new purchases aren't. It may take some time and research, but you might be surprised by just how many options there are for low-cost homeschooling!

If you prefer to follow a full curriculum, websites like Ambleside Online and Easy Peasy All-in-One Homeschool are a couple worth considering. While Ambleside is specifically a free Charlotte Mason-inspired curriculum, All-in-One Homeschool is more eclectic in its approach. Both are incredibly thorough and are a blessing to many homeschool families.

If a full online curriculum isn't a good match for your children, I recommend purchasing a homeschool planning guide such as Rebecca Rupp's *Home Learning Year by Year*. I borrowed it from our local library first, decided it was a keeper, and then purchased a used copy for around $5 on Amazon. I have used it countless times in our homeschooling years, but it made all the difference during the especially strapped times.

When you're not working with a curriculum, a book like *Home Learning Year by Year* can provide the foundation you need to plan your homeschool year. It provides suggestions for what to cover and when from preschool through high school, and many of the suggested resources can be borrowed from a local library. Having a guideline like this is a huge help when looking for free resources online and looking for inexpensive used materials for your children.

Obtaining materials when the budget is tight

Once you have your guideline of choice, you can create a plan for your homeschool. Having that guideline is important because it can give you a direction and a starting point for obtaining materials. Hunting and gathering resources can take time, but the reward is great. After all, this might be the very thing that allows you to continue homeschooling through difficult financial times.

For the most part, a good internet connection is all you truly need to homeschool for free or almost free. There are lots of options for free or low-cost resources that fit nearly every homeschooling style. Here are a few ideas to get you started:

Putting Pinterest to work. Think of it as a gathering place for countless ideas and resources for your homeschool because lots of parents, publishers, and teachers share free resources there. The key is to know what you're looking for before you get started. That way you don't get lost in the sea of new recipes and home decorating tips while you're trying to plan for your homeschool.

Frequent your local libraries. I can't stress this one enough. Many books used for homeschooling are only used while covering specific topics over the course of a few weeks. Borrowing these books from your local library is a no-brainer! Borrowing from your library is also a good way to preview titles before purchasing your own copy. An added bonus is that most libraries now loan out ebooks in addition to their physical circulation.

Put streaming to work for you. Streaming services like Netflix and Amazon Prime may seem like unnecessary expenses, but many homeschoolers find them higher on their priority lists than keeping cable or satellite services for their homes. Free channels like PBS Kids are also available to stream through streaming devices.

Plenty of documentaries are available for viewing; those are particularly helpful for supplementing science, history and performing arts. There are also lots of television shows that can be used to your advantage. These shows can be a part of regular TV time for your children or worked into lesson plans to reinforce what you're covering at the time. Here are a few good options to consider:

- Science can be covered (or supplemented) with shows like The Magic School Bus, Wild Kratts, and Popular Mechanics for Kids. These are good for covering specific topics.
- Martha Speaks, Word Girl, Reading Rainbow, and The Electric Company are just a few options that reinforce language arts.
- Preschool-friendly shows can be lifesavers! Episodes of WordWorld, Sid the Science Kid, Little Einsteins, Peg + Cat, and Super Why can go a long way in teaching basic preschool concepts and much more.

Buy used on Amazon and eBay. If you decide that curriculum purchases are needed, buying used is the smart way to go for many items. It's even worth considering for consumables like workbooks or student books. Be sure to read descriptions thoroughly so that you can know what condition the used items are in and how many pages from the consumables have been used previously.

Regardless of what you choose to use, be sure to preview before presenting it with your children. That applies to books, videos, educational games, and so on. That's the only way to know for sure that your resources line up with your belief system or if sensitive topics will be covered.

For additional ideas on how to make adjustments to your homeschool budget while going through financial struggles, you may enjoy my Make Over Your Homeschool Budget Series.

Cutting other expenses

The choice to homeschool comes with sacrifices for many families, mine included, from the very beginning from our homeschool journey. When I worked outside the home, I brought in more than half of our family's income. Turning in my notice to begin homeschooling meant we had to make big adjustments to our spending from the start. When our income took another hit a few years later, sacrifices were no longer optional. They had to be made so that we could continue this calling to homeschool. We've also learned that even when we're not struggling financially, homeschooling still requires sacrifice. Here are a few things we've done throughout the years to make room for the expenses that come with homeschooling and ease the blow from loss of income.

Cut the cable (or Dish package). One of the quickest ways to spend less is to make adjustments to your television packages. Between the many streaming options available and the quality of digital receivers for broadcast television, there's no reason to be tied down to costly contracts for hundreds of channels you'll probably not miss anyway. If you live in a rural area like I do, you may not be able to let go of the packages completely. Those digital receivers, as good as they are, don't pick up in our area. To make up for that, we have the lowest satellite package available. While we still have the service, we're still spending considerably less than even the next package up. That certainly gives us some breathing room in our budget.

Be disciplined about eating out. While it's tempting because of convenience alone, eating out adds up quickly. Even for our family of four, we're lucky to spend less than $20 in the cheapest drive-through. That's a big blow to our grocery budget! Add that to the fact that it's unhealthy and there's no real justification for it. Skip the fast food whenever possible and save restaurant visits for special occasions.

Clear and stock your closets through consignment and eBay. I'm still stunned when my children only wear an item once or twice before outgrowing it! It would make me sick to spend lots of money on clothing they barely get to wear. Instead, we usually purchase from local consignment shops and eBay. It takes some looking around and patience, but it always pays off for us.

When your kids outgrow their clothes, consider consigning them. You may not make much by doing this, but every dollar helps when you're facing financial issues. My favorite consignment shop would give consigners 60% of their sales if they chose to be paid through store credit or 40% to be paid for your sales on a monthly basis. That was a huge blessing for us in our most financially strapped times. There were times I made enough in consignment sales to completely cover clothing expenses for our kids because I used the store credit as my payment.

Buying and selling through eBay can also pay off. You can sometimes get an entire season's worth of clothing for less than a few items from the cheapest retail options. As for selling, do an eBay search for any items you would potentially sell and get a feel for how other sellers present those items. Once you've got an idea, get your items together and get them listed. While the payoff isn't instant, nor is a sale guaranteed, you can still use any money you make to help with other expenses when money is tight.

Use retail points programs for gifts. Kellogg's, Pampers, Swagbucks, My Coke Rewards, and lots of other companies have points programs that allow you to enter points and receive rewards. It takes time and dedication, but be sure to clip those labels, cut those codes, and search through Swagbucks. Then redeem your points for gift cards, magazine subscriptions, and lots of other things that can be used as gifts. The gift cards especially can be helpful for gifting when money is tight. You can simply gift the cards or use them to purchase gifts. Either way, you're not using money from your household to do so.

Be aware of Amazon's Warehouse Deals. In the past, we've saved money by purchasing diapers, wipes, household items, and several other things this way. You can get considerable savings on needed items through Warehouse Deals, usually because the original packaging was damaged.

Don't be afraid to do it yourself. From making your own laundry detergent to fixing an appliance and everything in between, do some research before you put it in the shopping cart or call a professional. For example, I started making our laundry detergent through a recipe I found on Pinterest years ago and saw the savings immediately. For about $25, I can make all the detergent we need for an entire year! We've also gone the DIY route for other household items like hand soap and body wash over the years to help lessen our spending.

As for the bigger things like replacing a car part or troubleshooting an appliance, you can save lots of money on labor costs by doing these things yourself. Sometimes you have call to a professional anyway, but some issues can be fixed inexpensively with some help from video tutorials or forums found online. It is always worth researching before calling someone else and spending that extra money!

In closing, it's absolutely possible to homeschool through financial crises and even job loss. It may not come easily and it may require a great deal of creativity and sacrifice, but it is possible. Don't let financial storms stop you from homeschooling! Be willing to ask for help, make adjustments to your homeschooling approach, and sacrifice in other household areas and you can weather the storm and come out stronger in the end.

Homeschooling While Pregnant

LaToya Edwards

Homeschooling during my last pregnancy was a lot harder than I expected. I always have hyperemesis when I pregnant. If you aren't familiar with it, think morning sickness on steroids. On top of being exhausted, I usually spend a lot of time severely dehydrated, sick and in the hospital. I'll be honest, not a lot of homeschooling gets done.

I struggle with perfectionism, and it was really hard for me to wave my white flag when it came to homeschooling. I really wanted to keep up with math, reading and spelling, but that's almost impossible when you can barely lift your head off a pillow.

Grace became the word of this tough season. I had to learn to give myself a lot of grace, especially in the first four months when I was feeling my worst. Your children's education is important, but that doesn't mean that you need to push forward at all costs.

The best thing that I did during my pregnancy was to scale back to the basics. When I had some energy I made sure that I covered Bible, reading, math and spelling with my boys. These are subjects that I call "non-negotiable." Just focusing on these things is a great way to move forward in those important subjects.

There were times when I had to let go of even those important subjects. There were those weeks when I was spending more time in bed, on the couch or at the hospital than I was able to teach. During these seasons I had to get creative about what school time looked like. When I wasn't able to continue our science read-aloud, I requested the audiobook from the library. We watched documentaries and the Liberty's Kids cartoons for history and Magic School Bus for science.

I wasn't able to read or teach reading for a while, but my boys could read to me. My oldest was also able to help out his younger brother if he struggled with a word here and there. It was nice to listen to my boys read and really warmed my heart to see them working together.

One other thing that really helped when I was pregnant was having my boys helping out around the house. They were able to fix themselves breakfast and lunch so I only had to worry about getting dinner in the slow cooker before 5 p.m. They were also able to keep the house relatively clean. Those months that I spent training my boys to wash dishes, clean their bathroom and vacuum were well worth it when I just couldn't manage the task myself.

Homeschooling While Pregnant

Dianna Kennedy

When I was a new homeschooling mom, I felt like I had it all together. I worked outside the home and managed to homeschool my kindergartener, as well as my twin preschoolers. Everything was smooth sailing... until I was pregnant with Baby #5.

That's when the wheels fell off my homeschooling bus and we hit a ditch. I'm not sure if it was being busy chasing many small children, or because I'm a little older, but that pregnancy knocked me for a loop. Between the bone-crushing fatigue and endless nausea, I felt like I was always behind from that point.

I'm certainly not the only mother to find herself in this challenge. I'll share my tips to what helped us weather the storm of homeschooling while pregnant.

Enter survival mode

Check your schedules and calendars, and eliminate the extra. Did you sign up to bring snacks to soccer practice? Graciously bow out. Learn the fine art of saying "No" to things that aren't essential.

Give yourself grace to rest and grow a baby. You may miss playgroups, co-ops or enrichment classes, but your body will thank you.

Enlist some help

I'm blessed with a husband who understands how rotten I feel during the beginning of my pregnancies. He's pitched in with cooking, cleaning, childcare, and keeping me supplied with drinks. Talk to your spouse and see how the division of labor in your home can be tweaked to make sure that you're getting plenty of rest and support.

Ask your mother, sister, or close friends for help. If your budget allows, a housekeeper or mother's helper may save your sanity, and allow you to get some rest.

Keep the fluids coming

It's easy to get dehydrated while pregnant, even in the early days. Symptoms such as nausea and headaches are compounded by mild dehydration, so keep your fluid intake up. Can't tolerate water? Try ice chips, popsicles, lemonade, fruit teas or sorbet instead.

Change up your schedule

If mornings get the best of you, why not teach in the afternoons or evening? Identify some times in your day when you feel the best, and try to get some schoolwork accomplished during those hours.

If you usually take the weekends off, you may have to juggle days around for a few weeks. You may be able to catch up on homeschool work during the weekend, if you've missed a day or two during the week.

Take a break

Part of the beauty of homeschooling is the fact that it's flexible. No one will give you demerits if you take a few days, or even a few weeks off. Wait until you feel better, then pick up where you left off.

Relish the season

Take advantage of this time in your life and enjoy it. We spent a lot of time on fetal development, health and nutrition studies during my pregnancies. My children learned how the baby was growing, and why it was important for mom to rest and eat right. They loved investigating how big the baby was, and took an active part in helping us to decide names.

I know it's hard when you're in the trenches, but trust me. One day, you'll look back on these days with love and even a little bit of longing.

When You're Longing for Quiet

Monica Lynn

As I anxiously waited for him to answer the phone, I could barely hold back the floodgate of tears.

The terrible weight of regret, shame and frustration was heavy on my shoulders.

Would he even answer? I desperately needed someone to talk to, someone who would reassure me that my actions weren't so bad, even though I knew better.

As soon as I heard his voice, the dam burst and out poured the tears and confession.

With worry he asked, "What's wrong?"

"I yelled at the kids!"

As the tears flowed I told him about the mess, the lack of following directions and the noise.

I couldn't take it a single minute longer, but instead of walking away from the situation to calm myself, I had allowed feelings of anxiety and frustration get the best of me and I had completely lost it.

The children just sat and looked at me wondering what was wrong with their mom.

How could I treat my children like that? Yes, I was on edge and frustrated, but what kind of mother was I to go and yell at them? As I continued to beat myself up over my behavior, my husband talked me down from the ledge of despair.

After I hung up, I proceeded to ask the Lord and my children for forgiveness. Thankfully, all are so graciously forgiving and proceeded to shower me with love I didn't deserve.

This is a scene I don't want to repeat. Although I'm not typically a yeller, when my anxiety level increases, I don't always handle it very well. I've had to take the time to reflect on some of the triggers and brainstorm solutions to keep from hurting the people I love.

Noise and mess-induced anxiety was not on my list of potential concerns when we decided to homeschool; however, it is something I struggle with. Some days the noise doesn't bother me, or there isn't much noise to be had, but other days, the noise affects me to the point that I feel completely agitated, stressed and I'd give just about anything for some peace and quiet.

I've had to find solutions to combat this problem and now, in our fourth year of homeschooling, I can say that I've found some calm. Not always, of course, but at least I have some strategies for keeping a quieter home and things I can do when I feel my anxiety level going up as the noise level increases.

There are actions you can take when you are in the midst of the noise. There are also some things you can do to try and prevent the noise level from ever getting to the point of permanent hearing loss. I'm not suggesting that our children need to be completely quiet at all times or that there aren't times where more noise is acceptable or even encouraged, but it needs to be at the appropriate time and at the appropriate level.

Children aren't always aware of how loud they are being, so we need to patiently teach them to become more aware of themselves and the noise they are putting out into the world (or the home). It can be frustrating when our children don't learn this self-awareness as quickly as we'd like and the loud voices continue, but many times it's a result of excitement. If we appreciate their energy and excitement for life, it will allow us to be a lot more patient as we work with them on becoming more self-aware.

The strategies we use are important for long-term success and oftentimes if we just tell our children to "keep your voice down," it's not going to do any good. None whatsoever. So, what should you do?

First, you need to determine what's contributing to their loudness. Do they need to burn off some energy, do they need some time to socialize, are they excited, are they hungry, are they tired, are they bored, are they looking for attention, or maybe there isn't a particular reason at all?

After you determine what might be some contributing factors, then you can quickly take action in order to bring the noise down to an acceptable level.

Immediately combat the noise

If you are in the midst of a noisy situation in your home and would like turn the buzz to a hush, then you need some strategies for getting the calm that you are desperate for. Here are some suggestions for actions that you can take. Depending on the reason for the roar, some of these may not apply to that particular situation.

- Allow your children to "get the wiggles out" and set the timer for one minute, or whatever amount of time you determine. Then, for that amount of time let the kids make silly noises while they wiggle around. When the time is up, then it's time to quiet down.

- Put on calming music and challenge your children to listen for certain instruments or listen to the words of the song. This forces them to close their mouths so they can hear the music.

- This idea is a fun way to let your children know their voices are too loud. However, you can't use this one too often because they'll catch on to what you are doing. Excitedly say "Did you hear that?!" They say "Hear what?!" Then you say "Shh! Listen!" and they'll want to know what you hear so they will quiet down. Of course they won't hear anything and then you can let them know that you couldn't hear anything either because their voices were so loud!

- For situations where the noise is simply due to the children being distracted by each other as they work on schoolwork, then you can move them so they are working separately.

- If the children are loud and wild, then of course you always have the option to drop everything and take them outside to allow them to burn off some energy (oh, the beauty of homeschooling)!

- Or, if the weather doesn't easily allow for going outside, then have them burn off energy inside. They can jump on a mini-trampoline, roll around on an exercise ball, do jumping jacks or run in place.

- And my favorite: Pick up a book you know will engage your children and just begin reading out loud to them.

If we are in the middle of a school day and the children's noise level begins to escalate, it's typically because we are in transition and they are making their own fun, which can involve loud, excited voices. In this case, my most common way of bringing their focus back and their noise level down is to just begin reading to them. I will pick up a picture book I know they will enjoy or continue a chapter book we are reading together and in the midst of the noise I will quickly gather them around and start reading.

My goal is to quickly engage the children in a story so that they are listening, not talking. Sitting down in the space we are already in and beginning to read before they've even quieted all the way down has proven to be very effective. Once they see and hear me reading they will quiet down so they can hear. In fact, this method has been nearly fool-proof for getting the children quiet and engaged within a matter of minutes.

The exception to this is when the children are arguing or someone is nearing a meltdown. In those instances, the situation needs to be handled differently. I won't be addressing meltdowns or sibling arguments in this chapter, so we'll have to save that discussion for another time.

Keep the noise (and anxiety) at bay

Even better than combating the noise when it comes is keeping the noise from ever getting to that point.

- Keep the schedule going during the day. On the days when I have my act together and I keep the schedule moving forward, the day goes a lot more smoothly. On days when I'm not as organized or get interrupted, that's typically when we have more problems with noise and mess.

- Catch your children keeping their voices down and praise them! It's easy to forget to praise our children when they are making the right choices or doing what we've asked of them, but try and keep it in the forefront of your mind (or keep a sticky note reminder nearby). Praise them when they are doing what you've asked of them and reward them with something simple like a hug, a sticker or a fun snack. This will help keep it firm in their minds that quiet voices are a good thing!

- Allow the kids to be physically active on a regular basis - take them to the park, take hikes, ride bikes, run around the block together or get them involved in playing a sport.

- Make sure you get enough sleep at night. Lack of sleep can cause irritability and agitation, which will be magnified when there is a constant buzz of activity and noise. From first-hand experience I know that getting enough sleep at night is huge for homeschool success. If I'm well-rested I will be able to handle anything that comes my way much more easily than if I'm tired.

- Keep the house tidy so clutter doesn't contribute to the anxiety. Designate a clean-up time(s) every day.

- Weave quiet time into your day (more to come on this).

Follow through on consequences for inappropriate noise

If inappropriate noise is common in your house, then you can set boundaries and follow through on consequences for overly loud noises. Let your children know what is acceptable and what is unacceptable, what the consequences are, and then make sure you follow through.

We've recently had some situations of all-out screaming. I mean like the kids are auditioning for a horror flick, ear-piercing, make-you-cringe kind of screams. I do not want them screaming like that, so I talked to the children and explained that it's unacceptable for them to scream at the top of their lungs unless they are in danger. That type of behavior now warrants a consequence in our home.

Remove yourself from the situation when needed

If you feel your anxiety level rising and you are in a frame of mind where you are unable to take any positive action, then immediately go do something that will help you gain your calm. It's much better to walk away, go into the bedroom, step outside, or lock yourself in the bathroom than completely blow up at your kids or have a panic attack.

Once you've removed yourself from the situation, you can then breathe, say a prayer, recite a Bible verse, or even have a good cry before going back to face the situation at hand.

You may not always be able to handle the situation perfectly in the moment and that's OK. Give yourself some grace and just do the best that you can. Remember that you are taking care of and juggling so much.

Make quiet time a part of every day

There are moms who have designated a quiet time from the beginning and they fiercely protect their daily quiet time. I admire the women that have done this and if that's you, congrats on a job well done!

Unfortunately, I didn't make quiet time a daily part of our lives, so when the naps ended, so did quiet time. Establishing it years later isn't quite as easy; however, it be done! Quiet time is so important because it allows us to recharge and give our senses time to rest.

Depending on the ages of your children, quiet time may be actual resting in your home where your children lay down in bed to rest or nap. Or it may be a time for quiet activities when children can sit and relax or work on something quietly.

If your children participate in quiet activities, you can consider designating a certain area in the house for quiet time. That way you can keep an eye on what's going on to make sure that quiet time stays quiet.

Decide ahead how long quiet time will be, especially if you are just beginning to establish this with your children. If everyone knows the expectation and how long it will last you are more likely to have a successful quiet time. You can start out with just 15 to 20 minutes if your children are resistant. Even getting a short period of quiet can be enough to calm your mind and senses so that you are reenergized and ready for the rest of the day.

Consider quiet time activities

There are many options for quiet time activities and you'll have to determine what will be best for you and your children. What works for one family may or may not work for another family.

Some of my suggestions won't be a good option for some children as they'd turn quiet time into all-out play time, noise and all. Other suggestions include screen time, which you may not want as an option.

Or you may decide not to give your children an option at all, and that's OK too. If quiet time in your home means reading time, then that's great. You can also rotate activities. For example, on Monday they can color, on

Tuesday they can read, on Wednesday they can put together puzzles, and so on.

If you'd like to establish daily quiet time with activities, here are some suggestions:

- Draw on a sketch pad or Boogie Board
- Color in a coloring book
- Read or look at books
- Put a puzzle together
- Build with Legos
- Play a single-player thinking game - ThinkFun has a wonderful selection of single-player thinking games
- Listen to an audio book
- Play an iPad learning game
- Watch a learning show on TV

Quieting the troops isn't always easy, but if you consistently teach your children self-awareness and what's acceptable, they will begin to automatically adjust their noise level without your prompting (at least that's the goal). The key to success is to have a plan in place and to follow through! This is true for establishing quiet in your home as well as other areas of homeschooling, parenting and life in general.

When Your Husband Doesn't Approve

Adelien Tandian

The idea of homeschooling came to me when my eldest son finished kindergarten in a private school. I was a teacher in a private school, and I felt it was weird for me to spend a lot of time with other children while I spent less time with my own children. It gave me a guilty feeling.

Thus, the idea of homeschooling came to my mind. Homeschooling was not popular at all at that time in our country. We didn't know anyone homeschooling their children except for celebrities or those with special-needs children. The law of homeschooling in our country was not readily available, and it was not clear at all. In addition, there are a lot of negative ideas about homeschooling around.

Given those conditions, it was not surprising that my husband rejected the idea of homeschooling our children. We ignored the idea of homeschooling our children at that time. It was very disappointing for me. It was four years after that when my husband approved my proposal for homeschooling my two elder sons. At that time, our youngest son was in kindergarten. I thought that my husband would automatically agree that my youngest son be homeschooled, but for the second time, he didn't approve. I was brokenhearted at that time; it seemed that he didn't trust me. The negative issues I mentioned before were even stronger at that time.

Three years later, he finally gave his approval to homeschooling my youngest son. It was a wonderful feeling; finally, we were a full homeschooling family. My husband's two disapprovals came from very different reasons. The first time, he was unsure about starting to homeschool; the second, he we unsure because of what he saw as I homeschooled our two elder sons.

After facing rejection twice from my husband, I learned some points that I will try to share about facing his disapproval toward homeschooling.

Is homeschooling really the best decision for your family?

Homeschooling is one way to educate your children. But there is no single best answer for anything. Homeschooling is not always the best kind of education. Your children's education is your decision.

It's not easy to decide whether homeschooling is the best form of education for your family. If you are a single mother, the decision will belong only to you. When the responsibility for the children's education belongs to both parents, there should be agreement and consistency about the decision.

How to know if homeschooling is the right decision will vary from family to family. There are many factors to consider, and a sudden move could lead to family discord. Remember, homeschooling is not the only issue that a husband and wife will have to take care of. There are many other aspects of family life to consider.

Be patient in waiting

Waiting was the best thing I could do to have my husband approve our homeschooling. Waiting patiently will show your maturity and your respect for your husband's opinion. This will help your husband respect your opinions about homeschooling.

Being patient will also give both of you more time to evaluate the idea of homeschooling. Even if your husband seems to ignore the idea at first, at least you will have informed him of the possibility. Hopefully, he will then want to find out more about homeschooling. He might also find some reasons to support homeschooling.

On the other hand, waiting is also a time for you to think further about the reasons behind his disapproval.

Why might your husband disagree about starting to homeschool?

If you're homeschooling some children, is there something about how you're going about it that your husband disapproves of? It is great to do some introspection and improve your own ideas and strategies for homeschooling.

Work harder to give better evidence

This is exactly what I had been doing before my husband approved our homeschooling. Having the idea of homeschooling disapproved of should make us more enthusiastic about building our knowledge and broadening our perspective. It should not make us more pessimistic.

If you have been homeschooling, try to think about what kind of things cause disapproval and discord, and how you can improve them to make things better for the children, yourself and your husband. Be honest with yourself and your husband, and talk about where you are able and willing to improve.

If you are not yet homeschooling but want to start, dig deeper and learn more about the theories and practice..

Involve Daddy

It is always advisable to involve your husband in any circumstance involving your family, which also includes homeschooling your children.

This will work best if it comes from the start. Including your husband in the decision-making is going to make your homeschooling stronger in the future. Therefore, respect your husband's disapproval and ask him to help you find what might work better for your children and the whole family life. The family belongs to all of you, so everything should be decided together.

Pray a lot

In any religion, praying is the most powerful weapon if you really believe in it. If your family is secular, you might have a kind of reflection about what you choose and what you have chosen. Let God show you the best choice for your family. You should see the answer in your daily life about whether to start or continue homeschooling your children.

Facing Judgment and Stereotypes from Outsiders
Kalista Sabourin

I was 20 years old when I had my first child and thanks to some very chubby cheeks and big, round blue eyes, I looked about 5 years younger than that. So I'm no stranger to judgment. I like to think that all of the hurtful comments and sideways glances made me a stronger person but in the beginning, I really let people get to me.

Homeschooling is funny in that everyone has an opinion on it. Even those who don't do it. Especially those who don't do it. If you take your kids to the grocery store during school hours, it's almost guaranteed you'll end up hearing someone's thoughts on how you choose to educate your children. Sometimes there are positive encounters. Sometimes, not so much. Once you accept that there will be negative encounters, it gets easier to deal with them.

Homeschooling can be so hard sometimes. I don't know a single homeschooling parent who doesn't doubt their decision from time to time. In my first year of homeschooling, a mean comment sent me into to tears and days filled with self-doubt. As the years have passed, I've learned how to best deal with these situations and I can, for the most part, leave those icky conversations with my confidence still intact.

First of all, there are the preventative measures that I take to fight the judgment. This involves taking care of myself: making sure I get enough time out of the house, doing things I enjoy, getting enough sleep and exercising regularly. When I am overwhelmed or stressed, those little comments become BIG ones and they become a lot harder to get past. Taking the time to fill my tank goes a long way in these situations.

I also keep a list of the reasons why we chose to homeschool and why we love it in my planner, where I see it every day. In the thick of our days, when there's a mountain of laundry where my bed used to be and a toddler stuck to my leg, it can be hard to remember why this seemed like a good idea. But it IS a good idea... even if I have to be reminded of WHY from time to time.

Find a good support network. Having friends that homeschool is always a bonus. That way, when you have an awkward encounter in the line at the bank, you can laugh about it with people who understand how silly the socialization argument really is! Once you're in a good head-space, it's easier to deal with those face-to-face conversations.

There are a lot a methods for handling people's judgments, and everyone will have their favorite. You can be very frank about the fact that it is a personal choice and that it is one that you aren't willing to discuss (especially with total strangers in the produce section). You can be very blunt about your reasons for homeschooling, though you should be prepared for some debate. You can also use my favorite method, sarcasm and humor. (I homeschool because getting four kids dressed and out the door before 10 a.m. seems like WAY too much work.)

There are some things that I would avoid saying or doing in these situations.

- **Don't rip apart public education.** We can discuss our reasons for homeschooling without putting down other people's choice not to.

- **Don't get overly emotional.** These conversations can get emotionally charged. People on both sides often feel very strongly about this issue. But getting emotional doesn't help people see your side or get them to change their opinions. It derails the conversation and it makes things awkward. Ask me how I know!

Regardless of how these conversations go, know that you have made the choice that is best for your family. No one else knows you and your situation. What they think they know about homeschooling isn't a reflection on you as a person. Their opinions are just that... opinions. They don't mean that you're doing a bad job or that you're ruining your children... or whatever else you may start to feel as you listen to people rant about the dangers of homeschooling.

You are doing a beautiful thing by homeschooling your children. It would be a real shame to let that be ruined by a stranger's opinions. So rock on, homeschooling mama (or papa). Keep being awesome!

When Your Heart Is No Longer In It

Alicia Michelle

A few nights ago, we had dinner with another homeschool family from our church. While the kids played happily outside (and the husbands talked shop over a smoky barbecue), my mom friend and I had a few quiet moments alone to sit at our kitchen table and talk.

Her oldest child had just turned 5 this year, so she and her husband were just starting their family's homeschool journey.

However, even in her short time thus far as a homeschooler, she noted that she saw so many homeschool moms who lacked true joy. She said that, although these moms may not have said so directly, she sensed that many of them felt trapped and alone by the demands of mothering and homeschooling. She told me of how she saw so many of them plaster on smiles and soldier through their homeschool day, whether or not their heart was in it.

This broke my heart to hear. Helping women discover a full, joy-filled life (even during the chaotic years of homeschooling and motherhood) is something I'm passionate about.

Why is discovering joy in the everyday so important (and more than just a luxury)?

Because, as the Bible says, "from the heart the mouth speaks" (Luke 6:45). Everything flows from the condition of our heart, and as women, we are the heart of our home! So if we are suffering, just existing and not living to our fullest potential, then everything (and everyone) else suffers.

Yet, I totally understand why so many of us operate in this manner. Some homeschooling and mothering seasons are plain grueling, and survival mode is the only way to get through.

While occasion survival mode is par for the course, I understand how easy it is to let that become the status quo. And yet, we can't let it become our family's "normal"! Why? Because once survival mode is just part of life, I can testify to the gut-wrenching emptiness that quickly follows.

And it's this emptiness that leads to overwhelm, disconnection from homeschooling, and ultimately, total burnout.

A glimpse into burnout: My story

In Fall 2014, I felt very much run-over by the marathon of motherhood and homeschooling —emotionally, physically and spiritually.

I knew that I was called to these noble tasks, but that didn't negate the seasons like this when I felt like I was just not going to make it.

Two of my kids were going through some really challenging seasons, which of course was exacerbating the condition. I was doing all that I could to encourage and guide them (but still felt overwhelmed by their ongoing needs).

There were many disappointing days when my kids just didn't get what I was desperately spending every last bit of effort to teach them.

There were more than a few moments where I found myself utterly confused and desperate for answers to really hard, ongoing situations.

It seemed like there was little that could relieve my deep heartache.

The most horrible part of these moments? There was no escape! Motherhood isn't a job any of us can call in sick for! Therefore, I knew each night that when I went to sleep I would have to get up the next day and face these issues all over again.

All of this put my emotions in a tailspin and brought old inner demons to light. Despite all that the Lord has taught me on discovering joy in motherhood and homeschooling, here I sat battling unreasonable thought patterns that I dealt with years ago when I struggled with depression.

Significance versus success

It would be naive to say that burnout and half-hearted living are completely avoidable. There is nothing perfect this side of heaven.

So first I want to free us from the paralyzing thought that the reason we suffer from lackluster living is because we're not trying hard enough or being enough.

Instead, I want to encourage us to do our imperfect best to focus on significance versus success.

"OK, OK, Alicia," you say, "I get it. Now comes the pep talk about how homeschooling and mothering is something significant and how we just need to focus on that."

Well, sort of... But not really.

Yes, I believe homeschooling and mothering are some of the most significant endeavors we can embrace as women. A mom's work in the heart of a child can change the course of nations and even the world, and we homeschoolers need constant reminders of how important are work is.

But what about our ability to change the world as individual women — through the other passions and God-given talents we may have outside of mothering and homeschooling? While we still must place our family responsibilities first, we moms cannot sacrifice our need to be significant outside of these core callings.

I feel that it is this great lack of significance outside of the arena of homeschooling and motherhood (combined with an over-committed family schedule that includes little to no time for rest and soul-replenishment) that leads many moms to less than joy-filled living (which eventually spills over into dull, lifeless homeschooling).

Ironically, by completely sacrificing ourselves on the altar of motherhood and homeschooling, we moms can actually bring damage to ourselves and to our families!

I'm convinced that if we took better care of ourselves, addressed the key homeschooling joy-stealers and allowed ourselves to pursue (even on a small scale) the great passions of our heart, great fountains of joy would fill our lives.

I know this is true because when I am able to do these things, it's like our entire family is released to bloom to its fullest potential.

Now... how much more effective and joy-filled could our mothering and homeschooling be when we're able to daily operate from this mindset?

Discovering your significance

How do we discover those passions that fill our soul and bring significance outside of our mothering and homeschooling?

While I can't give you a five-step formula, I'd say that a great place to start is to spend some time in honest prayer and soul reflection.

Ask yourself some key questions like:

- What do I really love?
- What makes my heart sing?
- What things in this world really anger me and I want to change?
- If money were no object, how would I want to spend my time?

Listen to what comes up — to what your heart says, and, if you are a Christian, to what the Lord tells you about yourself.

Then begin to explore how you could bring pieces of these passions into your daily living.

Please hear me: I'm not advocating that we place our families to the side and ignore our responsibilities so that we can go off somewhere and "find ourselves."

I'm also not dismissing the very real fact that our call to mothering and homeschooling will bring sacrifice — even sometimes a sacrifice of the fullest expression of our personal passions — and that's all right.

I'm just suggesting that we prayerfully ask these questions so that we can discover simple ways for us to explore our significance, while still keeping our family life a priority.

Our ultimate significance

No discussion on significance and meaning cannot be complete without mentioning our ultimate purpose — which is to be in relationship with God.

God has created a purpose for you, and if you're feeling "less-than," consider that nothing in this world can fill you up because it wasn't made to. You were made to be filled up first by God (through daily relationship with him) so that you can then go out and fulfill His great plans for you.

You are loved — fully and immensely — by the One who created you. All other significant endeavors must start and end from this fact.

What significant living can look like in this season

While there's no right or wrong answers for what significant living can look like in this busy season, I would encourage you to not discount the small things.

Here are some ideas of what I mean. Let's say, for example, that sewing or knitting is something that brings your soul replenishment, and you'd like to do something significant with that talent. What if you:

- gathered one day a month with other moms to work on a quilt for a local pregnancy resource center;
- worked as part of a team to create dresses for African orphans out of pillowcases; or
- worked with another mom friend to teach your daughter and her friends sewing basics?

Or maybe you're an awesome chef or just love to cook. Perhaps you could:

- provide dinners for the meals ministry at your church;
- help serve food at a local food kitchen; or
- work with your kids to gather canned goods for a local food pantry?

Do you have a heart to encourage women? What if you:

- reached out to a mom you knew was struggling and offered to have tea with her every few weeks;
- served as a small group leader for a church Bible study; or
- hosted a book study with other homeschool moms in your area?

These ideas are just off the top of my head. I know that you can come up with some awesome things that you'd love!

For me, creating (or experiencing) beauty fills my soul and empowers me to be a better woman.

Practically speaking, right now that can be anything from experimenting with new flavors in the kitchen to creative home decorating on a budget. Helping women by writing is a big part of this for me too. I love when God surprises me with unexpected chances to create beauty, such as the chance to serve a friend in need with an act of kindness.

Sometimes it's not necessarily creating beauty but instead partaking in it, such as by taking a walk with my family at sunset or watching a rainstorm. Savoring and treasuring these moments brings great significance to me, which in turn spills over into joy as a mom and homeschooler.

Significance in any season

Mother Teresa was famous for saying "Do small things with great love."

Small, passionate endeavors — things that replenish and fuel you as a woman — have significance. Explore your passions and see how you can express them (even in tiny ways) right now.

Keep yourself rested, replenished and fueled up so that you can excitedly live out your calling as a wife and homeschool mom!

When your Spirit is Eager but the Flesh is Weak

Lindsey Marie

Burnout.

We've all been there, right, my friends? (Right.) In fact, that's much the reason for this book. It's completely normal to have that late winter/springtime slump. Whereas once we were excited and bursting at the seams with innovative ideas and "blow your mind" projects, we're now staring longingly at the calendar... when will summer be here? Yes, our heart is with homeschooling, but our bodies are starting to give out.

But do we really need to go through that? Is there anything we can do maintain our integrity and strength throughout the school year? Sometimes it takes a strong self-examination to see what we can possibly do to alter this state we find ourselves in.

I'll be discussing a few things that I think would be very helpful in keeping up a strong spirit and strength when it comes to this beautiful journey that we're embracing. And just so you know, this chapter is as much for me as it is you!

Let's begin.

Avoiding the slump

First off, in order to fix something, you have to know what the cause is, right? So let's pinpoint some of the reasons we may burn out when homeschooling:

- Planning too many lessons or complicated lessons
- Scheduling too many outside activities and not considering limitations
- Not personalizing our experience
- Not maintaining a good schedule or routines

So let's attack these potential pitfalls with the following concept: Keep it simple.

Recently I wrote a series on K.I.S.S.ING your homeschool. (K.I.S.S. is an acronym standing for "Keep it simple, stupid" or, as we say, "Keep it simple, silly.") This year I am making a conscientious effort to simplify things.

Simplifying is my personal number-one weapon in avoiding burnout or maintaining endurance and motivation.

Simplifying takes reasonableness. We must be reasonable with ourselves and our limitations. How much should we plan? How much should we commit to? How much should we buy? How much time do we have?

Planning too many lessons or being involved in too many outside activities can easily begin to choke out your motivation and energy. Just think about it: do you look forward to and feel invigorated by complicated tasks or an overwhelmingly long list? And even if at times you enjoy a challenge, is this something you can keep up on a daily basis?

No, most of us cringe at the prospect of "climbing mountains," and it certainly isn't something that we can keep up with all the time. We may even begin to have the feeling that we are constantly "putting out fires," responding to one urgent need after the other. And when we do this, are we giving 100%? No. Most likely, we are barely making it through, just going through the motions.

When we have so much on our plate each day, it no longer becomes a focused effort. So simplifying is needed.

Simplifying our curriculum, schedule, home and mind help to relieve stress and preserve energy.

Let's take a look at a few ways we can do this.

We can maintain a simple mind when we keep our focus on our mission. Your mission is your final goal and what you ultimately want to accomplish. When you are aware of exactly what you want to accomplish in your home and with your children, you immediately can let go of all else that doesn't fit in.

We can simplify our curriculum by remembering our mission, thinking long-term, cutting back on the unnecessary, and by prioritizing our child.

Let's say, for instance, your mission is to raise disciplined students and critical thinkers. If you are tempted to add lessons, curriculum or activities into your homeschool that do not coincide with this mission, just say no. In the end, you will be thankful that you stayed the course.

Thinking long-term helps you to realize that you have several years to teach your child. You do not need to cover every continent and time period this year. You can make a long-term plan and list all that you wanted covered by graduation. This will allow you to simplify, take it slow, and really go deeper into your studies, enjoying them more. "Slow and steady wins the race."

Doesn't "slow and steady" just sound refreshing already?

And don't forget to prioritize your child. Sometimes we need to remember that we are teaching the child, not the books. Books become tools do to that, but when we focus on the child and what they are understanding or already understand, we realize that our intent does not need to be "covering" everything. Use your child's comprehension as a guide and remember that it isn't a race.

Remember that an important reason why so many homeschool is because it is not like public school. It is not "one size fits all" and we do not need to keep up with everyone else. All children are gifted in some areas, possibly different areas than their peers. When you embrace those differences you begin to go with the grain than against it, thus creating peace and "flow" in your journey together.

So take a deep breath, weed out what doesn't line up with your mission, focus on your child's strengths and limitations, and find curriculum that is in line with all that.

We can simplify our schedule by setting limits, working with our internal clock, planning what's important first, and planning for the unexpected.

How many times have you committed yourself to something only to regret it? How many times have you found yourself burned out and saying, "I'll never do that again!" Setting limits is important to avoid this predicament in our schooling.

If you don't make a clear goal of how much time you will spend on schooling, you can easily be overtaken. So consider all your obligations in life and pencil in what you realistically can dedicate as "school time."

Also, think "biologically." Are you a night person? A morning person? How about your kids? Just today I read a post on one mom's morning routine. She admitted that she doesn't wake her children until 11 a.m.

This made sense to me.

Her children are teenagers and many of us are aware that biologically (chemically, hormonally) teenagers often stay up later at night and sleep in. Even the public educational system knows this. So in an effort to avoid possible frustration and burnout, she created a schedule that went with the grain instead of against it. Smart mom.

We also need to prioritize and schedule the important. Let me ask you something: Have you ever spent your day responding to emergencies or urgent needs only to realize the most important tasks were never accomplished? Many of us have. In fact, many of us make it through most days doing so.

Think about your health: It's important. But weeks can go by without exercising or eating healthy. But what if you were to "make sure of the more important things"? What if you were to start your day off with exercise each day? Imagine the benefits. Imagine the satisfaction you'd experience and the domino effect it would have in all areas of your life.

That was a hypothetical question, but let's apply that to homeschooling. We can find ourselves "losing steam" and even motivation if we are not scheduling the most important things first. And again, this takes us to our mission.

If you really wanted to prioritize Latin this year, but find yourself giving more attention and time to worksheets, drills and science... what a bummer, right? But imagine your joy and sense of accomplishment if you were to prioritize, schedule and follow through with Latin each day. Then all else would fall into place. Perhaps that would mean you didn't have as much time for drills or science, but you would be on your way to "Mission: Accomplished," now, wouldn't you?

Have you ever seen the illustration of the jar, golf balls and marbles? Golf balls symbolize the important things. They are large. They mean a lot. Marbles are all the little mundane things that sometimes catch our attention whether we mean for them to or not. Or perhaps they are little tasks that we always seem to be distracted with. This could even mean the free downloads and shiny, colorful workbooks we find. (Oh, we get so excited, don't we?) But if you grab a jar of equal volume to the amount of golf balls and marbles you have, and you put in your marbles first, your golf balls do not fit. But if you put your golf balls in first, then your marbles on top, it all fits.

It's the neatest illustration/experiment with an important message: For greater joy and satisfaction, and to work toward your ultimate mission, put your golf balls in first.

We can simplify our home by staying organized with a home binder of some sort, creating routines, and getting the kids involved.

Having a home binder or control journal eliminates so much headache and misery. It is definitely a "simplifying" factor. Keeping track of what bills are due and when, what meals will be made on what day, what days you clean what, and having a control list of doctors, businesses, and companies you need to reach from time to time or on a consistent basis... I mean, can't you see the value in that? Absolutely. I'm sure you agree.

It can be stressful and even depressing when we cannot find that information at times we really need it. There are many free ones online, as well as those available on Etsy and other sites. It's worth it to have one.

Creating and maintaining routines vs. schedules has an incredible benefit as well. When you create a routine and practice that routine over and over, so as to make a habit, it becomes automated. Each time you perform that activity, your brain has deepened and solidified that pathway to the point where you don't even think about it any more. You have conditioned yourself to do these things.

Now wouldn't that make for simpler times and less stress? If you are running on automatic through these routines, your mind can be freed for more joyous and peaceful thoughts. Some women choose to pray during these times, or listen to uplifting music, or simply "think happy thoughts" as they prepare mentally for their day.

Getting the kids involved is important for two reasons: what it does for you, and what it does for them. For you, you have a helper. Finally comes the day when that baby is older and they can do for you! I couldn't tell you just how much I leapt for joy when my daughter first washed the dishes. My time had come!

But it is also beneficial for them. Not only is it part of life skills, but being competent increases their self-esteem. No matter how they may complain at first, their mind cannot deny that they are now becoming a contributing part of their family and environment.

I remember years ago when our before-dinner cleanup time took sometimes over an hour. It was mostly all on me, and such a pain at times, I'll admit. But with two children in middle childhood, we can now knock out our whole house in 30 minutes. It has definitely been a contributing factor in being able to reserve energy for more interests, pursuits, and recreation.

Strengthen your flesh

The flesh is weak, right? That could mean our actual flesh. Staying healthy is always a good idea. Now this doesn't mean you have to fit into your prom dress or join a gym. But let's discuss what it does mean:

- You keep your brain healthy.
- You get enough rest.
- You have energy throughout the day.
- You join your children in play, nature walks, or family outings.

It's ideal, isn't it? But it also can be a reality. Let's take a look at how we can accomplish this.

Boost your brain health

Your brain is the most important organ in your body. Without it, you couldn't function physically or mentally. Your brain controls all else. So wouldn't you say that this is a pretty good place to start when discussing your "flesh"? Oh yes. And building a healthy brain can be done in different ways.

- Feed it
- Use it
- Rest it

We feed our brain with different sources. We feed it nutrients through whole foods. We can feed it oxygen through exercising and spending time in nature. And we can feed it the right hormones through similar experiences.

(Please note: I am not a professional or medical doctor. The ideas expressed in this chapter are my own. Please check with your physician before attempting any of these suggestions, and I especially encourage you to research these statements.)

Whole foods are important because of the nutrients they give us. They contain building blocks for our bodies, enzymes for proper digestion, and help our bodies to thrive and to heal. Of special interest is oil, which contains essential fatty acids in direct support of mental health, like the ones found in fish oils. Without these proper nutrients, our bodies and brains begin to break down. This can be a direct reason our flesh begins to give out.

Oxygen is essential. It is a life force. We know that exerting ourselves and exercising is a great way to take in oxygen. But here's a neat little fact that I think you'll like: When you exert yourself, most of the oxygen is absorbed into your muscles. But a nice little stroll or 10- to 20-minute walk will actually allow more oxygen to go to your brain.

I'll never run again.

OK, not really. But this was definitely something I was thankful to learn and is right in line with our discussion on reasonableness and simplifying. I decided to use this information for our school. So perhaps you can identify a time when this would be helpful.

For us, we usually have an afternoon slump. So this year I am incorporating 15-minute neighborhood walks for the whole family before returning from our lunch break. And I love that our neighborhood is lined with trees, which give us extra doses of the oxygen we need. And we, in turn, give off the carbon dioxide the trees and plants need. What a beautiful thing to be happening.

Different hormones affect our brain in different ways. We want to find out which to avoid, and which to promote. Let's take a look at two.

Serotonin is the "happy hormone." How can we increase it?

- Take advantage of daylight. Rise earlier (if you can) and spend time outdoors in natural light each day.

- Exercise regularly. Start with reasonable goals. Aim for consistency over longevity.

- Eat foods containing tryptophan. These include beans, nuts, seeds, eggs and chocolate.

- Reach out and touch somebody. Yes, hugging and affection stimulate your happy hormones. Surround yourself with loving people and avoid those that stress you or bring negativity into your life.

- Smile. Yes, the very act of smiling (a genuine effort, not a fake smile) releases happy hormones into your system. Combined with intentional positive thoughts, they can slowly begin to turn your frown upside down.

Cortisol is the bad hormone, the "fear and stress" hormone. It's sometimes referred to as "public enemy number one." I agree. It is responsible for interference with memory, lower immune function, increased weight gain, high blood pressure, heart disease, a decrease in bone density, and interference with the metabolism of macronutrients, just to name a few. So what do we do to avoid this?

- Regular exercise is said to "burn up" this hormone, letting out the aggression that is related to fear and stress in our lives in a healthy way.

- Practice meditation and/or mindfulness. This may look different to you and me. For me, meditation is a time for prayer and reflection on spiritual things that uplift and center. For some, it may be a time for deep belly breathing or practicing mindfulness and gratitude.

- Laugh. I don't even think I need to explain this. We all know laughter is a great way to de-stress. Whether it's renting a comedy or joining a group of close friends, find a way to incorporate humor.

- Music has incredible healing powers. In my post on 5 Things Every Mom Should Do Every Day I talked about the effects music can have. One of its benefits is the proven way it lowers cortisol levels, and can be used to stimulate positive feelings.

- Connect with people... loving, kind people. Both romantic love and social bonding have relaxing effects on your nervous system. It also encourages mental health and balance. Think of the difference between coping with an obstacle with a friend vs. without one. Those who isolate themselves often have greater amounts of stress and unhappiness.

Ever hear the phrase "use it or lose it"? Much is the same with the brain. There are "brain-boosting" activities not involving food and exercise. Brain games are pretty popular now. There are apps such as Lumosity and games such as Sudoku that are rising in popularity. But these are not the only option. Old-fashioned board games or memory games are just as useful.

To maintain brain health, expose yourself to different activities. Learn something new. Try something new. Challenge your brain and improve your brain's "plasticity" or ability to shape and grow.

Just as important as feeding and using our brain is resting it. Without adequate rest, your brain slows down and affects all of your body's systems. There is an increased probability of accidents, a loss of memory and concentration, an increase in risk for disease, an increase in depression, an increase in weight gain, an increase in risk of death, an inability to assess situations accurately, and guess what – an increase in cortisol. Yikes!

It's worth really making an effort in having restful sleep, and getting enough sleep. Try these suggestions:

- Aim for 8 hours each night and research ways to make your sleep more peaceful.
- Avoid technology one hour before sleeping.
- Maintain the same sleep schedule, sleeping and waking at the same time each day.
- Dim the lights at bedtime.
- Take a warm bath a half-hour before retiring to bed.
- Research natural supplements like melatonin and magnesium that may be able to assist you.
- Talk to your doctor, if all else fails.

Maintain a fresh outlook

Let's just face it. Sometimes we're bored.

Yes, my friends, you know it's true. Sometimes we just need to switch things up to get motivated. Let's consider some ways in which we can create a fresh outlook and "jumpstart" our batteries.

- Days off from the normal routine (break in routines, planned fun, game days)

- Browsing Pinterest
- Find a tribe (co-ops, friends, homeschool bloggers)
- New scenery (parks, friends' homes, field trips)

One of the great privileges of homeschooling is the ability to schedule your own school year. I like to schedule adequate breaks and holidays.

Some have found it beneficial to schedule their school year in six-week rotations, with one week off between each set. It's never too long until they get a week off.

I've chosen a schedule somewhere in between a traditional school year and year-round school year, where we still have a "summertime" with July and August off, but because it's only eight weeks of summer, I can incorporate more weeks off throughout the school year.

Boy, does this help.

I especially schedule a three-week break in the springtime when I notice that I personally begin to "slump."

It's also fun to add activities that aren't part of your boxed curriculum or chosen textbooks and workbooks. For example, you might want to schedule days where the kids choose a project or activity found on Pinterest.

I have a special Pinterest board for children's games and activities and plan on using one Friday each month for us to choose from this board.

Variety is the spice of life!

It's also helpful to find your tribe. Collaborating, or just socializing, with other moms does wonders to rev you up. It can be so lonely, day after day, inside with the kids.

If you find you are "giving out," examine how much time you have for you, or with your girlfriends. Do you have a regular girls' night out? Do you have a date night with the husband? Do you join park days for homeschoolers? Do you take time to read homeschool encouragement from bloggers who can relate?

Being stuck inside is not always a bad thing, but without the change in scenery and surroundings we can start to have cabin fever. We may begin to feel stagnant and lack energy.

And here's a special tip that may sound simple enough, but, as I have recently found out, can be harder to implement than one may think: Schedule field trips.

The kids need it. Moms need it. Field trips can be what makes our lessons come alive. Actually seeing information being put to use is a motivation in itself. So make a list, call around, ask for suggestions, and get the kids out the door at least once a month.

Even if you have to take the bus. (Which I have to.)

Prayer

Not all of your readers will be Bible students, but for those of you who are, I wanted to write at least a paragraph on this invaluable tool we have: prayer. First and foremost, remember Philippians chapter 4, which reminds us in verse 13: "For all things I have the strength through the one who gives me power." When our flesh is giving out, remember He "gives power to the tired one." (Isaiah 40:29) Asking for His intervention in this area would be appropriate and beneficial before implementing practical methods, for He is ready to give and to assist.

Remember, when the spirit is eager but the flesh is weak, know that the flesh can always be "persuaded." We may find ourselves complaining of feeling "tired" or "unmotivated" without stopping to take a look at what we reasonably can do on a concrete level. As we see, there are both spiritual and practical suggestions we can put to practice (like grabbing a handful of almonds, taking a ten-minute walk, playing a game of Sudoku, scheduling a park day or field trip, and connecting with positive, encouraging people) that will help us to maintain our motivation in our homes and schools.

I sincerely hope that you found these tips encouraging and look forward to hearing about your successful homeschooling ventures!

Homeschool Moms Have No Down Time!

Karyn Tripp

I have always homeschooled my kids, so I have not had the experience of sending my kids off to school for eight hours and having the house to myself. I will likely never have that experience. If I am completely honest, sometimes I envy the moms who get so much downtime. I sometimes dream of what I would do with all of my free time. There are times when I just wish for an hour (or five hours) of alone time. I am NEVER alone! That may be one of my biggest hardships with homeschooling. I know a lot of moms who are just starting out say this is one of the biggest struggles for them.

I adore my children and I truly treasure our time together, but sometimes I just need to take a shower without someone trying to have a conversation with me through a closed door. There are times when I wish for nothing more than complete silence, or maybe just a little nap without a little person climbing on me during it. I also wish my house would stay clean during the day, but that will likely not happen for another 10 to 15 years! I wish I had time for my own hobbies. I wish I could go out to lunch with friends in the middle of the day.

Do you have this struggle? Do you share my frustrations? So, how do we deal with it? How do we survive having zero down time and not losing our sanity because of it? I want to give a few tips that have helped me through the past six years of homeschooling and mothering.

Change your thoughts

Nobody forced me to homeschool. I chose this course in life and I knew what I was getting into. I have to shift my thoughts to know that those lunch dates with friends are not really an option at this stage in life. I choose to just be OK with it and not get down when I can't go, or when they stop inviting me! When you hear others talk about how great it feels to drop their youngest child off at school for the whole day, remind yourself of the good you are doing for your kids. Don't let it get you down!

When I am really down about homeschooling after those terrible, horrible, no good, very bad days, I remind myself of the reason I am doing it. If you keep your thoughts positive it is easier to push through those hard times and get motivated to keep going the next day. Homeschooling is NOT easy. Nobody ever said it is. You are becoming a stronger person and strengthening your kids through the process, too. The benefits you get from homeschooling are worth the challenges you have to endure! Just try to remember that on the hardest days.

Making time for yourself

One of the most important things I have learned over my years of homeschooling is that I have to make time for myself. "Me time" is absolutely critical to my sanity. It may sound like an impossibility, but you have to carve out some time for just you. When you get busy with all of the school activities and kid activities, it may seem like there is no extra time left over for just you. Sometimes that is true, but I would highly suggest cutting back on something to make sure you get time for things that matter to you. Have you forgotten what that is among all of the homeschooling books and papers? Find it again!

My "me time" varies depending on my needs. My most important time alone is early in the morning. I always wake up at least an hour before the kids are up. This time is so precious to me. This is my personal devotional time, but also the only time I am alone EVER! I treasure it so much that I feel frustrated when I sleep in. It is peaceful and I can get so much done during this time. I read, pray, and often blog during these early morning hours. I am a morning person, but if you are late-night person, make it happen then.

There have been many nights when my husband comes home and sees that I need an outing. He is supportive of these needs and I love that! Some days, I just need to leave the house alone without buckling any seat belts or dragging along anyone in a cart or stroller. It feels so good to just go to the store alone! Do you know what I mean? Sometimes my alone time equals a long hot bath without any disturbances. Or maybe curling up in bed at 7 p.m. with that book you have been dying to crack open but haven't had time for.

I also NEED date nights with my husband. They truly help me keep my sanity. We try for a weekly date night, but many times there are other interferences with that. That time out with my husband gives me a chance to talk through issues with the kids or schooling. It gives me a chance to bounce ideas off of his brain. It gives me the chance to have uninterrupted adult conversation. If you are a single parent, find a way to have nights out with friends so you have this opportunity, too. Get a babysitter at least once a month so you can really refresh!

Don't give up your hobbies. My biggest hobby is music. I have been a singer all of my life. When I had kids it became much harder to perform or be a part of big productions. I decided to join a local community choir so I can keep doing what I love so much. There was minimal work and commitment, but I could still get out and do something for me. The times I get to go and practice and perform are special times to me, and I always come home so happy to have been able to do something I love so much. Whatever your love is, make a little time for it once in a while. Don't lose sight of who YOU really are among all the busyness of homeschool life.

Sometimes just spending time outside is enough for me to feel rejuvenated. I have noticed that 10 to 20 minutes outside in nature can be so refreshing. Find a shady spot and just sit for a few minutes. Let your kids play around you, or go for a walk together.

Set quiet time rules

If your kids are young, naptime may be your best friend. It gets harder when they outgrow nap time, though. You can still create a quiet time in your house even if nobody is napping. When school and chores are finished, my kids like to have a little down time of their own. We are all tired at the end of the day. This is the time when I let them watch a show or they read a book or play outside. It is also the time that I work on things that I need to do.

I know moms who make it a rule that their kids are quiet and in their rooms reading or playing quietly during a certain time of the day. If this becomes routine, your kids will know it and be used to it. This can give you some needed quiet, rest or work time that you desire.

How do I keep my house clean?

I have decided that I have sacrificed a clean house for being a homeschool mom. I like our home to be clean, but it never seems as clean as other homes I go to. I think the very fact that your kids are home all day makes it nearly impossible to always have a perfectly clean house. I am trying hard to just be OK with that! I have decided to worry less about mess and more about time teaching or reading to my kids.

I am definitely not the expert on this one, but we have a pretty good system going for our chores. The kids have a huge part in keeping our house clean and running smoothly. When they are home making messes all day, you have to involve them more than you would if they were gone all day. Pause school to make sure they clean their lunch dishes! Clean one activity or project before moving on to the next. Find a chore system that works well for your family and involve your kids in the work as much as possible. Teaching kids to work around the house provides important skills they need to learn anyway!

It is OK to ask for help!

If you feel overwhelmed beyond anything you think you can handle, ASK FOR HELP! Do not get down on yourself for not being able to do everything. Everyone has struggles that are beyond their control sometimes! Find a friend or family member or hire a nanny who help you fill in the spaces. Do not be ashamed to ask for help! We are all human, and life is just plain hard. Hang in there; I know you are strong enough!

When Family and Friends Turn Up the Pressure
Marlene Griffith

Peer pressure: It's not just for kids, it's for homeschooling parents too! And it's not any easier than it was back when you were in high school or middle school.

Homeschooling comes with a lot of unique qualities. From choosing what kind of approach you want to take (classical, Charlotte Mason, unschooling, interest-led, etc.), to choosing the curriculum. You're constantly faced with challenges along the way.

You're learning daily about this homeschooling thing, even if you've been at it for years. These are all normal challenges that come with the territory. Sometimes they are exciting and sometimes... not so much.

But we work through them and find a resolve because this is the path you and your family are on. It's just what you do, so you work through it.

And then the pressure of family and friends starts to knock at the door.

I just love how people who don't homeschool, and obviously know nothing about it, can have so much to say about it!

When we started homeschooling, I got so many side-looks with raised eyebrows from friends. People automatically assumed I was going super-religious and joining some cult of sorts. It was wild! I lost some friends after we made that decision, mostly due to them not knowing a thing about it... yet they chose to make assumptions. And we became the weird ones.

From family, things got a bit more vocal. Family members aren't as shy as friends can be when it comes to speaking their minds. I was bombarded with many of the same classic stereotypical questions like "How are you going to socialize them?" or "What about friends?" or "What about extracurricular activities?" These were also followed by comments that I wasn't homeschooled and should know better.

Then, as family began to embrace it, the pressure of perfectly including everything my child needed into their daily curriculum was put on. Granted, this what their perceived idea of perfect was, and their way of "helping" me make up for what the kids were going to miss.

The pressure will be there, and you'll need to face it head-on. You need to grow a bit of a thick skin when you are a homeschooler, and even with that, the pressure will sting a little.

There are a few things you need to try and keep in mind as much as you can. It's easy to set these things on a mental shelf and forget them. Then, when a situation arises, we're often caught between a rock and a hard place, which leaves us feeling either hurt or angry.

Keep in mind why you choose to homeschool. Your reasons may be different than my reasons, but they are still your reasons. You don't need to offer an explanation to anyone about your choices for your family, but chances are, you would like to at least attempt to work through those pressuring conversations with friends and family.

After all, we love the people we have chosen to be in our lives (our friends), and we love the family we were born into. It's natural to want to keep the flow of the relationships going, so you're going to naturally try and work through their curiosity.

That brings me to my next point. Oftentimes the peer pressure of family and friends comes from a place of ignorance. It doesn't mean they are dumb, it just means they have no clue about what homeschooling really is. And chances are, they remember what it was like back in the '70s or '80s! It's very different now. Homeschooling has grown massively over the last few years, and it just keeps growing. Families are choosing to homeschool all over the country and they come from all sorts of backgrounds too.

Help your friends and family learn about homeschooling. With my family, I started to email them articles about their most worrisome topic: college! Ironically, I have zero interest in pressuring my kids to go to college. But for my family, college is huge and a must-do. My kids will be prepared for college and will probably explore it as an option, but I'm not putting that same pressure on them.

But, to my family, going to college is huge. So I send them lots of articles about homeschoolers heading to college and how it is possible. I send them articles that talk about studies where it was found that homeschoolers generally score higher than the national average on the SAT and ACT, and they often enter college with more college credits. They also tend to do better during their freshman year than their peers.

That's just an academic example, but what I did here is help ease the concern they had with this particular area.

Once that is at ease, the walls begin to come down and interest begins to grow. My family now finds it fascinating that I homeschool. They love it and are genuinely excited to talk about it with me now.

So try to find out what the root of the problem is, what is causing them to put this pressure on you regarding your choice to homeschool. Then offer them up some information. This usually starts verbally, because the situation usually arises face-to-face. Then, you can offer to send them articles to read to help them understand homeschooling better.

As a society, we tend to put pressures on anyone who thinks or does something differently than we do. It's human nature. We stand so strong in what we believe in and we feel the need to fight for it at all costs.

So when you decide to homeschool, you'll find mixed reactions from family and friends. The best thing you can do is find out what their issue with homeschooling is, and try to address that issue. You aren't doing it because you have to, but because you want to. Address the most common concerns voluntarily; they may not even know how to express some of their concerns. So just go for it!

The grand-prize-winning question is: What about socialization?

Here's the truth about that one. Real life, adult life, isn't like school life. Not even college! You aren't grouped together with people of your own age ONLY. No, instead we interact with people of all walks of life, all ages, and all backgrounds. Daily we interact with a variety of age groups. Homeschooling offers up the opportunity to naturally interact with the world. Your children will, from the beginning and from there on out, interact with people of all ages. They will always know how to be around all kinds of age groups.

Maybe your family and friends are worried about your capability to provide your children with the proper education. Let's get real; you can provide them with the very best education they can have. You've raised them just fine up until this point, right? Maybe you didn't know some things along the way, or wanted to try something new with the second child, but you found answers. Right? It's the same with homeschooling; you are capable and you can provide your child with the education they need.

This pressure to provide a proper educations comes from not knowing anything about homeschool educational resources or methods. This is a great teaching moment that you can offer your friends and family, should they want it. Some people just don't care to hear anything outside of their lines of "perceived normal."

When I started homeschooling, I knew nothing about it. Zero. I mean, I didn't even know there were different methods of homeschooling. So, I did research on it and learned as much as I could. It's what should be done when we don't know about something that matters to us. I'm sure you did the same when you decided to homeschool, but your family and friends aren't making that choice, so they aren't as eager to search for answers as you are.

Be kind in your approach and try to understand that they simply do not know about it as much as you do. Trust your decision and don't allow anyone to make you question it. You as the parent are capable of doing this; you love this child more than anyone else. You will give them everything they could need and probably much more!

Be patient, be informative, but most importantly trust your decision to homeschool.

Spending So Much Time in the Kitchen

Jennifer A. Janes

My daughter lost dairy when she was 2 years old. Gluten and eggs followed a year later. In the years since then, she has lost shellfish and chocolate, and I lost shellfish myself and am now dairy- and gluten-free as well. In the early years of eliminating foods from my family's diet, I was overwhelmed and frustrated, and I felt like I spent most of my life in the kitchen. Since I was also trying to homeschool, write, and get my daughter to and from many appointments every week, this just didn't work. Convenience foods that met our dietary requirements were either not available or were too expensive. I had no idea what to do.

Fortunately, I have found ways to move myself and my family into a place where food preparation isn't a major ordeal. I can prepare meals and still have a life other than my kitchen.

Here are some of the things that have saved me.

Keep meals simple - and stretch them!

I used to be a lot more adventurous in trying recipes and preparing meals with lots of different dishes. Not anymore.

Now I favor soups or casseroles that can be served for more than one meal and that I know my family will eat. If there's not a pretty good chance that my family will love a new recipe, I don't even try it. Finding recipes that your family really loves and rotating through those on a regular basis will help you keep things simple. Talk to your spouse and kids and ask them what their favorite recipes are, what they crave when the weather changes, and other questions that will help you get a feel for what they really enjoy eating.

I make my work stretch for as many meals as possible. I make a double or triple batch of family favorites and freeze some for later or plan to stretch that one big pot over two or three nights. We may eat it alone the first night, and then prepare and serve it over rice the second night. The third night I might bake potatoes and "load" the potatoes with the little that's left. It's simple and much faster (and cheaper) than preparing another meal every night.

Supper is our big meal each day. I keep breakfasts and lunches simple, too. We usually eat cereal or homemade muffins and fruit for breakfast, and have lunchmeat or supper leftovers that won't feed more than one person. The bottom line is that I no longer cook three separate meals a day. If I need to make breakfast muffins or an occasional batch of pancakes, I often do it in the evenings after supper, while everyone is in the kitchen anyway to keep me company and to help wash the dishes I dirty in the process.

My slow cooker is also my best friend. On weeks that I know I will have crazy days full of more than the normal number of appointments, I plan meals that I can prepare in the slow cooker. Then I can be gone all day, and supper is still ready when I get home, with the possible exception of making a pot of rice or steaming some vegetables. It's a sanity and time-saver!

Enlist the kids.

Feeding a family three meals a day is a major undertaking, even if your family doesn't deal with food allergies. While keeping things simple and stretching meals helps, you still have to spend time in the kitchen every week. But when you're homeschooling, you can enlist the kids!

Helping with food preparation and cleanup is home education. It's a valuable life skill that they're going to have to learn at some point, so you might as well start early. My kids have been helping me in the kitchen since they were big enough to show an interest, and now my older daughter has some side dishes that she is primarily responsible for.

She has also set some goals for herself so that she can learn to prepare simple meals and handle herself safely and competently. She helps me several days a week, and it is a blessing to get to teach her, talk to her, and find out what she's thinking about. I look forward to our times in the kitchen together. If you're interested in teaching your kids to cook or giving them more kitchen tasks to help with, you can find lists of kitchen chores for kids by age on the internet.

When the kids really need to work on their lessons, but you have to be in the kitchen, they can still join you. Have the kids bring their lessons into the kitchen during meal preparation and cleanup. (We have a kitchen table, but even if you don't, you can find a way to make this work.) Kids can work independently on their lessons, with you there and available for questions, if they have any. Or a child can read a lesson aloud to you while you work, and you can discuss it. Another educational activity we enjoy in the kitchen is listening to audiobooks. Sometimes we want to talk, but if everyone is feeling quiet, listening to a great audiobook can give our minds a chance to escape to a world full of imagination and fun.

Plan.

For years I was resistant to planning meals. The problem was that I always had a pantry full of food and no idea what to fix with it. Or I couldn't think of anything to prepare, and it was almost time to serve supper and I was still trying to come up with an idea. A few years ago, my husband and I started meal-planning, and now I know why meal-planners talk so much about it. Having a plan has saved us time and money.

We start with a general plan for the week. We write down a main dish for each evening. Then we create a list for the week's groceries, and we focus on buying what we need to prepare those meals, along with fresh fruit and vegetables and other items that need to be replaced weekly. If there's a particularly good sale on canned goods or other items we use often, then we'll stock up as the budget permits.

Now, when I get ready to start supper, I know that I have all the ingredients I need to prepare a certain number of main dishes. If we want to change the night we make a certain dish, that's fine. The kids know that we'll be having the dish that got bumped later in the week. I no longer struggle with what to make for supper or whether I have everything I need. And we're saving money by not buying without a plan. It's definitely a win-win and helps keep things simple.

It is possible to homeschool, prepare healthy meals for your family, and not spend all day in the kitchen. With some advance planning, enlisting help, and a focus on simplicity, you'll find that your kitchen time becomes more enjoyable and less stressful – and should take you less time too!

Help! I'm No Good With Record-Keeping

Lindsey Marie

From time to time, I hear mothers mention that they are intimidated by the record-keeping needed for homeschooling. This, of course, will differ from state to state depending where you live because of homeschooling laws. But, in general, it is always good to have a certain amount of homeschooling records.

Record-keeping is an excellent way to gauge progress and to stay organized. Records include anything from Statements/Declarations of Intent to Homeschool, to attendance records, grade sheets, and lesson plans.

Possibilities can present themselves in the future. You may move from one state to the other and need certain documents, especially if the homeschool law has changed. There is also the possibility that your child may reenter public school. In rare cases, governmental authorities may require documentation. In any case, it's a good idea to have records – for you and, at times, for others.

Having said that, please do not be intimidated by this requirement. I know that for some of us – especially those of us who love to be flexible, spontaneous, and welcome a certain amount of clutter and/or unpredictably in our lives

– keeping records and charts and lists may just be one of those "mundane tasks" that seem to halt our creativity.

But that's where this chapter comes in, my friend. Do not despair.

I am a 30-something-year-old homeschooling mother with ADHD. If anyone understands the obstacle this often presents, it's me. Here are a few principles and practical ideas that I, myself, have employed.

Stay informed

First and foremost, you will want to find out what the law is in your state. There are states that require no notice or documentation. In that case, you may want to keep records only for your own satisfaction and awareness. But many states do have some requirements. In my state, California, we have to file on October 1 each year a Private School Affidavit Form. I file, and print out a copy for my own records. This goes into my homeschool lesson planner. But there are states that have moderate requirements and high requirements, so additional records are needed. Some of you will be meeting with teachers, so you will need proof in lesson plans and/or attendance records.

My point is this: Know what you will absolutely be required to prove. In addition to that, it's a good idea to have records for your own benefit.

Be prepared

The thing about keeping records is that, though they require time, they can most definitely be a helpful tool. Much homeschool success can be attributed to being prepared with a homeschool binder and lesson planner of some sort. Again, yes, it does take preparation and time, but the time it saves you is invaluable.

The other thing about being prepared is that you must prepare ahead of time. It is best to put together your records before the school year starts. If you haven't done so already, there is no time like now.

There are many, many homeschool lesson planners out there. Some are free; some cost money. It's fairly easy to find them. All you have to do is search for "homeschool lesson planner" and many will appear. You can also find a good deal of them on Etsy. Many times homeschool bloggers will offer their own homeschool lesson planners as free downloads, or to purchase for a small fee.

I have several homeschool lesson planners that I've either paid for or downloaded for free. My own homeschool binder is a mixture of files from different sources.

Your homeschool lesson planner can have the following sheets in it:

- Personalized cover sheet
- Yearly calendar
- Attendance record
- Monthly calendar
- Weekly lesson planner
- Progress report sheet
- Field trip planner
- Student information sheet
- Grade keeper

There are also lesson planners for different purposes, such as unit study planners or Charlotte Mason planners. There are also planners for unschooling. Even as an unschooling homeschooler, you may want a tangible record of what you have been accomplishing through the years. This is a great way to reassure yourself of progress and that you are making good use of your time.

Keep it simple

What I've noticed about this issue of "record-keeping" is that if you have too many records or papers to keep track of, or too much "writing down" that you need to do, it can be overwhelming and stop any progress. For me, I realized that planners are often a waste of time if things become too complicated. This is something you may want to consider. Here are a few things I've done to keep things simple in my life.

I've used an online homeschool planner and I see all of the many benefits of having an online planner. I like that it's efficient and doesn't require a lot of writing or scratching out or starting over. It also keeps the whole family "in the know" as it emails each family member their list or tasks for the day. Online planners can be an excellent way of keeping things simple and efficient.

Sometimes it's limiting the amount of planners, lists, or papers you have. For example, I started using a dry-erase calendar next to my desk. Instead of having to open a drawer, find a planner, open the page to this month's calendar and so forth, all I have to do is turn my head and I can visually see all that is going on this month. I did the same thing on the other side of my desk. I have a corkboard with a monthly calendar I make of my blogging tasks. I also have a clipboard on my desk that contains the most important papers I use on a daily basis (like my password log) so that I never have to go digging and flipping for information.

Keeping things simple and keeping it accessible is the key to having success using your records. If it's too complicated or not ready, chances are you won't want to use them.

Make it attractive

This may not seem like the most practical advice ever, but interestingly so many moms agree. When something is attractive and pretty, you are drawn to it and will use it more. It's that simple.

Having a binder you love or creating a personalized cover sheet does so much to emotionally attach yourself to such an inanimate object. Look at the fad of "glam planning." These use their planners like scrapbooks, filling them with stickers and Washi tape and sometimes lace.

I know that for me when I buy pretty pens in various colors, it just makes me want to use them. And I do! So really, making these items your own can do wonders to motivate you to use them.

Explore and ask

Another easy way of getting on track with record-keeping is to simply start exploring on the internet or asking around. Search for "homeschool records" or "homeschool planners." Read blogs about homeschooling. Ask your homeschooling friends or acquaintances what they use for record-keeping. Oftentimes, that is all it takes to get inspired and discover what would work for you. You might need to try a few different things but that's why it's good to keep looking and asking.

And you know what: I'll go first. If you stop by my blog at nittygrittyhomeschooling.com, you'll find posts and videos on how we organize our school and keep track of our lesson plans and homeschool records. From there you'll have a pretty good idea, but remember: Don't stop asking and searching until you find a system that works for you and your family.

Help! I Homeschool and My House is a Mess!
Kristi Clover

Some days I feel like I have to make a decision: Will we get everything done with our homeschool work today, or will I actually get my house clean? There doesn't always seem to be a middle ground. It feels like it's one or the other.

Balancing homeschooling and housework is very hard work. Overwhelming work. It probably shouldn't have surprised me that one of the top questions I was asked this summer at the homeschool convention I spoke at was how I kept up with my house and homeschooling. It just showed me that other homeschool moms were thinking the same thing.

Honestly, I don't always get to my housework. My house definitely does not stay as clean as it did before I started homeschooling. I should give myself some grace in that I now have five kids in the mix. I started our homeschool journey with three. I heard someone say the other day that trying to keep your house clean with kids is like trying to brush your teeth and eat Oreos at the same time! Ha! That was a perfect visual for me!

We have a 2-year-old in our house now, and we joke that she is our little tornado. She's always looking for adventure and that usually includes climbing up on something and dumping out whatever she can find! I'm sure her little mind keeps thinking over and over, "Will there be treasure in this box? In this drawer? Over here? Over there?"

I've been slowly learning to let it go — not the house so much as my attitude of perfection. It probably helps that some little person is singing "Let It Go!" at some point in the day — almost as though to remind me.

Please hear me in that you don't have to completely let your house go when you start homeschooling. There are ways to get things done that I'll discuss in a moment. However, it is so important to remember your first priorities and know that it's OK to not have a perfectly put-together house all the time.

It's OK for your house to look lived in. I find that the less I stress about making my house look perfect before people come over, the more they feel relaxed to let their kids play and make themselves at home. I joke that my mess is to bless people. I made a YouTube video about "keeping it real" and showed my homeschool room at the end of the day. It looked like school happened. :)

So, how do I get it all done? Well, you've already probably guessed — I don't!

I don't get it all done, but I do get what is most important done. It's a matter of prioritizing — more on that below.

Here are a few practical tips to help you survive the juggling act of homeschooling and housework!

Lower your expectations!

Know that something has got to give. You may not be able to keep the house as perfectly organized and tidy as you did before you started homeschooling. That's OK. You have to give yourself some grace! Homeschooling is a full-time job!

Mommyhood is a full-time job! Just make sure that you warn your spouse that you are lowering your expectations. He may not appreciate the surprise.

Prioritize!

As I already mentioned, I don't get it all done. I've had to learn to let go of perfection! It's a matter of prioritizing. Just like in life, you make the most time for your priority relationships; with housework you prioritize what is most important to you and your spouse to have done on a regular basis. Counters are important to my husband. Floors are important to me. So, we make those two things a priority to keep clean and tidy. Know that those are the two hardest things to keep clean and tidy in our home. But when it happens, usually at the end of the day... Ahh! It feels so good!

Get help!

Hire a cleaner! This was recommended to me at the first homeschool conference I ever attended by two different speakers. I remember thinking that every woman in the room was probably wishing her husband was sitting next to her so she could elbow him. Truly, if you can find money in your budget to hire a cleaner to come every other week or even once a month for a deep clean, it will be so worth it. I literally told my cleaners what my budget was and asked them what they could get done for that amount. I thought through what was the most important thing that I wanted done and what would help me the most — and had them do that. I've been really amazed at how much they can get done on the budget I gave them. (Please trust me that my house does not stay clean for long, so we still have to do plenty of housework here. But for one hour the house looks amazing.)

Train your kids to help!

We are a family, and our kids are part of our family unit. Housework is teamwork. It's not just about mom running around trying to serve everyone else. Everyone needs to be pitching in.

Even little kids can be a great help. I start training as young as 2 years old. This doesn't mean that my toddler can vacuum a whole room by herself, but she can hand her sister the clean spoons from the dishwasher to put away. Teamwork! Most little kids think that chores are fun anyway!

I actually train my kids to do the chores I dislike the most: laundry, dishes, and trash. :) My helpers definitely bless me tremendously (and they don't even know how much)!

By taking the time to teach them the most efficient way to do chores, you will bless them for life! Don't expect perfection as you are training them. It takes time. It took me over a year before I turned over the girls' laundry to my older boys. There were so many dresses that couldn't be put in the dryer, and I had a set way of hanging things. We just kept practicing and tweaking and eventually they were ready. I just tried to encourage them along the way. It's always a great moment when they say, "OK, Mom. I've got this."

Don't forget to praise them! I still remember my mom telling me that I was the best sink cleaner and made the sink shine better than she could. I always looked forward to cleaning the sink as a kid. I was so proud of my work. I asked her recently if she did that on purpose to get me to clean the sinks. She told me, "No, you actually were really good at making sinks shine." Her words encouraged the best from me!

Make a list!

It's important to figure out what is driving you the craziest! I literally go throughout the house and write down everything that needs to get done in each room.

Pile of papers? Endless pile of laundry? Focus on getting the most important things done first. What areas are driving you the nuttiest? What would be the best plan of attack?

I assign those things on my list to the family (and sometimes to the cleaners). Some jobs need to be broken down a bit into bite-sized pieces. I don't just say, "Clean the family room." We break it down into what specifically needs to get done, then we work together to make it "clean."

I love my whiteboards! I keep one in the kitchen so I can write down all the little things I see left out. I can't tell you how much this reduces stress in our home (and in me). Instead of me blowing my top when I see things forgotten or missed (again!), like reminding my kiddos for the millionth time to put away their shoes in their shoe bins as I trip over them, I just add it to my list! Then I add a child's name or initial next to it. This helps me remember to follow up, too. I often forget to check on beds or chores in another part of the house when I'm busy getting things done everywhere else. So, this board adds a bit of accountability. If you don't have a whiteboard, just use a piece of paper or a sticky.

I should note that we have an "Extra Chores" list. These are the things like baseboards, grout, windows, etc. that don't always get done. These projects are assigned to the child "needing" to have extra work.

Get organized.

Assign days to get specific work done. Create a checklist for kids and family — things that need to get done daily. Basically, we try to assign major tasks to certain days and daily tasks to certain times of the day. Keeping to this routine helps to ensure that things get done.

Plan your meals.

The question I get asked most often when I tell people that we have five kids — aside from "Are you crazy?"— is, "How do you feed everyone?" Meal planning is my secret to feeding everyone!

Simple meal planning can make such a HUGE difference in your day and save you the headache of trying to decide what to make for dinner at 6 p.m. when everyone is already hungry.

I actually plan out my meals for the week and do one big shop to gather everything I need. Now when my kids ask me what is for dinner, I just direct them to the list (usually because I've forgotten and the list keeps me on track). I've actually created a handy-dandy Menu Planner and Grocery List.

If you really want to make meal time easy, make your slow cooker your best friend! I pulled every recipe I could find that was Crock-Pot-friendly and did searches online for good recipes. I also asked my friends for their favorite slow cooker recipes. I took this precious compilation of recipes and put them all in one place — my Easy Meals list! This is just a list that holds all my easy recipes in one place. It is a life saver for me!

So, there you have it!

Housework doesn't have to go out the door when you are homeschooling — only your expectations of being perfect. Give yourself grace! Know that there will be a season when your kids are grown and out of the house. Your job as a homeschool mom will be done. Forced retirement. You can focus on keeping things in place then — even though my advice would be the same for you then, too: Grace!

I hope my tips helped you to get a glimpse into how we do things in our home to keep our sanity.

Cleaning While Homeschooling

Dianna Kennedy

Ready for a mom confession?

I'm not the best housekeeper.

With lots of little children underfoot, there are many days when my house looks like a disaster. After a few years of struggling to keep my head above water with cleaning, I've finally gotten to a point that my house isn't perfect, but it's reasonably clean enough. Here's how we juggle five small children, homeschooling and working outside the home while keeping life's messes under control.

Ditch the unrealistic expectations

Let's face it. I'm NOT going to have House Beautiful for at least a few years. Toddlers and preschoolers can wreck a room in moments.

Instead of wishing for different circumstances, I try to minimize the potential messes and damages as much as possible. You won't find fine art and white carpet in my house, but durable kid-friendly furniture and decor that stands up to the abuse of many small children.

Divide and conquer with your spouse

It takes a team effort to run a home. No matter who's working or who's at home with the children, you and your spouse are busy.

You both have strengths and weakness, so make a list of all the tasks that need to be done and devise a plan to get everything done.

Your roles will look different than other families, but the end result is working together.

Have a teaching spirit

It's easy to send your husband to the park with the children while you clean, but that could breed resentment. Take the time to teach your children how to do chores.

They're not going to be perfect, but with time, they'll learn all of the tasks they need to run their own homes one day.

Praise your children for their help

I KNOW it takes longer to do chores with children underfoot. I've been there, done that a million times.

Thanking them when they help is essential.

When my kids drag the laundry hamper to the kitchen, I tell them how strong they are. While they help me load the clothes into the washer, I explain to them that they are being SUCH a help to me.

Kindness goes a long way with children. Try your best to temper your words and spirit.

Less stuff means less cleaning

Take some time while you're cleaning to throw things out — broken toys go in the trash, outgrown clothes go in the Goodwill pile or sorted to be sold.

Mom Tip Keep a box by the front door for donations. When it's full, load it in your car and take it away.

Find some friends

Stressed about having the children home all the time, and not being able to clean? Chat with one of your friends about trading time.

Work it out where your friend takes your children while you tackle the housework that's piling up on you. Then reciprocate and take her children so she can get caught up at her house.

Make it a game

We set the timer in my house and see who can pick up the most stuff before the bell rings.

I like doing this especially before bed, since it means I wake up to a mostly clean living room. Ta-da!

Another fun tip? We put on "cleaning music" – fun songs with a catchy beat to keep us moving and grooving while we work.

Live by example

If my house is a mess, I can't think straight enough to homeschool (or find everything I need). Our rule is no school before chores, which also means my kids can't go outside to play if everything is in a shambles.

We get our work done FIRST, then we have fun.

Involve your children in age-appropriate chores

In our home, everyone is expected to pitch in and help keep the house picked up. Even my toddler and preschooler are capable of helping to put dirty clothes in the laundry baskets or helping to run the vacuum.

Having children involved helps them with taking ownership of their home, encourages self-worth with a job well done, and helps lift the burden on you.

Don't be afraid to hire some help

As a working mom who homeschools and has her own business, I've been known to burn the candle at both ends. Hiring a housekeeper allows me to get caught up on projects that I've left on the back burner (like organizing the pantry!).

Take some of these ideas and implement them slowly in your home to get things a little more under control.

The House is a Mess! Balancing Homeschool and Housework

Misty Bailey

Homeschool moms have a lot on their plates. We are teachers, nurses, cooks, moms, housekeepers and more. We run ourselves ragged, and too often feel like what we do is never enough.

Managing the home is an area that most women struggle with, regardless of their job status or method of educating their children. However, managing our homes well is possible; it just takes some work and planning ahead.

Get the kids involved

One of the first things you will need to do is realize that you cannot do it all on your own – and you shouldn't have to! If you have children over the age of 5, then you have built-in helpers.

Teach your kids to work from a young age. Even a preschooler can put his dirty clothes in the hamper. A 5-year-old is more than capable of picking up her room, and your 8-year-old is old enough to be responsible for unloading the dishwasher. Chores are a must-have in any home, and enlisting the help of your children is a given.

There are tons of printables and chore lists out there on the web that can let you see what may be age-appropriate.

Find a routine for homemaking

The next step in managing your home is to find a routine to help you in your homemaking efforts.

Right now my routine is pretty basic. Through the week, I do nothing but basic upkeep. A load or two of laundry each day, dishes, floors, etc. Then on Saturdays, I clean. It takes about two hours, but for now it is what works for me. Saturdays are the only day we don't homeschool, and I don't work; so it gives me a day to get up, get things done, and spend the rest of the time with my family.

When I had lots of little ones, I tackled one task each day. One day it was the bathrooms, another it was dusting, and another it was cleaning the bedrooms.

Everyone's homemaking routine will look different; you may need to break up the tasks into smaller pieces each day, like I used to. You may not want to clean on Saturdays and would rather have the day off. The key is to find a homemaking routine that works for you and then manage your home to the best of your ability.

Learn to prioritize

One of the biggest things we as homeschool moms need to do is prioritize. There may be days where little to nothing gets done in the house. Maybe the kids have been sick, you have been busy, or life has just gotten in the way. The house becomes a mess, and is overwhelming! At times like this, it is important to learn to prioritize.

Make a list of things that need to be done. What is the MOST important thing on there? Start with most important and work your way down.

For some, that may be tackling that pile of laundry so you all have clean clothes tomorrow; for others, it may be the pile of dishes, or cleaning the floors. When my to-do list is overwhelming, I go through and number the items based on what HAS to be done. The key is finding out what you need to prioritize, and working from there.

Remember to give yourself grace

As a busy homeschool mom, I have had to learn to give myself grace. My home will never be as clean as I would like it. We live here, every day. I will probably always have something on my to-do list, and that's OK. As moms, we have to learn to give ourselves grace. We need to realize that not everything HAS to be perfect, and my level of clean and organized may look different than yours.

When it comes to managing your home, there are three questions I want you to ask yourself:

- Am I doing my best? (Everyone's best looks different)
- Are my kids fed?
- Do we have clothes to wear?

If your answer to those is yes, then you are a success. Don't beat yourself up. Manage your home to the best of your ability, and everything else will fall into place.

The Stress of Choosing Curriculum
Tonia Lyons

Choosing the right curriculum for your homeschool can be stressful. When you make the decision to step out on your own and be the educator for your children, it's a momentous landmark in your life. You feel the need to do absolutely everything perfectly – which can put unnecessary stress on you, as a teacher and as a mother.

But I have a little secret I want to share with you. There is no such thing as the perfect curriculum. We all start out with that huge stack of homeschool catalogs, looking for just the right thing for our children. Perhaps we can't find what we want, so we combine 2 math programs or try to line up 3 different history books in the quest to find that perfect fit.

It doesn't exist. There's no perfect curriculum. Let go of that notion and take a deep breath. Choosing curriculum does not have to be filled with stress. There are a few things that you can do to ensure that your homeschool journey is successful and you find curriculum that will work for you and your children.

Find programs that make you an effective teacher

You should consider your child's learning style when choosing curriculum, but if you find a program that you are comfortable using, it will be easier to adapt it for your child. Once in a while, I find the program that just resonates with me, as a teacher, and it gives me the confidence to do my job well. That's so much more worthwhile than the latest math program or newest history text. So find something that makes you a fabulous teacher and stick with it.

Find what doesn't make your kid cry

When it comes to some subjects, especially math, you are better off finding one satisfactory program and sticking with it instead of hunting for something fun and interesting and new every year. If it's a good, solid program and your child doesn't break out in sobs whenever you put it in front of him, you've found a good fit!

Don't try to do it all

The more children you have, the longer your school day will take. Be sure to consider that when you are choosing your curriculum. It's OK not to cover every subject every year. Instead, focus on different needs each year. In the early years, that is usually reading skills, handwriting, and basic math. If you only do two science experiments in first grade, you'll be fine! As long as you are working on handwriting skills, phonics, and math, the rest can be done whenever you feel like it.

Set yearly goals and focus on those instead of getting stressed or burnt out over the things that may be fun but usually become burdensome about six weeks into the school year. As fun as all those extras can be, if you are stressed out trying to fit it all into your perfectly crafted schedule, no one is going to enjoy it.

Instead, decide on what important skills you need to cover this school year, find programs that will help you teach those skills, and use the other things as time allows. Don't get burnt out trying to cover everything. Choose your subjects and focus on those.

You don't need to teach everything to your child. If you give them the tools to learn – those basic skills you work on every year – they will be willing and able to continue educating themselves, long after they've graduated.

Let go of the thought of the perfect curriculum

Finding the one that is good enough and doing a little bit every day will be more successful than constantly searching for that elusive perfect curriculum. Set goals, find things that will help you teach to those goals, and let the rest go. Don't let the thought of perfect curriculum cause you stress. There isn't such a thing. But I can guarantee you will have a few things – some tears (from you and your kids), a program or two that is completely horrible, and maybe a few gems along the way.

The key to having a successful homeschooling journey is to find what works and do a little bit, every day.

Balancing Homeschool with a Special-Needs Child
Jen Dunlap

Parenting a special-needs child presents some unique and interesting challenges, and homeschooling certainly adds an extra dimension.

Keeping up with therapies and appointments can stretch the calendar, particularly in a large family. It's completely normal to feel overloaded, stressed and completely unable to conquer the task. I think knowing that we aren't alone in our struggles is half the battle. You aren't alone.

Have you ever heard the expression "a bad day of homeschool is better than a good day of public school?" I believe that is especially true with our special-needs children. My hat's off to families who are battling teachers and specialists for their child's IEP. While it's certainly not easy to manage everything at least we do have control and final say over the therapies and more importantly their school environment.

Tips to balance homeschool and family life

Plan therapies for the same day. Easier said than done, but if you are able to plan one day as your "out and about" day, your week will be so much more productive. Your days at home can then be more focused.

Get help from older siblings. Most of the time, older siblings love to help out. Recruit a sibling to read daily to your special-needs child. It is mutually beneficial. The older sibling gets reading practice, your special-needs child is listening to a great book, and you are available to help or work with another child.

Recruit a helper. For the first time ever, we hired outside help for this year. We have a college student from our parish coming over two times per week for a total of four hours to hang out with our daughter. They play outside, complete crafts, and do other various activities together. I can focus on completing schoolwork with my older children. We can get a huge amount of work done in four hours a week! I didn't realize how often I would stop working with my other children to check on her, redirect her, give her another activity, etc.

See the benefits to the family. Having a special needs child affects the ENTIRE family. That is not necessarily a bad thing. I believe we are teaching our children to be more compassionate and tolerant of others.

Make time for your spouse. This should be happening on a regular basis even if you don't have a special-needs child in your home, and is even more important with the demands of a special-needs child. Making time to reconnect with your spouse, while seemingly impossible sometimes, is so worth it. If you can manage to get away for the weekend once in a great while, even better! Parents of special-needs children are hypervigilant and have a constant underlying stress because often you can never fully relax. Taking time away is so restorative.

Make time for other children. Parenting our special-needs child or children can be all-consuming. We can't forget to make time for the children in our home that are not as demanding of our attention. Make a point to grab a child while heading out on an errand. Even a quick trip to the grocery store or hardware store can reap big benefits and an opportunity for some one-on-one conversation.

Homeschooling a special-needs child is extra-demanding, for sure. A worthwhile task, but we are not superhuman and need to remember to try and take time for ourselves, our spouses, and other family members and most importantly reach out for help.

Together, we can do this!

Trying to Balance Homeschooling with a Child with Special Needs

Jennifer A. Janes

I have no tiara, never wear heels, and definitely don't have a superhero cape. I am pretty good at juggling, though. Being the mom of a child with special needs, and a homeschooling mom at that, has taught me a few things over the past decade.

Time management is an issue for every mom, but when you add a child with special needs into the mix, things quickly get out of control. First, take homeschooling, extracurricular activities, field trips and sessions with your local homeschool group or co-op, church, and family — and then you add therapy sessions, doctor appointments, trips to various specialists (many requiring out-of-town travel), and medication to dispense multiple times a day. In my case, there are also weekly infusions to give and regular conferences with the immunologist and specialty pharmacy about those treatments, their effectiveness, and the number of infections she's having. And then there's the need to nourish a marriage, support a sibling, and sleep in the very brief 24 hours a day granted to me.

It's overwhelming. Do you constantly feel like you're not getting everything done? Do you feel like you're not doing enough — in your homeschool, in your housework, in your personal life?

What's a mom to do? It's definitely a juggling act. Here are some ways to juggle it all (and stay sane).

Realize you can't do it all.

That's right. If you feel like you can't get everything done, you're going to have to embrace that feeling and find ways to live with it. It is physically impossible to do everything we feel like we must get done every day. We expect too much of ourselves. We only have 24 hours in a day, and we really need to sleep seven to eight of those hours if we're going to be at our best for our families. You're going to have to figure out what your family's priorities are and plan your limited time every day to make those happen first. This applies to your homeschooling, housework, meal preparation, and extracurricular activities. Anything after that is a bonus.

Focus.

Forget multi-tasking. Most people aren't more productive when they multi-task, and some studies are coming out now that show that multi-tasking actually makes us less productive and can actually be bad for our brain function. We don't have time for that! Instead, focus on one activity at a time. When you finish one, move to the next one. If you're like me, trying to multi-task just leaves you with a lot of undone tasks because you flit from one to the other, never actually finishing anything. I'm beginning to think that years of trying to multi-task have caused something like ADD, and I'm having to retrain myself to focus on one thing at a time.

Accept help.

As much as I would like to be able to do everything myself, I have had to accept that I need help. I give my children age- and ability-appropriate tasks to help me with around the house. My husband helps me when he's not traveling for work. (See the chapter I wrote about flying solo when dad travels or works late hours for more on handling that.) My mom comes in once a week and pitches in when she visits. (Although I don't expect it, I don't turn it down when she does!) I have some friends who will step in and help out. I used to be humiliated by the idea of someone stepping into my mess, but I've come to realize that I need the help, and I can get along better by accepting it.

Say no.

You cannot do everything everyone asks you to do. It's not humanly possible. Prayerfully set goals for yourself and your family and say no to everything that doesn't fit those goals. I heard author Tricia Goyer speak at a conference a few years ago, and she said she and her husband wrote down everything that was on their schedule and categorized each item as 1 (things you MUST do), 2 (things you SHOULD do), 3 (things you enjoy and want to do), or 4 (things you do because you're afraid to say no or because you want to look good or have the kids look good). Cut out everything on the 4 list and some of the things on the 3 list. Later, some items on the 3 list can be added back in as you get a better handle on your schedule. I am still working on doing this, and it is difficult, but freeing!

Build margin.

As you whittle your schedule down as much as possible using Tricia Goyer's method, you'll find a little more breathing room. This will motivate you to continue looking for ways to build more margin in your life so that you and your kids have time to rest and participate in activities you enjoy — at home. Margin will also allow you some time to think and process everything that is going on in your life. Often, writing in a journal will help me to process things better, but I have to have white space in my schedule to allow that time for reflection.

Keep homeschooling simple.

Rotate subjects. You don't have to do every subject every day. We start with reading, language arts, and math every day. Then we work in and rotate the other subjects throughout the week. This makes the load much more bearable. Realizing that you don't have to do every subject every day will also build some margin in your schedule for fun activities like field trips and nature walks that everyone will enjoy.

Schedule time to work one-on-one with each child every day. It doesn't have to be long, but even the most independent learners have questions, need your input, and want to know that you're as engaged in their learning as you are in their struggling sibling's. When possible, combine classes like science and social studies to cut down on your prep time and having to teach the same subject twice.

Supplement curriculum with living books, documentaries, and activities that will provide multisensory learning experiences. Looking for learning opportunities in daily life is another good way for you and your children to bond, for them to learn valuable life skills, and to see how the subjects they're studying are used in real life.

My family also likes to combine out-of-town specialist visits with field trips. When we're getting ready for an appointment, we plan to spend the whole day, regardless of what time the appointment is. Then we spend half the day at a zoo or hands-on science museum (yearly memberships make this very affordable) and the other half at Children's Hospital. It gives all of us a chance to stretch our legs and get some hands-on learning done on an otherwise long and boring day. And it counts as school!

Finally, choose curriculum and resources wisely. Find what works for your family, and stick with that.

Schedule time for your spouse and other children.

It sounds funny to talk about making appointments to do this, but that's the only way I've found to make sure it happens on a regular basis. My husband and I have a monthly date night, and my older daughter and I get to have "dates" sometimes when my mom is in town to spend time with my younger daughter so we can slip away.

Making this time for your spouse and other children lets them know that they're important to you too, even during seasons where much of your time and energy is spent dealing with your child's special needs.

Use your time wisely.

Like to read? Take a book to therapy sessions and doctor's appointments. Waiting rooms are notoriously, as my daughter says, "wait-long" rooms. Have you been longing to learn to knit or crochet? Take it with you when you leave the house. Waiting for the kids to finish at an extracurricular activity gives you time to experiment. Want more time to write? Grab a tablet or netbook that will work offline. You can put all that time spent waiting to good use! Of course, there are times that there will be another parent who needs a listening ear and some encouragement, but many times, there will be time for you to do something you enjoy.

Balancing homeschooling with taking care of a child with special needs and the rest of the family is challenging, but with some goal setting and planning ahead, you can make it work.

Homeschooling an Unmotivated Student

Shannen Espelien

We all worry about it, and most of us struggle with it at some point: unmotivated kids. Whether that's an unmotivated first-grader or high-schooler, the stress is real. We all started this homeschooling journey for important reasons, and most of those reasons aren't met if our kids aren't doing any actual work. So, how do we light that fire and get them moving?

The first question I ask myself is if there's anything I can do to change. After all, it's easiest for me to change myself versus another person! So, I ask myself:

- Should this be more hands-on?

- Do they see the value in this work?

- Does this work really matter in the whole scheme of things?

We are fortunate there are so many options in terms of homeschool curriculum, so if something really isn't working, we can look for alternatives. Of course, we shouldn't be jumping ship every six months, but finding a nice balance of stability and flexibility is key. A simple search on Google or Pinterest can get those creatives juices flowing. Search for "hands-on geography" or "interactive math" as an example.

As for the value of the work, sometimes we can help our child see the value by showing them certain jobs and how the subject is used, or help them see how having a well-rounded education helps them think critically.

And sometimes we have to be real and admit that we are checking a box so they can have a better chance at being accepted to college by having it done, or we are meeting state requirements.

Other times we have to be real and admit that it doesn't actually matter very much in the whole scheme of things and let it go. For instance, I find the subject of logic extremely valuable, and being able to deconstruct illogical arguments a valuable skill for everyone. Since my teen daughter could not care less, we found a middle road and did logic for a year, and then left it to everyday conversations rather than a required course in her schoolwork.

"Do what you have to do before you do what you want to do."

My teenaged daughter hates this saying, but she knows it well. Some days we just need a "Get 'er done" attitude to get through the day, and the carrot to complete the day's work is the passion and interest that she can indulge in at the end of the day.

For us, that means a ride to fencing practice to prepare for upcoming tournaments, and meanwhile hanging out with friends. For other kids, that might mean screen time, or going to a friend's house for video games.

Especially for young kids, I don't know that I'd take away play time outside, especially since in Minnesota our beautiful days are quite limited. Instead of taking away time outside, if we have troubles getting things done, we use lunchtime like recess, and come back to finish work.

What's happening outside your home?

What distractions are there outside of your own home? You might underestimate how much a friend's parents' divorce affects your child, or how much a local news story resonated with him or her. Oftentimes when we give our children time to process and talk about their thoughts, they can get back to their tasks, or you may realize it's time to take a break and work through what distracts them.

The puberty and teen years are especially emotional, so we've had to learn how to have a bad day and still work through it, because, frankly, pubescent teens would only work half the time if they only did school when they were perfectly happy. During the teen years, they start to really notice the wider world around them, and it can be a scary place. Learning how to process that and still move forward is an important life skill. Maybe slant their work to fit in their feelings, like adjusting a writing assignment so they can write about what consumes their thoughts lately.

We don't want to teach our kids to bottle up their emotions, but with practice they will learn how to both process outside stimulus and keep moving forward with their own goals.

Take days off

In years past, we have followed a pretty typical school schedule, but what I've noticed in doing so is that the fall semester is marbled with days off from traditionally celebrated holidays, and spring semester seems to go on for months without much break.

Even though we want to push through and finish up the school year, we've learned that we need to schedule in more days off during the spring; otherwise all of us are dropping the ball toward the end of the year. That's never fun, and it's not teaching my kids any valuable lessons. It's better to take a few more days off and keep some energetic momentum.

Be positive

We want to build our kids up instead of breaking them down, but at same time we shouldn't be enabling them to slack off. It's a delicate balance to communicate with our kids that stuff needs to get done, and we love them regardless.

Some of my most used phrases are:

- I know you can do this.

- You are absolutely capable of getting this done. I wouldn't have assigned it to you if you couldn't.

Now when we've had to enact the natural consequences of not getting work done, I've tried to stick with phrases like, "This is how you chose to use your time." Instead of focusing on how missing out on fun stuff as a punishment, it is simply that there is free time available, and sometimes kids choose to use that free time during their school day, squeezing out the opportunity for free time in the evening, and sometimes squeezing out time during the summer.

Set goals

I saved what I deem the most important for last. Goal-setting is so important for kids of all ages, especially older students who are working more independently. I often see my teen daughter get overwhelmed with her task list in front of her, and in the past she has felt paralyzed by it. We've worked hard at learning how to break up her work into manageable chunks.

As the saying goes: How do you eat an elephant? One bite at a time.

Some goal-setting starter tips:

- Set your priorities; know what has to get done, and what can wait.

- Write it down! Writing it down makes it feel more contained. Plus, you get to check things off, and that's pretty great.

- In most cases, do the harder thing first; get it out of the way.

- For big goals, even if that's just staying on task all day, have a reward for completing it. Something simple like a movie night or ice cream does well, especially with younger students.

Reward ideas:

- Decorate a 12-oz. Mason jar. Put one marble in for each assignment successfully completed. When the jar is full, get some ice cream.

- Offer up a two-night sleepover with a friend if all schoolwork is done by Thursday night.

- Each assignment is worth 50 cents (or any amount you choose). Make a goal of an item they want to purchase and make a goal chart showing how close they are to meeting that goal, like a thermometer chart you typically see in fundraisers.

- Each assignment is worth 10 minutes of screen time.

- Your student gets to choose dinner for a night this week if they didn't have to be reminded to keep on task.

Sometimes school is downright boring, and depending on your homeschooling philosophy, you may give in to the natural ups and downs of homeschooling more or less than another family. I think everyone can agree that we want to see forward progress throughout the year, though, so I hope that trying to find ways to either get at the root of the lack of motivation, or to motivate your child toward a goal, helps you in your homeschool!

When You Feel Like Homeschooling is Breaking Your Marriage

Kara S. Anderson

I'm not going to lie. I cried. I sat in my big bed and cried, and then I whined a little: "It's just one night," I said. "It shouldn't be this hard."

I couldn't help thinking why is it this hard? Why is it ALWAYS so hard?

My husband and I had been trying to plan a night away. Just one night – to celebrate our anniversary. It had been a rough couple of months.

And so I texted my mom. I might have used the word "desperate," as in, "we are kind of desperate for a night away."

I shouldn't have made it sound so dramatic, but that was how I was feeling. We had gotten ourselves into a little ugly spot. We needed a reset. We needed to be reminded why we got married all those years ago (14!) – back when all we wanted was to be together and to always have a pizza in the freezer and not too many fees on our Blockbuster account.

My mom works as a night nurse, so it took some maneuvering, but we figured out a night. I would surprise my husband. Happy anniversary!

But no. I had forgotten about co-op. At the beginning of the year, we joined a new co-op, but the weekly meetings hadn't become part of our regular routine yet. I had completely spaced that our overnight would fall on the second co-op meeting day.

Blurgh. Stupid homeschooling.

3-and-1

Let's get this out of the way right away. Marriage isn't always a piece of buttercreamy triple-layer wedding cake. And I worry sometimes that homeschooling doesn't make marriage any easier.

In theory it should – homeschooling is all about family, after all. A lot of us do this to make family front and center, right? But in our house, it doesn't always look or feel like that.

Maybe it doesn't in your house either? Let me tell you what things do look like here:

- In the mornings, my husband leaves for work as the kids are getting up.

- He works for 9 to 10 hours or so. During the time, we do all the homeschooling things:

- We go to co-op. We read books together. We practice math.

- We take field trips. We go to plays and orchestra concerts. We see friends.

- We go to the park. We get ice cream. We study Ancient Greece.

- My husband comes home to a house where things have been happening all day. Big things. Little, but important things.

A life together... but without him.

Is that's what it's like for you too? Does it ever worry you a little bit? We have to be careful. Because over time, homeschooling can lead to a very 3- (or however many you plus your children are) against-1 sort of situation.

When we are with our kids all day, and our spouse isn't, I think it can create a kind of unhealthy separation. Spouses can feel left out. Homeschooling can feel like it's all on us, which can make it seem like parenting is all on us too.

All the everything is on us. As days turn into months and years, it can feel like this family life we planned on isn't very family-centric at all. Our spouses can easily become bread-winners and background characters. And our marriages can suffer.

I know this because it happens here sometimes. It sneaks up on us, and suddenly we're a million miles apart. One of us acknowledges it, and we make a plan to fix it.

Maybe that plan looks like a night away on our anniversary. You know, until co-op gets in the way.

The mistake

The mistake is thinking that this is all about homeschooling. I think homeschooling can contribute to these kinds of issues, but you know what else can?

Kids.

Yup. Those adorable people who look half like you and half like the person you married. Or the kids who look nothing like you at all, but who you chose to love. However you got them, they can rock your world, man.

Do you remember? Do you remember the first time you realized that kids can make marriage harder?

Do you remember yelling at your spouse because the baby would not stop crying and you just really, really needed a shower? Or your spouse snapping at you because you forgot to refill the wipes?

It's ironic. Kids, who are supposed to bring us together and make us a family can make us, turn us on each other like a couple of homeschool moms fighting over the stack of classics at the used book sale.

We don't want it to happen. We feel bad about it after. We vow to never do it again, until someone forgets to move the cloth diapers from the washer to the dryer and you have to engineer something out of a hand towel and shower cap for your wiggly, diarrhea-ing toddler.

Kids, man. They are stress-inducing little buggers sometimes. So we can't blame everything on homeschooling.

In fact, if we're being honest, shipping the kids off to the nearest public school could make things pretty complicated too, just a different kind of complicated.

But what about the responsibility?

But what about the responsibility of homeschooling, you're asking me.

"I constantly feel the weight on my shoulders of keeping our kids from turning into drug addicts and people who read ABRIDGED novels, and my husband is over there on his iPhone watching videos of cats falling over."

It feels like that sometimes, doesn't it?

First, don't worry about the abridged novels. Second, you're right – this shouldn't be all on you. So third, determine if your spouse is supporting your family's homeschooling, just maybe not in the same way you are?

(We have a tendency in all things to think our way is the best way.)

I recently sat down to make a list of ways that my husband does support us in this venture.

And it turns out, he's doing a lot. Things like:

- Attending parties and talent shows at our co-op.

- Never complaining when he has to clear owl pellets or LEGOs or art projects off the kitchen table so that he can eat a sandwich.

- Admitting to our emerging reader daughter that reading didn't come easily for him at first either and sitting up nights with her as she sounded out new words.

- Asking me almost every night if he can pick anything up on the way home from work (because when you're homeschooling, it can be hard to run out for milk or glue or a bag of cotton balls and a plastic bird to finish a stop-motion animation movie set).

- Selling old curricula on eBay, and helping me print things out, and dealing with all the other computer junk that makes me crazy.

- Helping to get us out the door on co-op mornings.

- Being protective of us and what we do; he even gave me a heads-up once that there might be a person at his company Christmas party looking for a fight, and I was able to steer clear of that person and instead become very involved in a conversation about The People's Court.

- Prioritizing homeschooling financially. He never says a word when yet another Amazon box arrives on our doorstep. He encourages us to go on field trips and to plays and orchestra concerts and museums and to have Adventure Days.

- Listening to me when I freak out. And I freak out a lot. I'd say I freak out enough that it's probably annoying, and he always talks me down without making me feel like I was over-reacting.

- Never questioning what we do. He has faith in me. I used to think that maybe he just didn't want to get involved, so I asked him — probably during a freak-out — and he said that he thinks I know what I'm doing because I read all the books and the blogs and I talk to other homeschool moms and the kids are fine. Well, OK then.

- Stepping in when things get hard. If I tell him about a significant worry, he'll help me address it.

- Showing the kids that he supports what they do. He chooses his words carefully about school and learning, and never makes them feels like homeschooling is different or odd.

- Keeping me out of trouble. When our co-op got yucky, for instance, he suggested I step away. Then, when it kept getting yuckier, he told me that he needed me to step away because he was really worried about me.

- Sharing his own interests with the kids. He isn't a huge reader. (OK.) He doesn't do Latin for fun. (That's fine too.) But he connects with our kids through shared interests (like presidents!), and the kids learn a lot that way.

That's a lot of things, and certainly not the actions of a person who doesn't think what we're doing is important.

Are you saving room?

So I'm going to bring up something tricky. I'm going to say it carefully. And if you are raw right now, and frustrated about your marriage and overwhelmed with homeschooling, you might not like it very much.

But I am going to ask anyway, because I think it's a pitfall for us taking-care-of-business homeschoolers.

Ready?

I'm wondering if you are saving room for your spouse to be part of homeschooling?

I only ask, because I realized recently that I wasn't. Instead, I was giving the appearance of having it all together, until I would get so underwater that my concerns came out as an incoherent rush of fear and anxiety.

I couldn't articulate what I needed. I don't think I even knew what I needed. It took many a late-night conversation for my husband and me to identify where I could use some help, and how he could become more involved in homeschooling. Right now, that looks like him teaching a presidents unit study to the kids on Saturdays.

It was his idea, because he loves presidents. But it also came about because I was willing to let go entirely. Like, I do NOTHING. I don't put president books or videos on hold at the library. I don't ask what he's got planned.

So are you making room? Or are you trying to do it all? Or are you just used to doing it all? Are resentment and frustration building and making you angry? Because anger doesn't bring you closer to your love. But you knew that already.

It takes work

So maybe, if your marriage doesn't feel super-great right now, the last thing you want to hear is that you need to work at it. But we know that marriage takes work, right?

And maybe, if we are homeschooling, and our spouse is feeling left out, or we're feeling burdened, we need to work at making homeschooling a little more marriage-friendly.

It might not be easy at first. It might start with a conversation. It might be a conversation that has to stretch over three nights after the kids are in bed. It might seem too exhausting at first.

But if you are reading this chapter, you want to make your marriage better, right? So let's buckle down. We've already talked about making room. Let's talk about some other ways to include your spouse, and bring him or her into the homeschooling fold:

- You can text a few times a day with little updates.

- You can take pictures to share via text, via email, or after he or she gets home.

- You can save some news for dinner. In fact, you can give everyone a chance to share their day at dinner. You can make this a routine, and eventually a tradition.

- You can save field trips for weekends or days off.

- You can begin a family project – genealogy is GREAT for this.

- You can read a book together after dinner. Save that next read-aloud for your partner to enjoy too.

- You can share the tough stuff, but you can be sure to share the good stuff too – especially the moments when you are feeling grateful for the opportunity to homeschool, or for your spouse's support

- You can talk about homeschooling. Talk about parenting. Talk about worries. At least once a day – for five minutes. Schedule it if you have to. But don't let days and weeks go without talking about real things.

- And you can talk about your marriage.

Because this is what you have to remember when homeschooling feels like it's coming before your marriage: It all starts with the two of you. It isn't selfish to work on your relationship, because a strong marriage is only going to make homeschooling easier. (Everything easier – ahem.)

So if you have a marriage worth fighting for – fight for it. Put it first. Your kids will thank you later.

As of this writing, my husband and haven't gotten our night away yet. But we did have an anniversary dinner date. And it helped a lot.

We had a chance to talk about some big things without anyone asking us to tie their shoes or find their toothbrush.

But we're still planning to take an anniversary trip sometime soon. Because it's important.

And so we're going to make it a priority, before it's too late.

Help! How Can I Discipline My Children?

Lindsey Marie

I can still remember the first week of our homeschooling journey. It was an exciting week filled with new books and new ways, but what stands out in my mind more than anything was the stress and exhaustion... of getting the kids to behave.

It was evident they did not view me as a teacher. I was Mom, and they were going to test me as usual. It was evident that they did not view our home as a classroom. It was home, and they were going to wander around as usual.

Fast-forward four years, and I have to say that it's still a challenge, but not one that is overwhelming, or that has not been successfully managed and contained.

There are many aspects of discipline, and so much we can talk about, friends, but I'd like to highlight a few of my thoughts about this issue and present a few ideas that I think can greatly improve this struggle.

Shall we begin?

First off, let me just say: If you are looking to read about a "quick fix" on how to get your kid to "be quiet and sit down and do their work," this may not be it. I am not the Super

Nanny, though she had some pretty good tactics, but I do believe deeply in bonding, connections, and communication that can flourish. Proper discipline and *lasting results* come from good relationships and good communication. And that takes time, introspection, hard work, and parental sacrifice.

Having said that, let's explore the first side of this conflict that can happen with our children: *us.*

The four parenting styles

In college, my favorite class was on "Guiding Young Children," and my favorite unit we studied had to do with parenting styles. We must control ourselves before we can influence our children.

I learned that there were four main parenting styles, and each style influenced whether or not the children would grow to thrive and have proper self-esteem.

The four parenting styles are as follows:

- Permissive
- Authoritarian
- Authoritative
- Uninvolved

How do we know which type we are? Well, each type was tested in four areas of parenting, and whether they scored high or low in these areas. Let's take a look at the four areas.

- Warmth: How comforting and affectionate a parent is
- Communication: How well a parent communicates and reasons with (not yells at) a child

- Control: How well a parent can stick to or enforce logical or natural consequences
- Expectations: How reasonable a parent can be in what they expect of their child

A Permissive Parent often is high in warmth. They love to love, they love to give hugs, and may dole out compliments. They may be very lenient and allow the child a lot of freedom so as to not disrupt the "peace." However, permissive parents are often low in communication, control, and expectations. They do not always reason at length with their children, enforce consequences that are consistent, and may not have high standards or expectations for their child. As a result, the children often grow up with low self-esteem.

Sure, they were hugged and kissed and allowed to do what they wanted for the most part, but without a good amount of direction, control, and expectations they will often struggle with competency and follow-through in life. Another issue with permissive parenting has to do with the resentment that may build in the parent, because leniency often does not earn respect. At times, this can come out as eruptions. A normally lenient parent can sometimes "burst" and come down hard on the child, interrupting the child's sense of security. Life becomes unpredictable, so to speak. This takes a toll on the child.

An Authoritarian Parent is high in control and expectations, but low in warmth and communication. These are the "Because I said so" parents. They are not going to have a back-and-forth discussion about it (communication). They said so; you do it. They enforce control, even possibly using physical punishment, and they have high expectations, sometimes even beyond the child's ability. They are often not very warm parents. Some may be, but their "authority" will reign in most situations. As you can guess, the authoritarian can produce children with low self-esteem, as well as the permissive parent. Some situations become outright abusive, and so you will have children that behave out of fear, but may rebel later in life. They will have self-control issues as well, not having been taught to control themselves through proper reason, but having been controlled with fear.

An Uninvolved Parent is low in all four areas. They are sometimes simply not around, or if they are, they are emotionally unavailable. This is very destructive and damaging to a child. The child may feel unloved and uncared for. Left to their own devices, these children may have trouble with the law, or may act out with attention-seeking behavior.

If the prior three paragraphs leave you feeling slightly down, or seem negative (especially if you identify with any or all of these), please listen: We are often a combination of these. As imperfect humans, we are all striving to better ourselves but are inevitably going to have things to work on. But take delight in the fact that most of us as parents do have a very strong love for our children and work hard to bond with them and steer and encourage them to growth.

Having said that, let's take a look at the fourth type: the Authoritative Parent.

Authoritative Parents are high in all four areas. This is what we all strive for. We want to have a warm, loving, open and honest relationship with our kids where we can communicate often and freely and respectfully with one another. We also want to encourage our children to strive higher and be productive, competent individuals. And as "overseers" of their childhood, we often set them up for success by managing them with control and expectations. But that "management," when combined with high warmth and positive communication, becomes such a positive thing, quite different than how the authoritarian parent may manage or use an unhealthy amount of control.

As you may guess, the children of authoritative parents grow up feeling loved (from the warmth), competent (from the expectations and control), and knowledgeable and wise (from the communication).

So what does this mean for a homeschooler that needs to discipline his or her children?

Showing warmth in your homeschool

Let love reign. First and foremost, let your children know you love them and are on their side. There are many ways you can do this. I'm sure you can get creative.

Here are a few things I try to do personally:

I begin each day with a "greeting." We hug one another, briefly check in with each other and how we are feeling or how we slept, and the three of us hold hands and say a prayer. I openly express my love for my children in my prayer and make sure they hear me ask for help to show my love in even greater ways. I also name my children individually and openly praise them.

But I don't just do this in prayer. I look for ways to do this with my children throughout the day. Children need praise, but they need the right kind of praise. "Good job" may be too vague for them. What was good about it? Be specific. This is a great way to reinforce good behavior. When you see your child working diligently, notice it and name it. "Johnny, you are working very hard. I bet it's really important to you to do a good job."

Treat them as if they already are what you want them to be. If you want Lucy to be more focused, notice when she is focus and commend it. It will be imprinted in her mind that it feels good to be focused because of the positive attention she receives when she does that. Think of animal trainers: They use positive reinforcement and constantly reward the behavior that they want. It feels genuine and it lets them know that they are being noticed and cared about.

Communicating in your homeschool

Let me ask you: How often do you talk to your children? You know, it's not uncommon for parents to spend all day with their child, even teaching them in different subjects, but realize that the day, even week or month, went by and they didn't really "connect."

Communication can be telling a child what to do, but we are talking about real heart-to-heart here. Do you know how your child feels about homeschooling? Do you know your child's insecurities? Do you know how your child likes to learn? Do you know their personality type, type of intelligence, or their temperament, and do you discuss this with them? Do they feel personally noticed and responded to?

Moreover, when there is conflict, do you view this as an opportunity to communicate? *Moments of conflict are great ways to bond with your child.* These are moments where real growth can occur if you take advantage of that moment and talk things out... calmly, reasonably. Resist the urge to get angry, or wait until the anger passes and you can be calm and listen. Talk to your child and listen to your child. What were they thinking and feeling during this conflict? What could they have done differently?

Just as an example, here is what I do with my children when there is conflict (usually between the two of them):

- Each child states "their side of the story." I allow the most upset one to talk first. This storytelling almost always involves their opinions, anger, and frustration. (Letting them do this helps the flood in their right brain to come out so that they can begin to integrate their left brain – the hemisphere responsible for logic and reasoning.)

- I ask them what they could have done differently to create more peace or a better outcome. This, again, engages the left brain. Now that their feelings have been released and acknowledged, they can begin to think clearly and engage their problem-solving skills. Sometimes, I have to help in this area, but I try to allow them to brainstorm solutions first. This step usually involves the children deciding to apologize and make amends.

- Praise and reassurance. I reassure them that they are normal, loved, and their feelings in the matter were heard. I also thank them for any humility they showed. For example, in our last "episode" my son admitted that he sometimes knows he is wrong, which makes him act out worse, because his conscience is bothering him. What a profound thing for an 11-year-old to say! I made sure to make a big deal of this, acknowledging his humility. Most adults won't even acknowledge such things. But when we bring this to the attention to our children, it will most likely invoke that response the next time.

Expectations in your homeschool

Do your children know what is expected of them? Do you talk before, during, and after an assignment or activity?

It can be very frustrating to anyone to not understand what exactly is expected. And children need reminders and repetition. So always keep that in mind.

In your homeschool, it's good to have rules and instructions repeated and discussed. But speaking of rules and instructions...

Who makes them? You do, of course. And caution and care is needed when making these. It is wise to take a look at what you expect and whether or not it is reasonable. Consider the child's age, interests and limitations. Do you expect too much? Do you expect too little?

If it is an academic problem you are having, do research on where your child should be. Trying to make your second-grader write cursive? You may want to research that. Letting your sixth grader write a one-page essay, instead of two or three? Think they can do more and that you should be "moving them toward excellence"? Research that.

If it is a behavior issue you are having with your child, educate yourself as much as possible on that issue and what you can do first to understand your child and influence the situation. There are many child development books that cover the abilities and needs of children at different ages. It is very rare for children to have "wicked" or purposefully bad intentions. Many things can play a part in misbehavior: health concerns (such as diet or sleep), neurological issues (such as autism or ADHD), and emotional issues. Your child can be experiencing depression or simply be feeling insecure. And if there is a big change in the household, or a traumatic event that everyone is recovering from, further patience may be needed.

Any expectations you have in your school and home should be researched, analyzed, and then communicated on a regular basis.

Control in your homeschool

Control is a funny thing. It can be bad; it can be good. The right degree and the right motive are key here.

Most of the time, people associate control with fear. We are afraid of not having a certain outcome, so we blow through with control and an adamant spirit, instilling fear in a child, and therefore controlling their behavior. They will do what we want them to do because they are scared of the consequence or scared of us. This does nothing to give them self-discipline and thinking ability.

You catch more bees with honey. (I'll explain this soon.)

Using logical and natural consequences, we can display a healthy amount of control in our home. Our purpose for control is ultimately to teach them self-control.
Natural consequences are consequences that happen naturally without force or interference. You forget your raincoat; you get wet. Or, if the bee doesn't get in the jar, it doesn't get honey.

I've been using natural consequences with my child. He likes to bring his sleeping bag into my room and sleep on the floor, but lately he's been complaining his back hurts and the floor is hard. I remind him each morning that if he wants to sleep nicely, he can always bring his mattress into the room, like he used to. He says no, it's too much work, and he continues to hurt his back. I could interfere and make him bring his mattress in, but honestly, I don't want to be "in the picture." I want him to become self-disciplined and self-regulated. I want him to associate his own behavior with his own outcome; not "Mom intervened, that's why."

How can you use natural consequences in your homeschool?

Sometimes a natural consequence in school-aged children is to allow them to fail if they do not study or perform well. Many overprotective parents these days choose to get involved with their children and the teachers, often dashing in to be their children's hero and prevent their children from suffering any consequences. This is detrimental to the child's growth, and is responsible for the entitlement that is so prevalent today.

Allow your child to reap the consequences of their actions. This is natural. This is good for them.

My children had to school into the summer. When other children were out of school and playing, my children had to complete their math program because of the time they wasted during the school year. Another natural consequence.

Prior to an assignment or activity, you should review the expectations with your child. Hold them to these expectations (unless you deem them to be unreasonable and need to alter them) and *do not give in.* Your children need to learn that their actions have consequences, for others and for them. This is how they learn responsibility. Giving in will only lead to further frustration for you and for them.

How can you use logical consequences in your homeschool?

Again, let your expectations be made known. When your children do not meet these expectations, consequences are needed, and it is often logical consequences that have a great impact. This is especially true if the well-being of someone was threatened, or if your child was blatantly disobedient or disrespectful.

I do not advocate physical punishment or unjust punishment; please do not think I am saying that. But logical consequences can take many forms.

You may have started this chapter hoping that I would provide a list of tactics you can use with your child. I haven't done this because truly you know your child and your home better than I do, and I trust you to be creative in your responses. But there are ideas and principles that will help you and guide you that I am discussing. So just know this: If you do not provide appropriate consequences for your child, misbehavior will continue.

For me, I often tell my children that I will not reward bad behavior. I have a child who loves Minecraft. When they are disrespectful or do not fulfill their obligations in a reasonable way, I take away their privilege of playing Minecraft and remind them that misbehavior is not rewarded. I reason with them, letting them know that I won't force them to behave, but I won't ignore it either. They do have a choice, but not one without consequences. Before you are quick to criticize or belittle your child, make sure you are willing to examine the root cause of the behavior and remind yourself of your child's innocence and possible unawareness. Keep in mind, too, that if you have a general feeling of disgust or disappointment in your child (especially on a regular basis), this can be felt, seen, and heard intuitively by your child and lead to further acting out.

Let love be your guide. See moments of misbehavior as opportunities to teach and to bond and to help your child use their "left brain" and grow to maturity.

Children need those boundaries and those "rails" as guides. They are not born with complete control over themselves. They are born dependent and looking to us as guides. So we have to be mentally strong, consistent, and inspiring examples.

By building a loving and warm relationship, communicating openly and often with our children, having reasonable expectations, and using logical and natural consequences to solicit obedience in our home, we can begin to enjoy a smoother and more cooperative atmosphere in our homes and schools.

When the Kids Don't Obey
Adelien Tandian

Obedience is a character trait that people should have to be received well in society.

Society consists of some hierarchy and tradition that requires people to respect each other. That state of being respectful is also shown by the ability to obey others. Some occupations demand obedience toward those of a higher rank, including the military, science and business.

Obedience is not only about the relationship between people, but also includes the ability to follow the law and instructions. For me, obedience is important in a religious sense. Most religions teach people to obey God and religious teachings. And as citizens, everyone also needs to obey the law.

However, character can be quite hard to instill in your children's nature, especially in the modern world where freedom is more and more available. Freedom is usually the symbol of maturity, while obedience is usually grouped with being under pressure or being conquered. Many children become obedient because there is something they're afraid of.

Training children to be obedient is one of my goals in educating them. The message of being obedient is sent to them in a variety of ways.

Before we started homeschooling, I always thought homeschooling would give us as parents more time to build the character of our children, including obedience.

Unfortunately, that idealistic assumption seemed more like a dream when we started our homeschool. There have been many times when the children became so wild and didn't obey what I said, or what they were supposed to do, or what the rules were. My jaws and my throat are often tired from reminding them what to do and getting them to follow the rules and routines. I often feel that my three boys have eaten me alive. I often cry and pray when they don't want to listen. I felt like it was the end of the world that they didn't pay attention.

Well, there are various contexts for kids being disobedient. I am not a psychologist or any certified advisor in parenting. I am just a homeschooling parent of three sons; two of them are teenagers, and one is still 8 years old. Every child has different unique characteristics to deal with. There are also different situations when they avoid obeying me. Those are very painful experiences for a mother.

Do you have any experience being ignored by your children? If you don't have any, then you must be a very lucky mother. However, if you are, like me, ignored sometimes, I would like to share some tips you might want to use when it happens. They are not always successful, but they work most of the time.

Silence is golden

One day, I was desperate because my three children didn't want to finish their schoolwork and their chores. I know we are homeschooling family and need to be flexible. However, it has been in our vision that obedience is very important for the future of our children. We just cannot follow everything they want to do.

Can't you imagine what happens in the future when people don't want to obey each other?

I was very exhausted from having to talk a lot to them about their lack of motivation to obey me. I was thinking about what made that happen. Were they also exhausted from hearing my voice asking them doing something? I prayed about this, and it came to my mind: the idea to get silent and see what they would do.

I did the silent action without any planning or thinking. I just told them that I was exhausted from talking a lot. I was surprised to see what happened. They just did everything that they needed to do. They finished all of their schoolwork and chores as well.

I am not sure why they did it well when I was quieter. The most important lesson for me was that my kids might be as tired as I was. From there, I tried to find some ways to get them to be more obedient without getting myself tired and noisy.

Be firm

- Obedience is a very important requirement in real life, as I mentioned. Therefore, we should not be easily discouraged by the disobedience of kids.

- Stay with your principles. Once you forget your principles and follow what the kids want, you will open the door for your kids to bargain with you next time.

- Find some ways to "persuade" them to listen to you.

- Tell them what obedience is by giving examples.

- Make a cue so the kids know when they cannot avoid your words.

- Don't forget to give kids "rewards" when they obey you. Rewards don't have to be some special physical thing. Praise can also be a reward for kids.

- Being firm doesn't have to mean you're confrontational with your kids, but just that we stick with what we know they need to do. Get your kids to know your expectations and how to stay within them.

Self-evaluation

Teaching your kids to obey you firmly is a must. However, you should think further about whether your expectations toward them are reasonable. An unreasonable expectation will make your kids mistrust you, and finally they will ignore you.

When you aware that you have made some wrong expectations about your kids, you can either apologize or direct them to the right way indirectly.

Here are some self-evaluation you can use when your kids don't obey:

- Is my expectation reasonable for my kids?

- Is there any alternative way for my kids to meet the expectation?

- Is the expectation for the kids appropriate for them, or is it for myself? (Make sure that the expectation is not only merely for your ego.)

- Discuss and negotiate

- Getting kids to obey should not always be tense. I'm not saying that I never have tension with them. I usually had tension every day to get them obey me. This is a very honest confession of mine.

- People think that disobedience might be happening because we are a homeschooling family. They would start to tell us stop homeschooling our kids. Thinking about this, I told them that even parents with kids who go to public or private school might have the same problem. In addition, it is not academic problems that cause our struggles most of the time.

- Nevertheless, I try hard to minimize the debate about obedience with discussions:

- Why they need to obey in this particular situation.

- Why they are expected to obey me as their mother.

- What will make them obey what I say in the future.

Show your love

Getting kids to obey you doesn't always need to be serious and tense. Lately, I'm learning that persuading the kids will work better than giving commands. This is the best way, and what I try to do often with my kids. This is a very precious lesson I have had from my kids. How unfortunate I have been that I just got this lesson when they are teenagers. It is very late, I think. However, I just feel lucky to know this simple way to win my children's hearts to listen and to obey.

When Homeschooling Looks Like Climbing Mount Everest

Crystal Wagner

"Start by doing what is necessary;
then do what is possible;
and suddenly you are doing the impossible."
St. Francis of Assisi

Sometimes it seems like homeschooling is a mountain impossible to climb. As soon as you see a clearing ahead, a boulder falls right in front of your path that you have to climb over or around or slowly chip away. I have faced many such boulders in our seven years of homeschooling.

Boulders can be short-term distractions, such as illness during the winter months when it seems like your family just cannot kick that cold. You can only complete a fraction of your scheduled lessons because you also need to care for the sick children or they don't feel up to doing any lessons. You miss connecting with friends and participating in extracurricular activities.

They can also take the form of a serious illness. My youngest daughter was born six weeks premature and was on a heart monitor for six months. God was faithful and she is now a healthy 8-year-old, and you wouldn't know by looking at her that she struggled during her first six months of life. But during those six months, my older daughter and I did lots of snuggling and reading on the couch, playing games, and playing in the backyard. I did not plan lessons. We did not take field trips. In fact, we only left the house at night when my husband was home to care for our infant daughter so we didn't risk her getting sick. This season required a shift in my mindset.

We have overcome other boulders, too, including moving three times. For one of these moves we only took one small U-haul trailer of belongings for one year in another state while my husband completed fellowship training.

Several years later, we welcomed two foster children into our home for a time. That was quite a disruption, but an incredible learning experience of a different kind. We also travel often with our work. Even though this is an enjoyable disruption, it is still a disruption that requires planning and a good attitude.

I keep the following strategies in mind when it seems like we continue to face obstacles to homeschooling.

Have a good attitude

Having a good attitude through an arduous experience can be the difference between just surviving and growing. It can be the difference between accomplishing the necessary or staying in a fog. The year we spent away from friends and family during my husband's fellowship training was one of the most difficult years of my life. It was a huge boulder! Instead of feeling sorry, depressed or angry, I approached the year as an adventure. It didn't change the circumstances, but I can look back on the year grateful for the experiences and new perspectives I gained.

Look for small blessings

"Gratitude as a discipline involves a conscious choice... It is amazing how many occasions present themselves in which I can choose gratitude instead of a complaint."
Henri J.M. Nouwen

There are blessings in all situations. Even though the challenges you face may seem monumental, there are reasons to be thankful. I find it helpful to keep a gratitude journal and write down why I am thankful. I am not consistent at this because journaling does not come naturally to me, but when I do keep a gratitude journal, I find my perspective is always a little brighter. I looked back through my gratitude journal from our year in fellowship to find a few examples of how a bad day can still have sunshine. (These were written as prayers of thanksgiving.)

- We went to the Farmer's Market today. I was thrilled that we found some garlic scapes. Thank you for the beauty of your creation and for local farmers that still respect your land.

- Thank you for creating me with resilience. I was reflecting today on the many situations, moves, etc. throughout my life. I thank you that you are, always have been, and always will be right beside me.

- Thank you for the experience of this year. I am learning to be grateful for what I have and what you have given me.

- Thank you for gentle reminders.

- I have found many benefits of this neighborhood even though at first my complaints about it seemed overwhelming.

- I do not know where to begin tonight. I do not know all of the reasons you have for this year, but I know that you are holding us. I know that you are teaching us to rely on you more. Please hold me tight tonight Lord. I need your loving arms around me extra tight.

Approach the situation with an adventurous attitude and humor

The six months my youngest daughter was on a heart monitor were stressful. I remember cutting apart game pieces for my preschooler with my infant sleeping in a baby carrier, and I couldn't move far because her heart monitor was plugged into the power outlet. We called this time our hermithood months. I had been praying that we would find a way to slow down because we were too busy. I still chuckle at God's humor.

My prayers during this time went something like this, "Thank you that we have an opportunity to bond as a family and spend time playing and resting at home. I asked for guidance as to how to accomplish that, but I didn't ask to be a hermit. Something a little less drastic would have sufficed."

Our year of fellowship was approached in much the same way. Since we lived in Wisconsin that year, we decided to use the Little House on the Prairie books by Laura Ingalls Wilder as the spine for our history studies. After all, the first book in the series was set in Pepin, Wisconsin. We even made a miniature covered wagon from moving boxes for the girls to play pretend. I remember one particularly cold morning in our rented house that used a centrally located pellet stove. My closet was nowhere near the pellet stove, and thus quite cold on that morning with single-digit temperatures. As I dressed as quickly as possible and with teeth chattering, I remembered thinking, "This must be how Laura felt." Tackle your challenges head-on with an adventurous attitude and humor, and you will find ways to keep going.

Focus on forward progress

Your child is able to advance at his own pace when you homeschool. Progress during challenging times is no different. Your child may not make as much academic progress when your family is dealing with a stressful situation, but he is learning valuable coping and life skills. He is probably making more academic progress than you realize. Focus on what he is learning instead of what you are not covering.

Regardless of the boulders you face in your homeschooling journey, it is important to remember that education, and life in general, is not a sprint. Keep the long-term perspective in mind. It is OK if your child does not reach the milestones right on time.

Take a break

Sometimes it is best to just take a break. Your children will not be behind because of a break now and then. What is "behind," anyway? Every child progresses at his own pace. Spending time focusing on family relationships or serving others will prepare him for life in more ways than trudging through the schoolbooks will anyway.

Ask for help

Sometimes you just need an outside hand. Friends are usually ready to step in at a moment's notice, but they may not know that you need help. Swallow your pride and just ask. When we had foster kids living with us, life was crazy. I asked for help supervising the preschool-aged boy on every field trip. I just couldn't keep up with him and his baby sister at the same time. One friend in particular always stepped up to be his "buddy." What a blessing that was. I also remember a particularly difficult day that I called friends until I could find someone that could come over for just an hour so I could shower and have a few moments alone. They would not have known that I needed help if I didn't ask.

Set realistic expectations

When you face yet another mountain to climb, you might need to lower your expectations. If you need to take a nap most days because you have a newborn or an illness, you might be able to listen to an audiobook instead of reading one after lunch. If you don't have the time or energy to help your children through individual history studies, combine everyone into one time period and read a living history book together. Spend the time focusing on the basics. The basics will be different for every family, but many families consider reading, religious studies, and mathematics important.

Redefine school

School does not need to be done sitting at the kitchen table. It also does not need to be bookwork for hours every day. We have taken lessons with us on a three-week trip to Maine, to grandparents' homes, and to dance class. We have completed our lesson work in the morning, during a younger child's nap time, or on the weekend when we needed to catch up. You are not limited to the physical boundaries of a schoolroom or a traditional school schedule. Fit in the lesson work when and where you can.

Reduce outside activities

This strategy seems obvious, but can be one of the most difficult to implement. It is hard to pull back from time with friends, especially when you have already committed to an activity. Remember that your family's well-being comes first, and sometimes you need to make the difficult decision to stop attending co-op, park days or dance class.

Remember that this is more like a sabbatical instead of a permanent change.

Just as St. Francis of Assisi said, focus on what you can do to get through this season. It is a season, and it, too, shall pass. Once you feel the ground under your feet again, start to add in a little more, and before you know it you will be doing the impossible.

404

Homeschooling in Hard Times or Through a Death in the Family

Ticia Messing

As I prepared to write this chapter, I counted up the number of funerals I've been involved in over the past 13 years (I count from then because that's when my Dad died). I stopped at 10. It can be hard homeschooling through a death in the family, or a major illness.

I have homeschooled through the death of 2 grandparents, a step-father, a friend who was like a brother to me, death of friends' parents, death of friends' children, and they all have unique needs. As I type this up, I just realized most of this comes in the last five years. That's an even scarier thought.

Make a schedule

You will get nothing done if you don't have a schedule. I do not mean from 8 to 8:30, I will do this. What I'm thinking of is probably more of a to-do list.

I could not have gotten anything done without my Illuminations schedule. I printed out what needed to be done and worked my way down the checklist.

Because of my schedule I did not have to think in the midst of grief. I just went down the page and completed the next box, and then the next box. That's all I did. The same thing is even more true when you have a major illness and are faced with doctor's appointments. Write down everything you must do that day and check each item off. Know when to throw the schedule out

You will not get everything done on your schedule. Planning a funeral takes a lot of meetings. There's the meeting with the funeral home, the meeting with the church or the pastor, there's picking up out-of-town family from the airport. It takes a lot of driving around.

Get books on tape, or watch Magic School Bus videos. You will need something to keep your kids busy as you drive from place to place and as they wait for meetings to be done.

The schedule you made earlier will help you know where to pick up and what you need to finish.

Know when to stop school altogether

Back when my best friend Sam was dying of cancer, there were a few times I got phone calls from Tara along the lines of "I need help now." School was done for the day; I didn't worry about it; and that was OK. It all worked out.

But my kids were in early elementary at the time, and that's more manageable than high school. A high school student will be much more likely to need to make up the time later.

Keep in mind, if you were going through this major event and in public school, they would not expect you to get a thing done. The teacher might give you work to do while you are out, but quite likely they'll say, "Just do what you can, I understand."

Know when to ask for help & when to accept it

There are a lot of details to plan for a funeral. It's like planning a wedding, but you have less than a week to do it. People are upset and emotional, and they will say things they don't mean. Remember that. A few quick words of advice:

- Accept all offers of help. People want to show their love for you, and they want to do something. Let them. When I traveled to Colorado for my grandma's funeral, the kids stayed with four different people because that many people wanted to help, and that's how the schedule worked out.

- Write down what needs to be done, and when. When someone calls and asks what they can do, look at your list and name some of the tasks there. Other homeschooling moms often want to help but can't do the task, but they can watch your kids while you do it. That is a HUGE help.

- Accept offers of meals.

- Remember that everyone grieves differently and processes grief differently. Some people won't cry for weeks because it hasn't hit them. Others will fall apart at random things. There are some movies I still can't watch almost 13 years after my dad died.

- Assume the best of those you love. They probably did not mean what they said to be hurtful.

- Remember the Ring Theory; you cannot complain to someone closer in to the circle than you. Find another person to vent your frustration and hurt to; don't heap more pain on that person.

- It will get better. It takes time, but it gets better.

Homeschooling with Bickering Kids
Ticia Messing

Do you have more than one kid? If you just answered yes, than I'm willing to bet you a million dollars your kids have started bickering at some point or another. I'm sure you've seen it; here's how it often goes in my house.

Kid 1, looking bored, pokes Kid 2. Kid 2 ignores them for the first minute or two, because Kid 2 is an angel, and also Kid 2 knows the kid who makes noise is usually blamed for the problem. Eventually, however, Kid 2 snaps and yells at Kid 1, or hits Kid 1, or does both and then runs to Mom. Either way, your kids are all angry at each other, you're frustrated because they're bickering, and you're done with the whole thing. You want them to stop the whole silly mess.

I have three kids who are all within two years of each other. The two oldest are twins, and the youngest is convinced her older brothers are out to get her.

I write all that to say, "Hi, I'm Ticia, and I have three kids who I love to pieces, and there are some days I would gladly give them to the first taker."

In my experience there are three primary reasons kids fight: out of boredom, for attention, and because of too much time together.

Boredom

Let's talk about boredom. First, if your kids are in the habit of looking to you to solve their boredom, you will always have this problem. So train them to find ways to alleviate their boredom.

- Cut down on screen time. For my kids, the more screen time they are allowed, the more often they will come to me saying they are bored. I know this is counter-intuitive, but trust me, once they are used to entertaining themselves, you will thank me.

- Create a BORED jar and fill it with suggestions of things to do: put together a puzzle, color a picture, make a craft, play with toys, walk the dog, etc. This is an intermediate step, because it still requires some of your involvement. Your goal is for them to be self-entertaining.

- Give them free access to board games. My kids' access to games directly corresponds to how often I get the "I'm bored, Mom" statement.

- Rotate toys. I'm not good at this one, but I've seen many moms say this helps keep toys entertaining.

- Assign chores. My kids' willingness to admit being bored goes down a lot once I start assigning chores.

The key place my kids get bored is standing in line. It's boring, I find it boring, and I solve it by bringing a book or reading stuff on my phone. My kids have not figured that out. So I come up with simple standing-in-line games.

- For preschoolers, the touch game is a huge hit. It's a lot like Simon Says, but you're not trying to get them out. You just call out a body part and they touch it. (Touch your nose, now touch your chin, and that's the way the Touch Game begins.)
- I've been known to have my kids stand in separate squares and do jumping jacks or run in place. It works, and burns energy. It also gets you comments from the cashier as she watches in amusement.

- Practice math facts or spelling words. Added bonus: You're getting school work done. My boys are terrible at spelling, so they can always use extra practice.

Attention

My kids fight when they feel they haven't gotten enough attention from me. Usually that comes down to acting out and then getting negative attention. There's a very simple solution for this: Spend extra time with your kids one-on-one.

I used to do better at this, and I need to get back into the habit of it. Once upon a time, I would do one special activity with each kid once a week. It didn't have to cost money; most of them didn't. With my daughter, I would do small crafts. We'd pick out something she'd seen and we would work on that. With my sons it consisted of playing a level of a video game. They are crazy for Lego Batman, and will happily play it with me as often as they can.

Keeping up with this idea meant happier kids, and less bickering.

Too Much Time Together

The final reason my kids fight is too much time together. It's one of the side effects of homeschooling. If your kids were in a classroom, they would all be in different rooms and have more than 8 hours apart from each other. But while homeschooling, they are together all day long almost every single day. Almost anyone who spends that much time together will end up feeling oppressed and like they are tired of the other person. In this case, here's my number-one tip to help the kids:

ASSIGN THEM ALONE TIME. Occasionally I turn to the kids and say, "You are fighting too much, go find different places to play in." Then they each choose different areas of the house to play. One might go play in their room, another might play outside, and my last kid will play in the family room. After a good thirty minutes to an hour, they suddenly like each other much better and are quite happy to play together again.

Sometimes the kids who are fighting the most need structure. In that case, I set a timer and pick one kid to be in charge. Until the timer goes off, that kid is in charge of what they play; when the timer goes off, I reset it and the next kid is in charge.

One final thing that can help tremendously when the kids bicker is to stop and think of what they like about their siblings. This is most effective once your kids are able to write. Then I set them to writing about their sibling until the timer goes off. They write down as many things good things they can think of about their sibling. This can be especially helpful on a later day when they're fighting again and you can remind them of what they like about their sibling.

When You Feel Like You're Doing a Terrible Job
Sallie Borrink

Every mom struggles from time to time with the thought that she's doing a bad job of parenting. Motherhood is a big responsibility that involves constantly learning how to do it well. It's normal to feel overwhelmed and have doubts.

When you throw the responsibility of homeschooling into the mix, you are presented with even more opportunities to feel like you're failing. Not only are you the mom, but now you are also the teacher. It's a lot to juggle at times.

It's easy to feel like you are doing a terrible job.

Is it possible you're actually doing a terrible job? Perhaps. There are some parents who truly neglect their child's education. There are some parents who frankly should not be homeschooling. The fact that you purchased a book about what to do when you want to quit tells me you probably aren't one of them. Parents who are truly doing a terrible job generally don't seek out help and information like you will find in this book.

So let's try to figure out why you feel like you're doing a terrible job and then see what we can do to fix it!

Identify the source of the feelings

One of the first things we should do when our child starts acting up is ask ourselves if it is due to a HALT (Hungry, Angry, Lonely, Tired) feeling. Any one of these can push a child over the edge.

Well, guess what? The same thing applies to moms!

If we are hungry, angry, lonely and/or tired, it can have a tremendous impact on how we view our lives. So the first step is to decide if any of these common reasons are a factor.

- **Are you eating poorly?** Everything will seem worse if you are run down. Being a homeschooler demands a lot of mental, physical and spiritual stamina. You won't have stamina if you aren't eating well.

- **Are you angry?** Is there conflict in your life that you need to resolve? It might not even be conflict with your children. It could be conflict with your husband, a friend or relative that is overshadowing your homeschooling.

- **Are you lonely?** This can be a real problem for some homeschooling moms. As much as we love our children, they don't meet all our needs for social interaction. Do you need some time with another adult or friend? If our emotional well is empty, we won't have anything to give to our child.

- **Are you tired?** Are you getting enough sleep? If you have a baby in the house, this can make it very challenging. If you are an introvert, are you getting enough time alone to recharge? Are you burned out from too much life?

So go through this list first. If any of these ring true to you, then that is the first place to start. If it isn't any of these or not just these, keep going.

Is it life or your neglect?

It's important to differentiate between whether your struggles are due to the realities of life or your own neglect.

Sometimes life simply overwhelms our best efforts. Illness, family emergencies, new babies, travel, church conflicts and more can have a significant impact on our families. Any of these circumstances can overwhelm us emotionally which can then spread over into our homeschooling efforts.

This is different from neglect. Neglect is when you have the time and energy to homeschool properly and you simply choose not to do so. If it is neglect, then you do have a problem. But if it is more a case of life overwhelming this season of your family's life, then take a deep breath and know that this will pass eventually.

The burden of unrealistic expectations

Are you staggering under the weight of unrealistic expectations? Are you trying to do too much? If you set goals that are simply not attainable, you are going to feel like you are doing a terrible job.

Every homeschool family needs to operate under realistic expectations. It doesn't matter what any other families are doing. You need to do what will work best for your family. If you've taken on too much, then ask yourself what you can let go of.

Keep your eye on the long-term goals

It's so important to keep our eyes fixed on the long-term goals. Yes, this week or this month might have been a disaster. It happens to everyone. Dust yourself off and start over again.

Some years are going to be less than great. They might even end up being just adequate. That's reality. Remember that even classroom teachers have bad years with challenging classes when they have to focus daily on just getting through the year. It happens in school and it happens in homeschooling.

Remember why you decided to homeschool. If you need to, make a list of all the reasons and all the pros to homeschooling. Take note of all the good things coming out of your child's homeschooling experience. Keep the end in mind.

So what's the verdict?

Are you really doing a terrible job? Or are you human and facing normal human struggles? If you can identify the source of the discouragement, you will be well on your way to getting back on track!

When Your Kid Hates School
Alicia Michelle

In late fall of 2014, it seemed like I woke up every morning with a pounding headache.

As the alarm went off, I would feel my neck and shoulders crunch up, knowing the drama that awaited me each day. My body anticipated the intense, ongoing fight that would rage the second my son woke up, and it couldn't help but react.

I would get out of bed, turn on the shower and stand in the warm spray, praying again and again for relief from the pain.

And although the hot steam would relax my muscles somewhat, the shower's steam couldn't remove the real source of the pain: the mounting anger and frustration I had toward my 11-year-old.

This kid suddenly hated school and had seemingly made it his life's mission to fight me on anything education-related. This not only made him nearly impossible to teach, it greatly limited my ability to help my other three children.

Like a donkey that had set in his heels and refused to move, my son's defiance and uncooperative spirit kept him locked into this mindset: I will not do school, no matter what you say.

And this spirit was not only destroying him, but causing our entire family to suffer.

Assessing the source of the pain

"Where in the world is this all coming from?," my husband and I wondered.

Since this wasn't the first time we'd seen our son dig in his heels, this behavior wasn't completely out of context. There had been several times when our son's immutable, "you-can't-make-me" spirit had caused family upheaval.

And yet, we'd never seen battles like this.

But as we looked closer, the motivation behind our son's heightened defiance became clearer.

You see, along with an iron-clad will, our son deals with Asperger's Syndrome, which means that he doesn't always understand the bigger picture of why certain things need to happen. And in this situation, he'd decided that his homeschool assignments were not his favorite and therefore he didn't want to do them.

We realized that it was this mindset — coupled with the onset of puberty and tween hormones—that proved to be the impetus behind the immense, daily battle-of-the-wills withour son.

While that fact didn't bring relief from the drama, it did bring insight and allowed us to really see what we were dealing with.

Being real about the pain

Next, I began examining my own thoughts. Why was I really angry about this — so much so that my body was showing physical manifestations of the stress?

I was surprised and saddened by my answers.

First, I felt like a complete and utter failure, both as a teacher and as a mom (which is a hefty combination). Why couldn't I help him through this? What was I doing wrong? What did I need to change? Things had always worked so well up to this point and I didn't understand why they suddenly weren't.

Second, I felt helpless and trapped by something completely out of my control. What was I supposed to do with this situation? Ignore it? That was impossible since it was in my face every single day. Let him not do any school? No, he had already fallen behind in math. And besides, I didn't want him to learn that if things were too hard than he should just quit.

So was learning to persevere the real issue for him? Or did he need a curriculum switch? Perhaps it was time to consider different schooling options? My heart was torn as the battles raged on each day.

In addition, my soul was grieved and concerned for my son. Yes, I knew embracing difficulties was harder because of his diagnosis. And while we were always trying to be sensitive to this, we also tried to equally balance his need to be prepared for the "real world."

My husband and I believe that choosing to embrace responsibility (whether or not that responsibility is our "favorite") is essential to all areas of life success. If I did not push him to his greatest potential at this critical juncture, would he learn in the future to simply give up if things get too hard or if they weren't his "first choice?"

Lastly, I hated how much energy this struggle took from our entire family's day. I was emotionally spent after each encounter with my son and felt like I had nothing left to give my other kids. In fact, a friend of mine noted that since I was giving 90 percent of my time, energy and attention to my oldest son, I was trying to parent my other three kids on that measly 10 percent.

Something needed to change. But what? And how?

Steps to discovering solutions

How could we get over this hump when my husband and I felt like we'd exhausted all solutions?

We began by asking some basic questions.

First, we asked, "What can we change?"

Answer #1: We could change the curriculum.

I wasn't sold on this one. Our curriculum was solid. I was willing to change (and have changed things up on multiple occasions for our kids).

But I sensed that it wasn't the fact that he didn't like this style of learning, but that instead he just didn't want to do anything related to school. This became especially evident when we allowed him to choose different ways to learn the material (and he still fought us). When we noticed that we also got similar pushback around doing chores, it was pretty clear that he didn't want to do anything related to hard work.

And now that he was in sixth grade, his educational needs required something more rigorous in order to prepare him for middle school, high school and eventually college. I couldn't let him slip by.

Answer #2: We could change how we did school (in terms of daily rhythms and location).

We played with this one for a while. We wondered if perhaps (as a child approaching puberty) he needed additional sleep? So we let him start school a little later. The problem was that he didn't sleep later! Asking him to stay in bed so that he could sleep longer actually became a new point of contention.

Another option we tried was to allow him to do his schoolwork in different locations around the house (and even outside on our patio). We thought giving him additional freedoms might warm him up to the idea of learning, but no dice. This just distracted him further from his tasks. Now he was wasting time being distracted and pitching a fit about the schoolwork. Super fun, right?

Answer #3: We could move him to a different schooling option.

This was the biggest and most drastic of the options, but as the other alternatives continued to not pan out, we began to look more seriously at possibly putting him in a traditional school.

We knew this wasn't a decision to make lightly. We'd planned to homeschool even before we married! However, we decided that our son's best interest was far more important than our need to force the homeschooling mold if it was no longer a good fit. We needed to help our son through this and, therefore, all schooling options were on the table.

Next, we asked "What can we not change?"

Ultimately, that came down to one answer: We couldn't change his behavior.

We could pray about it (which we did daily and fervently) and we could talk to him about it. And, yes, these are powerful.

But ultimately, we realized that our son is in charge of his own decisions. He has the power to respond differently to school and to embrace the responsibility... or not. This was a very hard pill for us to swallow, because it reminded us of how powerless we parents are when it comes to helping our kids grow into who they need to be.

We couldn't do the maturing for him or change how he interacted with us.

However, we could control how we interacted with him:

- We could continue to do our best to stay calm and to not respond in anger.
- We could continue to pray regularly for him and ask for specific guidance.
- We could continue to stay united as a couple in helping him through this.
- We could accept this circumstance with joy and believe with all our hearts that God was going to use it for our good.

So that's what we did.

Other survival tactics for the battle

As the main teacher and caretaker of our children, I dealt with the brunt of my son's challenges during this season. And as I felt the stress rising (and sensed that the situation was probably not going to be short-term), I began to develop personal strategies for survival.

For one thing, I made sure that I was not only praying for my son but for myself, the other kids and for our marriage to remain strong.

And, because most days I was mentally exhausted by 9 a.m., I took time each day for a 20-minute or 1½-hour nap. I tried to make time for basic stress relief and soul care.

Third, my husband and I shared with our pastor (and a handful of other families in our church) about the utter hell our family was enduring. We trusted them to pray us through on those moments when we had nothing left.

I also asked myself, "What other things can I let go of in my life so that I can focus on being triumphant through this?" How I can get off the merry-go-round and simplify things?

Lastly, I chose to believe with all of my heart that good would come from all of this pain. I chose to believe verses like Psalm 126:5 that say: "Those who sow with tears will reap with songs of joy."

What finally happened for our son

This was a long, hard battle for our family that lasted around nine months. So many tears were shed. So many "end-of-our-rope" prayers were lifted up.

And yet, nearly a year later we stand in awe at all that God has done.

Three of our kids (including our oldest son) are now enrolled in a hybrid homeschool where they attend classes with other homeschool kids two days a week. They are just flourishing there, and oh, it is so beautiful to see.

My son loves school. And I do mean "loves" school. I can't think of the last time he fought me on having to complete an assignment.

Ironically, his workload has actually increased since we started at the school! And yet, I watch him dutifully complete his school, most of the time without me having to motivate him through it. Truly his attitude and maturity levels have changed dramatically.

In fact, words cannot express what an incredible change this has been. Tears of gratitude are probably the only way to express it. Without a doubt, God did a miracle in my son's heart.

My encouragement to you

If you have a child that "hates school," I want to let you know that you're not the only one that has gone through this. If we were having coffee together and you were sharing your story with me, I'd be crying alongside you because I understand the deep, debilitating pain.

Friend, can I encourage you to assess the source of the defiance; to be honest with yourself about what you're experiencing as a result; and then develop some tangible solutions based on the questions, "What can I change?" and "What can't I change?"

Be real with yourself and others, and hold on tight to God through the battle. Most of all, ask him daily for specific wisdom on how to parent — and homeschool — through this challenge. Let Him lead you step-by-step to victory and to the best solution for your family in this season.

What If You Feel Like You're Doing Too Little?

Jen Dunlap

We have been doing this homeschooling gig for a long time. Our oldest is in his first year of high school and we have homeschooled him from the beginning. It's the blink of an eye and forever all at once!

One thing I have learned through our homeschool journey is that no homeschool mom is completely free of feelings of doubt. Am I doing enough? Am I doing too much? Are we following the right course of study? Are we schooling with the right method?

I know I personally struggle with knowing if we are doing enough. I considered myself to be more of a relaxed homeschooler. I know I don't want my house to look like a school classroom, but I also want my children to be well-prepared for life. I know what I don't want for my everyday life:

- Rigid schedule

- A bunch of random subjects to complete each day

- Follow someone else's scope and sequence

- Learning that only happens during "school" hours

Although I wouldn't mind a lunch lady!

What do I want my day to look like?

- Time for my children to play and just be kids
- No push to read/write at a certain age/grade
- An excellent education in a relaxed environment
- A routine for the day, but the flexibility to "go with the flow" as needed
- Learning, not tears – mine or theirs
- My children to be excited about learning
- Curious kids

Knowing what I know about how we want our day to look, a rigid course of study is not going to work for my family. Writing out these "truths" helps to keep me focused on the overall goals for our homeschool. What are your truths for your family? Making them clear and concrete will go a long way toward your peace of mind.

"Comparison is the thief of joy"

We've all heard the quote and know it to be true. Yet, even the most seasoned homeschool mom can have moments when it feels like we are spinning our wheels and not making any progress. Then we start Googling and Pinteresting, and before you know, it we feel like a BIG fail.

We forget that those blog posts and gorgeous photos of well-behaved kids in clean houses are the ESPN Sports highlight reel and not everyday living and learning. We all have the good moments and the not-so-great moments too.

Every family is unique. The needs of the children and parents are unique as well. Have faith that what you are doing for your family is what you need to be doing, not the curriculum or schedule of Susie Homeschooler down the street. Value the environment that God has created and is calling for you and your particular family. Of course, we can learn and grow from each other, but keep your eyes on your own work and you will find peace.

Am I Pushing My Kids Too Much or Too Little?

Ticia Messing

When my boys were in kindergarten, they weren't reading. Then we went to a service project with my church, and a boy the exact same age was reading the cans of vegetables we were sorting. I was sure right then my boys would never learn to read.

Fast-forward three years, and my son randomly picked up a chapter book at the book store, and as we sat waiting for our car to be fixed, he read the entire thing. That was the day I realized I no longer had to worry about reading.

Now I'm worrying about writing. My boys are horrible at writing. My daughter is a prodigy; she writes far above her grade level and routinely gets comments on her word choice. This makes it worse because she's two years younger than my boys.

All homeschool moms have this worry

We all wonder, did I teach my kids enough? Did I push them too hard? Do they know enough math? Am I going to cause my kid to have a mental breakdown when they graduate high school at 14 because "I knew they could do it" and I pushed them? Will my daughter get to college and fail all of her classes because I didn't teach her how to cope?

I'm sure you have all of those questions and more. I know I do. But we don't have to ask ourselves those questions.

We can know, or at least have a fairly good idea of, the answer to all of these questions.

Am I pushing my kids too little? Am I teaching them enough?

A very quick and easy way to determine if your kids are learning enough is to have them take a standardized test. But what if you're like me and you don't want your kids stressing over a test? Then the answer becomes more complicated.

First, look at the scope and sequence of curriculum you are using. What are they expecting a child in the same grade as yours to know? Do they expect a fifth-grader to know long division by hand? If so, then can your child do it?

I want to emphasize looking at the scope and sequence of the curriculum you are using. We use Math-U-See, which uses a mastery approach and covers one topic each year. In this program, kids don't cover fractions until approximately fifth grade. If I looked at the third-grade scope and sequence for Saxon math, it covers simple fractions in third grade.

I could very easily start thinking my kids are behind because they don't know it yet. But they're not behind. They are completely on grade level for their curriculum.

Now, if you're constantly changing curriculum due to different circumstances, money, change of teaching style, it wasn't working, what have you; this method becomes more difficult. Then you have a couple of different options.

First, are you completing roughly one year's worth of curriculum in a subject area? Most curriculum is designed to be completed in one school year. It's a good rule of thumb that if you have successfully completed one year's worth, you should be on level.

But you might have missed something in skipping around. That's where the next way of checking if your child is on level comes in.

Look into the standards for your state. What do they expect a fourth-grader to know? Every state that I know of has their education standards posted somewhere on their website. It may be difficult to parse their legal language, but you can usually figure out "A first-grade child is expected to read short vowel words of 2 syllables and silent e words."

Next, there's a book series called "What your [grade level] needs to know." It's a good, solid book series for giving you a general range of what is expected in each grade level. It also has some suggestions of books to read that year, and social skills in your child should have. As a warning note, this series is aligned to Common Core standards, in case that is important to you.

What if I'm pushing my child too hard?

I'll be honest; this is a much harder one to diagnose. I'm quite frequently guilty of this with my daughter. She is crazy smart, and is fully capable of doing the same work as her brothers, who are two years older than her. I no longer differentiate between her schoolwork and her brothers.

This hasn't happened without a few missteps. I've had more than one day where she sat crying as we tried to complete math together. She was capable of doing the math, but the sheer number of problems was overwhelming.

Signs you're pushing your child too hard:

- Your child cries during a particular subject.
- Your child is taking an extra-long time to complete a subject.
- Your child starts saying "I'm so stupid."
- Your child just gives up.

Those last two can be the most heart-breaking. If you're answering yes to these questions and saying, "It's like you're in my house," there is hope, and you can still keep the high standards you're going for. Here's what has worked with my daughter.

- **Take a break. We** took a break from math for a month. My daughter was fully capable of doing the work, but she had convinced herself it was hard, so I took a break. Then, when we came back a month later, she suddenly figured out it wasn't too hard.

- **Set a time limit.** Last year we covered long division, and those problems can take a long time to complete. My daughter would sit there and cry for 5 minutes, "It's too hard, I can't do it," and would take 10 minutes to complete one problem. Then I had a flash of insight and told her she only had to work for 20 minutes. I wasn't expecting her to finish during that time, only work as hard as she could. Suddenly she was completing quadruple the work she completed before.

- **Reinforce how smart your kid is.** Sometimes when my daughter is freaking out about math, we talk about how far she has come in her abilities; how two years ago, she thought adding 5 + 7 was hard.

Now she can multiply big numbers together and add three-digit numbers together. As we slowly walk through how much she has learned and is learning, and her confidence is restored.

Sometimes you are pushing too hard

Sometimes you are pushing too hard. Your child does not really need to graduate high school at 14. Are you trying to complete two years of school in one year? Or are you competing with another parent whose child has a natural gifting far and above the normal child in that area? Maybe you need to slow down.

Instead, enjoy the time you have with your child. Homeschooling is a precious gift for you to enjoy with your child. Take the time to enjoy. Stop your curriculum for a week and explore that one topic your child is fascinated with. Suddenly your child's love of learning will explode!

Homeschooling is hard. We don't have specialists hired by the school to tell us what to do and when, and most of us didn't get teaching degrees to know exactly what our child's developmental stage is. But we've been given a charge to raise our children, and that is wonderful blessing.

Authors

Adelien Tan is a mother to three awesome boys and a wife to a great husband. They are a home education family living in Surabaya, Indonesia, where home education is still very rare. English is her foreign language, but she tries to use it in blogging. You might visit her at **BlessedLearners.com**, where she shares thoughts, experiences and information about homeschooling, family, parenting, blogging and personal growth. She also created an e-book, 100+ Notebooking Page Templates, to equip families for notebooking activities.

■■■■■■■■■■■■■■■■■■■■■■■■■■■■■■■■■■■■■■

Alicia Michelle writes about living a beautifully imperfect journey through homeschooling, parenting, marriage and all family-related matters at **YourVibrantFamily.com**. She has been married to her best friend for 14 years and together they spend their days lovingly guiding their four passionate and creative kids. Alicia is the author of Plan to Be Flexible and the Back to School Survival Manual, and the creator/producer of the online video courses "bloom: A Journey to Joy (and Sanity) for Homeschool Moms" and "rhythm: Guiding Your Family to Their Ideal Learning Flow." She believes each day offers new opportunities to grow in grace and to trust God in unexpected ways; and that "acceptance with joy" is one of the hidden secrets to a full, contented Christian life.

■■■■■■■■■■■■■■■■■■■■■■■■■■■■■■■■■■■■■■

Brenda is a work-at-home writer and mom to two girls. Brenda has a background in writing and education and is the author of several homeschooling courses. She spends most of her days balancing homeschooling and writing or editing for numerous clients. Brenda believes that homeschooling doesn't have to be complicated. She shares simple ways to make homeschooling easier on her website, **SchoolingAMonkey.com**. Brenda currently lives in Dallas, Texas.

Ann is a 40-verysomething (ahem) homeschooling mom of five. She has been married for 26 years to her never-boring husband who travels three weeks per month; and she has homeschooled all of her children since pre-kindergarten, graduating three of them so far. Doing this while living in the boonies very rurally outside of Branson, Missouri, she has had to find ways to simplify her life in order to keep her sanity! At **AnnieAndEverything.com**, she blogs about making any and everything as easy and cheap as possible – frugality, homeschooling, and a bit about homemaking, motherhood, marriage, and other aspects of being a woman thrown in for good measure.

■■■■■■■■■■■■■■■■■■■■■■■■■■■■■■■■■■■■■

Cait is a school psychologist, mom to three, and unexpected homeschooler. She blogs about the journey at **My-Little-Poppies.com**, where she also discusses her passions: education, parenting, literacy, and nature. She is founder of Granite State Gifted, a support group for families of gifted children in the NH and MA area and co-founder of Raising Poppies, an online community for parents of gifted children. Cait is a Year Round Homeschooling contributor, where she writes about special needs and literature. She has been published by: Simple Homeschool, Gifted Homeschoolers Forum, Secular Homeschool, Raising Lifelong Learners, MindPrint Learning, and Doing Good Together.

■■■■■■■■■■■■■■■■■■■■■■■■■■■■■■■■■■■■■

Crystal Wagner is a homeschool mom of two, author, speaker and blogger. She has a passion to share her research and experience with parents in a way that equips them to train the hearts, minds and souls of their children. She encourages parents through her blog, workshops and published resources. You can find out more about Crystal at **TriumphantLearning.com.**

Dianna Kennedy is the Catholic homeschooling mother of six, juggling working outside the home with pursuing a classical education for herself and her students. You can find her resources for Catholic homeschooling and laugh at her misadventures at **TheKennedyAdventures.com**.

Emily Copeland is a homeschooling mother of two children and minister's wife. She blogs at **TableLifeBlog.com** where she shares encouragement and ideas for homeschooling, family life, ministry, and living with purpose.

Erica Arndt is a Christian, a wife, a mom, and a homeschooler. She authors the homeschooling website **ConfessionsOfAHomeschooler.com**, where she offers tons of free printables, resources, ideas, and homeschool curriculum. She likes to spend time with her family, and dabbles in graphic design in her *free* time. Feel free to drop by her site for a visit anytime!

Jennifer Dunlap blogs at **ForeverForAlwaysNoMatterWhat.com** and chats about homeschooling and large-family living. In her copious amounts of free time, she can also be found at your favorite social media sites Facebook, Twitter, and Pinterest

Jennifer A. Janes and her husband homeschool their two daughters in Arkansas. Jennifer loves connecting with people both online and off, and she has a heart for encouraging special needs families. She writes about faith, family, and parenting and homeschooling a child with special needs at **JenniferAJanes.com**.

Kalista Sabourin is a Canadian homeschooling mama to four awesome children. She can frequently be found snuggled up on a comfy chair with her knitting and at least one child under her arm. Her homeschooling philosophy is to keep it simple and enjoy the ride! She blogs about homeschooling, crafting and simple living.

Kara S. Anderson is a work-at-home, homeschooling mama to two amazing kids. She takes too many pictures and never leaves home without a notebook. You can find her at her blog, **QuillAndCamera.wordpress.com.**

Karyn is a homeschool mom to four kids 11 and under. She is a former public school educator who decided that she could do the best job at home! Karyn loves music, running, baking and reading the best books! She spends half of her life these days writing her blog, **TeachBesideMe.com**, where she share hands-on learning ideas, curriculum reviews, and other homeschooling and family-related topics.

Kristi is a follower of God, wife to her high school crush, and mom to five blessings ranging from teens to tots. Aside from her family, she's also passionate about homeschooling, creating family traditions, and finding new ways to run a more efficient home and school. Not surprisingly, you can usually find her at home trying to bring some order and fun into the mayhem of daily life. Kristi is a down-to-earth writer and energetic speaker who loves to share insights from her wonderful, yet sometimes challenging, experiences of being a homemaker and homeschool mom. Her tips are creative, practical, and help bring back some simplicity in the chaos of life and homeschooling. Kristi blogs about her adventures in wifehood, mommyhood, and the fun to be found in homeschooling at **RaisingClovers.com**.

■■■■■■■■■■■■■■■■■■■■■■■■■■■■■■■■■

LaToya is the author of Beautifully Broken: Finding Joy and Purpose in the Pain. She traded in a law degree to homeschool her children and be home full-time to serve her family. Through trials of divorce, depression, death and more she has learned how to find joy in motherhood and broken circumstances. As a certified life coach it is LaToya's desire to encourage and equip other women to do the same. You can find her online at **LatoyaEdwards.net.**

■■■■■■■■■■■■■■■■■■■■■■■■■■■■■■■

Lindsey Marie is a passionate writer eager to touch the hearts and minds of her readers. As a devoted mother to two, happy homeschooler, and scatterbrained housewife, she's on a mission to find love and joy in "the simple life" and invites you to join her! She shares this journey with you at **TheNittyGrittyMom.com** where you will find information on real life parenting, homeschool encouragement, resources, and a place to connect as inspired women.

Marlene is a wife to an amazing husband and a mom to three kiddos. Her days as spent making her home a haven for her family and homeschooling their kiddos in between hugs and snuggles. In her not-so-spare time, she enjoys crafting, painting (canvas, not walls), or just relaxing with a cup of coffee and a good book. You can find her blogging over at **ADiligentHeart.com**.

■■■■■■■■■■■■■■■■■■■■■■■■■■■■■■■■■

Michelle Cannon is a single mom who has been homeschooling for 16 years. She's a public speaker, parenting and homeschooling consultant, and gives support to families living with bipolar disorder. You can find her blogging at **HeartOfMichelle.com**.

■■■■■■■■■■■■■■■■■■■■■■■■■■■■■■■■■

Michelle Morrow is an author and publisher of homeschooling books and resources. She can be found at **HomeschoolingDownUnder.com**. Her experience as a homeschool mom means that she understands what works (and what doesn't) in homeschooling. She wants to help homeschoolers to homeschool. Her resources, advice and curriculum ideas are there to make homeschooling easier. Michelle lives in Australia with her husband and 4 children. Her oldest son is studying to be a doctor; her daughter is at university studying communications; and her 2 youngest are finishing their homeschool high school studies.

Misty Bailey is a work-at-home homeschool mom. She loves helping new homeschoolers and has a Homeschool 101 eBook for those getting started. She shares her struggles with time management, becoming unglued and finding joy in the everyday moments on her blog **FindingJoyInTheJourney.net**.

■■■■■■■■■■■■■■■■■■■■■■■■■■■■■■■■■■■

Monica Lynn is a Christian homeschool mom to three lively children, including a set of twins. In 2010, she left her career as an HR professional to become a stay-at-home mom and began the adventure of homeschooling in 2012. She writes about their learning journey and shares children's learning activities at **EnjoyTheLearningJourney.com**.

■■■■■■■■■■■■■■■■■■■■■■■■■■■■■■■■■■■

Nicole is a homeschool mom to six children (five boys and one girl) for the last 10 years. She lives in Michigan with her children, wonderful husband of 16 years, 14 chickens, three cats, and whatever insects might be found that her kids are studying about. Two of her children are intense and have continued to make her think outside the box when it comes to teaching them. Nicole uses lots of Charlotte Mason principles in her homeschool. She blogs at **MamaOfManyBlessings.com** about her homeschool journey, slow-cooker freezer recipes to make monthly, essential oils, parenting, special needs, and anything else life throws her way.

Sallie and her husband, David, enjoy home educating their creative and spirited only child, Caroline. A former elementary teacher, Sallie now creates education materials and writes about learning topics at **SallieBorrink.com**. Sallie enjoys reading and following her beloved Michigan State Spartans in her free time as well as working with her husband in their home business, artsandletters.biz. When not enjoying the four seasons from her corner office, she likes to explore the back roads around the cute little town they call home in beautiful West Michigan.

■■■■■■■■■■■■■■■■■■■■■■■■■■■■■■■■■■■■■

Sara Dennis is a homeschooling mother of 6 children ages 5 through 19. After much research into homeschooling in 2000, she and her husband fell in love with classical education and use it as the foundation for their homeschool. Their oldest son graduated high school in June 2015, after homeschooling the entire way through. With two children still in high school, one in middle school, and the youngest two just beginning their homeschool journey, Sara looks forward to many more years of homeschooling. She blogs at **ClassicallyHomeschooling.com**.

■■■■■■■■■■■■■■■■■■■■■■■■■■■■■■■■■■■■■

Sara began blogging at **EmbracingDestinyBlog.com** in 2008 as a way to share encouragement and ideas with other moms on the homeschooling journey. She writes about purposeful living, especially in the areas of homeschooling, raising daughters, faith, and marriage. She is also the owner/editor of The Homeschool Post, a website dedicated to encouraging, informing, and connecting the online homeschool community.

Selena is a homeschooling graduate and a veteran homeschooling mother of four. She and her husband, Jay, use an eclectic homeschooling approach to encourage their children to learn throughout their lives. Selena blogs about her family's homeschooling adventures every week at **LookWereLearning.com**.

Shannen is in her eighth year of homeschooling, now with a preschooler coming up the ranks after sending her teen to college. She enjoys knitting, quilting, tatting, and healthy living. You can find her blogging about homeschooling high school, preschool, faith, and family life at **MiddleWayMom.com**.

Ticia is a homeschooling mom to three elementary kids, twin boys and a little girl. She loves to make their learning hands-on, and delights in making history fun. You can find Ticia at her blog **AdventuresInMommydom.org**.

Tonia is a homeschooling mom to one daughter, married to her college sweetheart, and owner of one crazy beagle. You can find her reading a book when she isn't busy homeschooling or keeping up with her blog, **TheSunnyPatch.ca**.

Made in the USA
San Bernardino, CA
25 August 2016